# Modernization, the State, and Regional Disparity in Developing Countries

# Modernization, the State, and Regional Disparity in Developing Countries

## Tunisia in Historical Perspective, 1881–1982

Ezzeddine Moudoud

Routledge
Taylor & Francis Group
LONDON AND NEW YORK

First published 1989 by Westview Press

Published 2018 by Routledge
52 Vanderbilt Avenue, New York, NY 10017
2 Park Square, Milton Park, Abingdon, Oxon OX14 4RN

*Routledge is an imprint of the Taylor & Francis Group, an informa business*



Library of Congress Cataloging-in-Publication Data
Moudoud, E. (Ezzeddine)
Modernization, the state, and regional disparity in developing countries: Tunisia in historical perspective, 1881–1982 / by Ezzeddine Moudoud.
p. cm.—(Westview special studies on Africa)
Bibliography: p.
Includes index.
ISBN 0-8133-7709-9
1. Tunisia—Economic conditions—1956– —Regional disparities.
2. Tunisia—Dependency on foreign countries. 3. Economic development. I. Title. II. Series.
HC820.M68 1989
338.961'1—dc19

88-38119
CIP

ISBN 13: 978-0-367-01295-3 (hbk)
ISBN 13: 978-0-367-16282-5 (pbk)

à la mémoire de mon père
à ma mère

pour Chantal, Fadhel et Fathi

## CONTENTS


List of Tables and Figures xi
Foreword, *Dennis A. Rondinelli* xv
Acknowledgments xvii

**PART ONE**
**DEVELOPMENT, UNDERDEVELOPMENT AND THE TRANSITION'S DILEMMAS** 1

1 INTRODUCTION 3

Regional Disparity and the Problem in Tunisia, 4
Methodology, 6
The Data Used, 8

2 MODERNIZATION, DEVELOPMENT THEORY AND THE QUESTION OF "TRANSITION" 15

Introduction, 15
Theories of Development, 16
Modernization and the Transition at the National Level: Modernization Theories, 17
Modernization and the Transition at the Sub-National Level: The Growth Pole Approach, 33
Regional Disparity and Alternative Approaches of Regional Development and Planning in Developing Countries, 40
Conclusion: Regional Disparity, the New Debate and the Transition's Dilemmas, 46

**PART TWO**
**REGIONAL DISPARITY AND THE QUESTION OF TRANSITION IN TUNISIA** 59

3 GROWTH, DEVELOPMENT, REGIONAL DISPARITY AND THE TUNISIAN DILEMMA 61

Introduction, 61
Growth or Development? The Tunisian Dilemma, 61

Regional Disparities: The Nature and the Magnitude of the Problem, 75
Conclusion, 89

4 THE HISTORICAL ROOTS OF REGIONAL DISPARITY 103

Introduction, 103
Precolonial Tunisia: An Historical Background, 104
Regional Disparity and the Legacy of French Colonization, 109
Conclusion, 122

5 REGIONAL DISPARITY AND REGIONAL DEVELOPMENT POLICIES IN THE POSTCOLONIAL PERIOD: 1960-1980 135

Introduction, 135
The Regional Policy During the "Ben Salah" Period: 1960-1969, 136
Regional Policy During the "Nouira" Period: 1970-1980, 155
Conclusion, 168

**PART THREE**
**TOWARDS RETHINKING THE REGIONAL QUESTION** **175**

6 THE IMPOSSIBLE "JACOBIN" REGIONALIZATION 177

The Central Tunisia Development Project, 177
Conclusion, 187

7 CONCLUSIONS: RETHINKING THE REGIONAL QUESTION 193

Epilogue 201
Bibliography 209
Index 227

# LIST OF TABLES AND FIGURES

## TABLES


| | | |
|---|---|---|
| 3.1 | Structure and Growth of Production by Sector, 1960-1980 | 65 |
| 3.2 | Evolution of the Labor Force Distribution by Sector, 1960-1980 | 65 |
| 3.3 | Distribution of Exports by Sector, 1964-1980 | 66 |
| 3.4 | Evolution of "Absolute Poverty," 1961-1980 | 67 |
| 3.5 | Population Distribution and Population Density by Region, 1980 | 80 |
| 3.6 | Employment Distribution by Economic Sector and by Region in 1980 | 81 |
| 3.7 | Distribution of Employment in Public and Private Sectors, 1980 | 82 |
| 3.8 | Employment in Industry by Region, 1980 | 83 |
| 3.9 | Employment in Tourism and Tourist Capacity by Region, 1980 | 85 |
| 3.10 | Population by Milieu and by Region, 1980 | 87 |
| 3.11 | Rate of Urbanization by Region, 1980 | 88 |
| 3.12 | Distribution of Cities by Size and by Region 1980 | 91 |
| 3.13 | Infrastructure Indicators by Region in 1981-1982 | 92 |
| 3.14 | Labor Force by Economic Sectors and Regions, 1980 | 93 |
| 3.15 | Household Cash Consumption, Population in "Absolute Poverty" and Unemployment Rate by Regions, 1980 | 94 |
| 3.16 | Basic Socioeconomic Indicators by Region, 1980 | 95 |

| | | |
|---|---|---|
| 3.17 | Employment Structures in the Gouvernorat's Capitals | 97 |
| 4.1 | The Tunisian Urban System Before and After the French Protectorate | 123 |
| 4.2 | Evolution of the European Population Distribution in Major Tunisian Cities, 1936-1956 | 127 |
| 5.1 | Distribution of Industrial Investments by Region, 1962-1971 | 140 |
| 5.2 | Employment Distribution in the Industrial Sector by Region, 1972 | 141 |
| 5.3 | Growth of the "Coopératives de Production" | 145 |
| 5.4 | Net Migration by Region, 1970-1975 | 151 |
| 5.5 | Population Change of Some Cities and Towns in the Interior, 1956-1975 | 153 |
| 5.6 | Importance of the Employment in the Tertiary Sector in Five Cities in the Interior in 1966 | 154 |
| 5.7 | Regional Distribution of Investments, Projects and Job Creation Under the Law 72-38 of 1972, 1973-76 | 157 |
| 5.8 | Regional Distribution of Investments, Projects and Job Creation Under the Law 74-74 of 1974, 1973-76 | 158 |
| 5.9 | Regional Distribution of Industrial Investments Between 1962-71 and 1973-76 | 160 |
| 5.10 | Growth of Industrial Employment by Region, 1972-1980 | 161 |
| 5.11 | Net Migration by Region, 1970-1980 | 167 |


## FIGURES


| | | |
|---|---|---|
| 3.1 | Local Political/Administrative Structure | 73 |
| 3.2 | Economic Regions | 79 |
| 3.3 | Employment in Industry by Region, 1980 | 84 |

3.4 Employment in Tourism and Touristic Capacity by Region, 1980 86

3.5 Gouvernorat Capitals 96

4.1 The Urbanization of Tunisia during the Roman Period 106

4.2 Tunisian Circulation System in the XIth Century 107

4.3 The Railway Network in 1920 120

4.4 The Road Network in 1930 121

4.5 Tunisian Circulation System in 1880 124

4.6 Tunisian Circulation System in 1956 125

5.1 Growth Poles Location during the 1960s 138

5.2 The Structural Organization of the PDR 163

6.1 Central Tunisia 180

# FOREWORD

Achieving some degree of equity in economic growth and social progress among territorial regions has been a goal of governments in less developed countries since the late 1950s. Many governments have divided their nations into territorial administrative regions in order to focus development activities on the diverse needs of people living in different parts of the country. Many have created regional planning or development agencies to carry out development plans. But few governments in the developing world have succeeded in reducing the disparities among regions or in stimulating development in economically lagging areas.

The infrequency of their success, however, has neither discouraged Third World governments from pursuing regional development nor undermined the rationale for regional planning. Indeed, regional planning and development remain an integral part of development strategies in nearly all Third World countries. The reasons are not difficult to discern. Subnational regions can provide convenient units of analysis for disaggregating national development goals and objectives, and for devising policies and programs that can attain more balanced and widespread economic growth. Regional planning can help national and local government agencies to tailor their development policies to the diverse needs of people living in different parts of a country. Regional planning can also provide greater opportunities for local groups who will be affected by development programs to participate in their identification, design, and implementation.

Regional planning also allows governments to test innovative economic and social programs that are appropriate for one area without having to justify them for the whole country. Regions provide convenient geographical units for coordinating the investments of a variety of central ministries in the services, facilities and infrastructure needed to stimulate economic development and meet basic human needs. Finally, regional planning can guide the spatial allocation and location of development investments that influence population distribution and the pattern of human settlement.

Given these advantages of regional planning, why have so few governments in developing countries been successful in implementing their development plans? Why have so few sustainable benefits accrued to people living in economically lagging regions?

Ezzeddine Moudoud's analysis of regional policy in Tunisia begins to answer these questions. His book provides an historical context for understanding why regional disparities emerged in Tunisia and why reducing those disparities has been so difficult. Moudoud shows that the disparities between the littoral and the interior regions of Tunisia cannot be attributed to natural or accidental causes. They were the result of deliberate policies during the colonial period that favored the littoral zones and that drained resources from the interior. Post-colonial economic policies in Tunisia reinforced the pattern of development that enriched the ruling elite and its political supporters and that consolidated the power of the State.

Regional development does not occur simply because governments make plans for their growth. Development requires the investment of economic resources in productive activities, the enhancement of human resources, the creation of incentives that motivate people to work toward development goals, and the empowerment of local communities to identify their objectives and mobilize resources for their attainment. Resources must be invested in specific communities with growth potential, guided by a spatial strategy that takes into consideration the distribution of population and the comparative advantages of settlements. In countries where policies have favored the development of some regions over others, development in the lagging regions usually depends on State policies that ensure some degree of redistribution.

Moudoud implies that the failure of regional development in Tunisia does not lie in the concept of regional planning. His analysis concludes quite clearly that although the central government made regional plans, regional development was never seriously tried in Tunisia. The actions needed to bring about a more equitable pattern of economic development never received serious political support. In what Moudoud calls the "Jacobin" tradition, the central government attempted to impose technocratic solutions from above. It had no spatial strategy for developing the interior. It had little interest in reforms needed to redistribute economic resources between the littoral and interior areas. Most important, the government failed to enact or implement policies that would redistribute political power between the State and the regions.

In this study of Tunisia's experience with regional planning, Moudoud sheds light on the dilemma inherent in the "regional question" in many other Third World countries. Underlying the inefficacy of regional planning is the lack of political commitment to reallocating economic resources and political power in ways that will enable local communities to fashion their own economic and social destinies.

These tensions between the State and the regions are ironic: history suggests that few political regimes have sustained their power under conditions of severe economic disparity, yet few regimes are willing to redistribute the economic and political resources needed to promote widespread economic growth and social progress. It is this dilemma that Moudoud explores in his study of Tunisia. It is this dilemma that must be resolved before the efficacy of regional planning and development can be tested fairly in the Third World.

Dennis A. Rondinelli, Senior Policy Analyst
Office for International Programs, Research Triangle Institute
Research Triangle Park, North Carolina

# ACKNOWLEDGMENTS

The undertaking of this book would not have been possible without the support of many institutions and individuals.

First and foremost I would like to thank the Ford Foundation, the International Development Research Center of Canada and the Population Council for providing me with a generous research award (Middle East Research Award). I wish to express here all my gratitude to Dr. Frederic C. Shorter, Dr. Huda Zurayk (respectively former and current director of the Population Council's Cairo Office), and to Ms. Beth Orson, Fellowship Secretary (Population Council, New York) for all their support and encouragements during the research as well as during its preparation for publication.

I also wish to thank Syracuse University and the Tunisian Scientific Mission at Washington for their contribution.

The generous help and faith of my family and several friends in Canada, France, and the United States are also most gratefully acknowledged. In Tunisia, I owe much debt to all those who granted me interviews and shared much of their time and insight with me. Their contribution is also most gratefully acknowledged.

In addition to the above, several special acknowledgments must be made. First and foremost, I wish to express my heartfelt gratitude to John Agnew, John Nellis and Dennis Rondinelli, whom as colleagues and friends have been from the inception of this project and throughout my research at Syracuse of a great support and a constant source of inspiration.

Several other people have played a similar vital role in the shaping and evolution of my ideas through the last decade or so. I wish to thank all my colleagues and friends of the Institute of Urbanism of the University of Paris VIII. I owe a special debt to Annick Osmont, Michel Coquery, Anatole Kopp, Khelifa Messamah, François Ascher, Stephane Yerasimos, Charles Goldblum and Yves Lacoste (Geography). I also wish in this regard to express all my gratitude to Paul Claval, Pierre Flatres (Institute of Geography, University of Paris IV); to Jean-François Gravier (Centre National des Arts et Métiers); to Clyde Weaver (Urban and Regional Planning, University of Pittsburgh) and to my good friend Rolf Wesche (Geography, University of Ottawa, Canada) for all their encouragements at different stages of the project. Special thanks are also due to Minion K.C. Morrison (Chair, Department of Afro-American Studies), Louis Kreisberg (Sociology) and Jim Duncan (Geography) of Syracuse University for their helpful comments and suggestions on an early draft of the study.

My final debt is to Jerry Peek, whom with care and patience has skillfully transformed it into its present format. Special thanks are also due in this regard to the editors at Westview for their support and advice. In particular, I wish to thank Dean Birkenkamp, Amos Zubrow and Peter W. Kracht. My sincere gratitude to Kristina Ferris, Marcia Harrington and Todd Logen for the map preparation.

Last but not least, I owe most to my wife, Chantal, for her constant support and for surrounding me with the emotional support I needed throughout the whole project.

Ezzeddine Moudoud
Syracuse, New York.

# PART ONE
# DEVELOPMENT, UNDERDEVELOPMENT AND THE TRANSITION'S DILEMMAS

Chaque société, chaque civilisation doit trouver en elle-même sa voie; chercher dans ses traditions, dans ses valeurs propres, dans ses expériences politiques concrètes d'avant la colonisation, ce qui peut revivre aujourd'hui et constituer le noyau à partir duquel peut s'élaborer un système cohérant, socio-politique, économique, culturel, spirituel...un système enraciné dans la vie même de cette société, dans ses réalités, et qui soit ressenti sien.

Ahmed Baba Miské
*Lettre Ouverte aux Elites du Tiers-Monde*
(Ed. Le Sycomore, 1981, p. 87)

# 1
# INTRODUCTION

Among the many problems presently facing Third World countries, regional disparities and rural poverty are perhaps the most important. Despite many programs, considerable investments and a large number of institutions and actors involved in regional development and planning, rural exodus, rapid urban growth, and inequalities between rural and urban zones continue to be sources of social, economic and political problems.

There are at least two reasons for this.[1] First, in many Third World countries during the last three decades, regional development policies have not received a sufficiently high priority in their strategies of development. The spatial dimensions of development have been neglected.[2] Strategies were based on theories of development in which "urban bias?"was deeply rooted.[3] The point is that mainstream "modernization" development theories were deficient; they did not adequately recognize or emphasize regional development issues.

A second important reason for the persistence and, indeed, the aggravation of regional disparities and rural poverty is that even when some explicit concern with regional problems existed, the resulting policies were based on unsound theories of regional development and planning, which have in most cases failed in Western countries,[4] and where, again "urban bias" was deeply rooted.[5] Among the spatial models developed in Europe and in North America in the early 1950s, the "growth pole theory," the most popular, was given a major role by Third World regional planners.[6] During the late seventies, with the disenchantment with modernization theories in general and with growth pole theory in regional development and planning in particular, there emerged, with growing evidence, the need for new approaches and alternatives for promoting economic development and spatial equity.

Recently, new theories of regional development and planning have replaced the more conventional growth pole theory and have challenged the older center-down paradigm of modernization theories. But despite these changes in regional development theories over the last decade or so, there is a pressing need for more work to offer concrete solutions to regional problems in Third World countries, because, despite this theoretical progress, government policies continue generally to be based on older theories and the conventional center-down paradigm. Government bureaucrats still find it difficult to accept "basic needs," "agropolitan development," and decentralized spatial policies that advocate economic integration from "below" rather than from "above." For many practitioners, these new theories advocating rural and regional development from "below" are not development, but rather, a new and unacceptable form of *utopianism.*[7]

## REGIONAL DISPARITY AND THE PROBLEM IN TUNISIA

### Introduction

By conventional measures Tunisia has been particularly successful among Third World countries in stimulating economic growth. Per capita GNP has passed US$1,400 in 1981, with an average growth rate of close to 5 percent per annum between 1960 and 1980.[8] Social and regional disparities, however, remain crucial. The Tunisian spatial system reflects a traditional "center-periphery" model. Historically this system is an artifact of French colonialism, and it has been only marginally altered since independence in 1956.[9] A geographical axis divides the country from the south to the north, separating the richer regions of the coastal littoral from the poor regions of the west in the interior. The failure of past regional policies to restructure the Tunisian spatial system, to reduce urban-rural disparities and regional disparities in general, a failure that reflects in fact the limits and the impasse of past and present Tunisian development strategies, places Tunisian leaders today in a dilemma.[10]

For, the persistence and even the aggravation of regional disparities as are seen among the most important problems facing the country and are considered today as a serious threat to its stability and unity. Some recent political events, such as the "Gafsa Affair"in 1980 or more recently, the "Bread Revolt" from December 1983 to January 1984 (a revolt that began, interestingly, in the poor regions of the south and the west and then spread to the coastal regions) have clearly shown the gravity of this threat.[11] Aware of this danger, Tunisian leaders appear to have, since the "Gafsa Affair" a new commitment to reduce and eliminate regional disparities.

A key document of the Ministry of Plan and Finance published in November 1980, almost one year after the "Gafsa Affair," stated that one of the most important priorities of the Sixth Five Year Plan (1982-86) and the Third Decade of Development is *social justice* between *classes* and *regions*, in order "to assure social peace and consolidate *National Unity*."[12]

President Habib Bourguiba himself, in a speech at the end of the National Consultation period before the final adoption of the Sixth Five Year Plan (1982-86), indicated that regional development is now a "patriotic obligation."[13] The Sixth Five Year Plan itself states that the "development of the least favored regions and the quest for a better inter-regional equilibrium are among the most important priorities of the Sixth Plan and the next decades," in order, it was indicated, that "Tunisia—the land of moderation and balance, would be a structured, balanced country, a non-dual economy, a harmonious society, and a human civilization that avoids *violence.*"[14]

Another indication of this new commitment to regional problems and social justice is the creation in August 1981 of a new institution: "The Commissariat Général au Développement Régional," the main task of which is to improve and strengthen regional development and planning.[15]

## Regional Disparity and the Failure of Past Policies

Over the last three decades, Tunisian leaders have attempted to restructure the Tunisian spatial system inherited from the French protectorate in two different ways. In the early 1960s, the first stage of Tunisia's approach to reduce regional disparities was based, first, on the then conventional growth pole theory. Several industrial units were created in the lagging regions of the country. These industrial units were meant to constitute "real growth poles capable of radiating over the whole regions where they are located and to induce the development, of several related activities."[16] Second, in the rural areas, the approach was based, on the other hand, on the modernization of 'traditional' agriculture through a centralized and comprehensive rural cooperative program.[17] But, as many doubts were raised about the correctness of the growth pole approach,[18] and as the Tunisian development strategy itself shifted in 1969 from direct State control and centralized economic planning towards a market-oriented economy, the Tunisian regional development approach entered a new era. In the early 1970s the growth pole approach and the cooperative program were abandoned. A new approach was based first, on a policy of subsidies—industrial decentralization legislation—to marginal activities in marginal regions and, second, on a less centralized rural development program.[19] But soon many doubts were raised about this second approach as well.[20] In an official report published in 1979 by the "Direction de l'Aménagement du Territoire," Tunisian planners have admitted that

> The industrialization of the country has first of all benefitted the region of Tunis, second, the other coastal regions; and the development and modernization of agriculture have only slowed the rhythm of the widening of the gap between the interior regions and the coastal regions, but did not, however, succeed in reversing the tendency towards the aggravation of the disequilibrium. ...In other words, if the jobs creation continues to be regionally localized as in the past, we will reach very rapidly a situation that could be characterized as explosive.[21]

A year later, in 1980, a study of the World Bank states that despite its good economic performance, the country remains characterized by "great regional disparities in general and substantial urban-rural differences in income level in particular."[22] More recently the Sixth Five Year Plan (1982-86) notes that despite all the actions undertaken and the investments made during the last two decades,

> Whatever the indicator one can choose (per capita private consumption, the proportion of poor families, the unemployment rate, water or electricity consumption, the illiteracy rate, health facilities per capita, km of road/km$^2$...) one can observe that the Western and the Southern regions of the country are behind the coastal regions and below the national average.[23]

In brief, the least one can say is that, as of 1982, the impact of the past two policies on reducing the regional disparities inherited from French protectorate has not been impressive at all.

Regional Disparity and the Objectives of the Study

Considering the persistence of regional disparities and the growing evidence that past Tunisian regional development policies have failed, this study has two specific objectives. The first is to answer the following questions: why didn't the overall good economic performance of Tunisia during the last three decades benefit all regions of the country? Why have past regional policies in Tunisia, whether they were centralized or liberal (based on economic laisser-faire), failed? Based on the answers to these questions, the second objective of the study is to draw some conclusions from the Tunisian case and to provide a new framework for rethinking what is called in the literature, the "Regional Question" in Tunisia and hopefully elsewhere.

## METHODOLOGY

The first premise of this work is that regional underdevelopment has nothing to do with "mother nature," but can be *historically* explained.[24] In other words and contrary to the basic tenets of modernization theories, that regional underdevelopment is not the result of the lack of resources or whatever "attributes of development" in the underdeveloped regions themselves but is fundamentally the product of historical development resulting from certain policies which create and perpetuate it.[25]

The second premise of this work is that all societies have their own productive systems and related spatial organizations that have to be analyzed, understood and planned for in terms of their proper structural logic and "rationality."[26] Dualistic models such as "traditional vs. modern" or concepts such as the "Asiatic mode of production," "oriental despotism" and the like only confuse the situation.[27]

The third and final premise of this research is that the major causes of the perpetuation of regional underdevelopment today in most Third World—at least in Tunisia—are not the lack of natural or human resources. They are rather the continued polarization of political power by hegemonic political elites and bureaucracies organized on regional bases. In other words and as far more than a mere "economic" problem, regional underdevelopment can be politically explained.[28]

Based on the three premises stated above and within the framework of the problem and objectives of the study, the book is comprised of three parts. Part One provides a general discussion of the evolution of ideas and theories about development and the question of "transition" at the national and the subnational levels. Because of their dominant role during the last thirty years or so, modernization theories are the focus of Chapter 2. The objective here is to see how and why these theories have come, during the last decade or so, under constant criticism from a conceptual as well as from an ideological point of view. This criticism has led, in many parts of the world, to the reevaluation of the "question of transition" at the national as well as at the sub-national levels.

The Chapter is divided into three sections. The first will focus on the issue of "transition" at the national level. Then, and because of its use as the basis for regional development policies for so many years and in so many countries, the growth pole approach is the focus of the second section. Here, too, the objective is to look at the major and now well-known problems with the application of the approach.

Finally, and as this study is mainly concerned with Regional Disparity, a brief survey of major new theories of regional development for Third World countries that have emerged during the late 1970s in response to the failure of the growth pole approach and to that of modernization theories in general, will be presented.

Part Two will discuss the "question of transition" in Tunisia. Chapter 3 presents an overview of Tunisian economic performance in terms of growth and development. Then, in a second part, it will provide a descriptive analysis of the nature and the magnitude of regional disparities.

In order to have a thorough understanding of these disparities, Chapter 4 analyzes their historical roots. The objective here is to re-place the "regional question" in its historical context. The analysis is focused, therefore, on the policies that have transformed the precolonial socioeconomic and spatial structures of the country during the colonial period and that have therefore "created" the disparities.

Chapter 5 will then document and analyze the policies that, during the post-colonial period, have attempted to reduce or to eliminate the inequalities. Because they have constituted the major components of these policies, special attention is given to the following areas: (1) the growth pole policy and the rural cooperative program, the two major components of regional policy until 1969; and (2) the industrial decentralization legislation policy and the "Programme de Développement Rural," the two major components of regional policy between 1969-81.

Finally, Part Three will conclude the study by first looking at the lessons that can be drawn from the Tunisian case. This is the objective of Chapter 6. Based on these conclusions the final chapter (Chapter 7) will then attempt to propose a new framework for "rethinking the regional question," in order to contribute to the progress of the debate—which seems locked in a dangerous impasse—on this very sensitive question.

## THE DATA USED

### Official Data

The use of official data included administrative documents such as development plans, area studies, sectoral studies, project evaluations and national censuses and surveys. These have been the major sources of information for Part Two, especially Chapters 3 and 5.

### Secondary Data

Secondary data have been used whenever necessary to supplement official data. For example, the analysis of the historical roots of regional disparities (Chapter 4) is based on the work of geographers, historians and urban planners. This type of data has also been used, and constitutes, in fact, the main source for all of Chapter 2. Statistical information, such as the World Bank development reports or country studies, has also been used to supplement official statistics and administrative documents.

### Other Sources of Information

The analysis of regional policies during the post-colonial period, did not focus only on how government policies have attempted to reduce the disparities, on how much money was invested and where, but also and especially on the political and institutional mechanisms of the conception and implementation of the policies. In other words on who decides and conceives the policies and on who implements them. An attempt was made to obtain this kind of information through several interviews with various Tunisian planners and officials at the national as well as at the regional levels.

### The Problem of the Data

Three major problems have been encountered in using some of the above data. As in other parts of the world, the reliability of official data has been the major problem of the study (see Chapter 3). Official statistics exist but are not reliable or are kept secret. The second type of problem is due mainly to the nature of planning in Tunisia. Very centralized and concerned until recently, with only the national level, it did not need statistical information for a wide range of subnational territorial units. And even when there is some statistical information on the subnational territorial units, it does not cover a long period of time, so a series of comparative statistics for different territorial units is nonexistent. The third major problem is the constant changes over the last 15 to 20 years of the administrative limits themselves. So, even when the data exist, this makes it difficult to have reliable comparison over a long period of time. All of these factors have rendered a precise analysis of interregional disparities over time out of the question. However, and due to the whole range of available data in recent years, it is possible to measure their evolution in the last ten years or so. Also, I must add here that the major concern of the study is to look at the profound and lasting changes that affected the country, with regard to regional disparity, over a very long period of time: since 1881, year of the official colonization of Tunisia by France. Moreover, and although of a far less historical significance than 1881, 1982 is, however, of some importance. First, it marked the launching of the Sixth Tunisian Five Year Plan (1982-1986) the end of what was called the "Nouira Period" (1970-1980) and the beginning of the "Mzali Period." Secondly, by 1982, Tunisia has had five consecutive national development plans since independence in 1956, the implementation of which covered a period close to a quarter of a century in the post-colonial era.

In brief, and whatever limitations the data has, in view of the objectives of the study and analytical perspective used here, we have a time span that allows us to analyse those historical-structural changes, our main concern here, with a very "reasonable" data basis.

## NOTES

1. On the general problem see: D.A. Rondinelli and K. Ruddle, *Urbanization and Rural Development: A Spatial Policy for Equitable Growth* (New York: Praeger, 1978); W.B. Stöhr and D.R.F. Taylor, eds., *Development from Above or Below? The Dialectics of Regional Planning in Developing Countries* (New York: Wiley, 1981).

2. E. Brutzkus, "Centralized Versus Decentralized Pattern of Urbanization in Developing Countries: An Attempt to Elucidate a Guideline Principle," *Economic Development and Cultural Change* 23, no. 4 (July 1975): 633-52.

3. M. Lipton, *Why Poor People Stay Poor: Urban Bias in World Development* (Cambridge, MA: Harvard University Press, 1977).

4. For discussion of this issue, see: W.B. Stöhr and F. Todtling, "An Evaluation of Regional Policies: Experiences in Market and Mixed Economies," in *Human Settlement Systems*, ed. N. Hansen (New York: Ballinger, 1977), pp. 85-119; J. Friedmann and C. Weaver, *Territory and Function: The Evolution of Regional Planning* (Berkeley and Los Angeles: University of California Press, 1979).

5. See J. Friedmann, *Urban Bias in Regional Development Policy*, C.U. 29, School of Architecture and Urban Planning, UCLA, Los Angeles, 1981.

6. A. Mehretu and D.J. Campbell, "Regional Planning for Small Communities in Rural Africa: A Critical Survey," *Rural Africana*, nos. 12-13 (Winter-Spring 1981-82), pp. 91-110.

7. C. Weaver, "Legitimizing Use-Value Production in a Mixed Economy," (U.B.C. Planning Papers, D.P. #1, School of Community and Regional Planning, University of British Columbia, Vancouver, May 1982).

8. World Bank, *Report on World Development 1983* (Washington, DC: World Bank, 1983); see also J.R. Nellis, "A Comparative Assessment of the Development Performances of Algeria and Tunisia," *The Middle East Journal*, no. 3 (Summer 1983): 370-93.

9. See E. Moudoud, "L'Urbanisation et la Politique du Logement Social en Tunisie," (MA diss., Institut d'Urbanisme de l'Académie de Paris, Université de Paris VIII, Mai 1980); and E. Moudoud, "La Politique du Logement Social en Tunisie," *Revue Algerienne des Sciences Sociales*, nos. 4-5 (October-November 1980), pp. 169-98.

10. For discussion of this issue, see Ch. Bernard, ed., *La Politique de l'Emploi-Formation au Maghreb 1970-1980* (Paris: Centre National de la Recherche Scientifique, 1982).

11. For the analysis of the causes and the consequences of these events, see: K. Chamari, "L'Alerte Tunisienne," *Le Monde Diplomatique*, no. 312 (Mars 1980); P.R. Baduel, "Gafsa Comme Enjeu," *Annuaire de l'Afrique du Nord* 19 (1980): 485-511; J.R. Nellis, *Decentralization, Regional Development and Local Public Finance in Tunisia*, Occasional Paper, no. 79, Metropolitan Studies Program, the Maxwell School, Syracuse University, March 1984.

12. Republic of Tunisia, Ministry of Plan and Finance, *Note d'Orientation sur la IIIème Decennie de Développement et le VIème Plan* (Tunis, 1980), p. 2 (Emphasis mine).

13. Republic of Tunisia, Ministry of Plan and Finance, *Sixth Five Year Plan 1982-1986* (Tunis, 1982), p. 183.

14. Ibid., pp. 183, 206 (emphasis mine).

15. Ibid., p. 187.

16. Ibid., p. 183.

17. See E. Moudoud, *Modernisation, Centralisation and Destruction de l'Economie Rurale: L'Expérience des Cooperatives Agricoles en Tunisie 1962-1969*, U.B.C. Planning Papers, CS #2, School of Community and Regional Planning, University of British Columbia, May 1983.

18. Ph. Aydalot, "La Structuration de l'Espace Economique Tunisien," *Revue Tunisienne des Sciences Sociales*, no. 5 (1966), pp. 65-93; H. Attia, "L'Evolution des Structures Sociales et Economiques dans les Hautes Steppes Tunisiennes," *Revue Tunisienne des Sciences Sociales*, no. 6 (1966), pp. 5-41; J. Poncet, "La Régionalisation en Tunisie," *Tiers-Monde*, no. 55 (1972), pp. 597-614.

19. For discussion of this political shift, see: J.R. Nellis, "Decentralization in North Africa: Problems of Policy Implementation," in *Decentralization and Development: Policy Implementation in Developing Countries*, eds. G.S. Cheema and D.A. Rondinelli (Beverly Hills: Sage, 1983), pp. 127-82; and D.A. Rondinelli, J.R. Nellis, and G.S. Cheema, *Decentralization in Developing Countries. A Review of Recent Experiences*, World Bank Working Papers, no. 581 (Washington, DC: World Bank, 1983), pp. 92-93.

20. See for example: J. Poncet, *La Tunisie à la Recherche de son Avenir* (Paris: Les Editions Sociales, 1974); H. Sethom, "Les Tentatives de Remodelage de l'Espace Tunisien depuis l'Indépendance," *Méditerranée*, nos. 1-2 (1979), pp. 119-25; P. Signoles, "Les Deséquilibres Urbains en Tunisie," *Aujourd'hui l'Afrique*, no. 20 (1980), pp. 21-30; A. Belhadi, "Le Programme de Développement Rural: Les Illusions et la Realité," *Revue Tunisienne de Geographie*, no. 7 (1981), pp. 9-45; D. Kamelgarn, "Tunisie (1970-1977), le Développement d'un Capitalisme Dependant," *Peuples Méditerranéens*, no. 4 (1978), pp. 113-45.

21. Report published by the "Comite de Reflexion sur l'Amenagement du Territoire et de la Decentralisation Industrielle," (Tunis: Direction de l'Amenagement du Territorire, 1979), pp. 17-19 (translation mine.)

22. World Bank, *Tunisia: Social Aspects of Development* (Washington, DC: World Bank, 1980), p. viii.

23. RT, MPF, *Sixth Five Year Plan*, p. 185.

24. See J. Bugnicourt, *Disparites Regionales et Amenagement du Territoire en Afrique* (Paris: Armand Colin, 1974); R. Matthews, *The Creation of Regional Dependency* (Toronto: University Press of Toronto, 1983).

25. For discussion of this issue, see: T.G. McGee, *The Urbanization Process in the Third World* (London: Bell and Sons, 1971); M. Santos, *Les Villes du Tiers-Monde* (Paris: M.Th. Ghenin, 1971); A. Gilbert, ed., *Development Planning and Spatial Structure* (London and New York: Wiley, 1976), pp. 1-19; Rondinelli and Ruddle, op. cit.; B. Granotier, *La Planete des Bidonvilles: Perspectives de l'Explosion Urbaine dan les Pays du Tiers-Monde* (Paris: Le Seuil, 1980); R. Matthews, op. cit.;

26. C. Weaver, op. cit., and for a thorough analysis see, C. Weaver, J. Jessop, and V. Das, "Rationality in the Public Interest: Notes Toward a New Synthesis," in *Rationality in Planning: Critical Essays on the Role of Rationality in Urban and Regional Planning*, eds. M.J. Breheney and A.J. Hooper (London: Pion, 1983); K. Zamiti, "Les Freins Ideologiques au Developpement," *Cahiers Internationaux de Sociologie*, 41 (Juillet-Decembre 1966), pp. 105-15.

27. See on this issue: S. Avineri, *Karl Marx on Colonialism and Modernization* (New York: Anchor Books, 1969); I. Sachs, *The Discovery of the Third World* (Cambridge: MIT Press, 1976); J. Suret-Canale, "Les Societes Traditionelles en Afrique et le Concept du Mode de Production Asiatique," *La Pensee*, no. 117 (1964), pp. 21-47.

28. For further discussion of this so vital and controversial issue, see for example: T. Michalon, *Quel Etat pour l'Afrique?* (Paris: Les Editions L'Harmaton, 1984); J.R. Nellis, "Decentralization in North Africa: Problems of Policy Implementation," in *Decentralization and Development: Policy Implementation in Developing Countries*, edited by G.S. Sheema and D.A. Rondinelli (Beverly Hills, CA: Sage, 1983); E. Moudoud, "L'Impossible Regionalization 'Jacobine' et le Dilemme des Disparites Regionales en Tunisie," *Canadian Journal of Regional Science*, no. 3 (1985), pp. 413-38; see also: M. Paillet, B. Maximim, and S. Schaudel, *Etudes sur le Developpement Regional en Cote-d'Ivoire* (Bordeaux: Centre d'Etude d'Afrique Noire, Universite de Bordeaux, 1976); World Bank, *Amenagement du Territoire et Developpement Regional: Quelle Approche pour les Pays en Developpement* (Washington, DC: World Bank, 1982).

For discussion concerning developed countries such as France for example, see: J.F. Gravier, *Paris et le Desert Francais* (Paris: Flammarion, 1947 and 1972); idem, *La Question Regionale* (Paris: Flammarion, 1972); R. Laffont, *Decoloniser en France* (Paris: Gallimard, 1971); J. Hayward, "Incorporer la Peripherie: L'Essor et la Chute de la Regionalisation Fonctionelle en France," *Pouvoirs*, no. 19 (1981), pp. 103-18; J.C. Perrin, *Le Developpement Regional*, Chapter 3, "L'Incidence de la Centralisation et de la Decentralisation Institutionelles sur le Developpement Regional," pp. 174-202 (Paris: Presses Universitaires de France, 1974).

# 2
# MODERNIZATION, DEVELOPMENT THEORY AND THE QUESTION OF "TRANSITION"

## INTRODUCTION

Debates on development strategies have been going on for at least 30 years, involving scholars, development experts and policy makers.[1] Not that scholars and experts have never debated these issues before; they have, at least since the industrial revolution in England.[2] But the debates have become more violent and more acrimonious since what Ignacy Sachs has called the "discovery of the Third World" by Western scholars and experts.[3] After the Second World War and the disintegration of the colonial system these debates have generated questions about how Third World countries can cope with their economic problems and about how the developed countries can "help" them in this task. As a result of these debates, a deluge of research, publications, and conferences at the international and regional levels has followed.[4] This deluge indicates obviously that these debates are not nearly finished; on the contrary, they are more and more controversial.[5] To illustrate this, I would like to present in the first part of this chapter a discussion of two major plans for African development in terms of the "theories" of development upon which they are based.

The first plan was adopted by the Organization of African Unity (OAU) in April 1980: the "Lagos Plan of Action for the Economic Development of Africa 1980-2000." The Lagos Plan was presented to the United Nations General Assembly at its eleventh special session in September 1980 and is now an integrated part of the "International Development Strategy for the Third World Nations Development Decade." The second plan was formulated by the World Bank, requested by its African governors, entitled: *Accelerated Development in Sub-Saharan Africa: An Agenda for Action.*[6] It is not my intention to make an in-depth comparison of the two documents.[7] The concern here is simply to point out the main characteristics of the theories underlying the two documents, which since their publication have generated much debate and many polemics on the one hand between African governments and the World Bank and on the other between scholars and experts.[8]

It is hoped that this very brief comparison will enable us to see how and why "theories" of development were discredited and how, therefore, the question of the transition at the national level was reopened in the late 1970s, early 1980s.

Then, and in the second and final section, the discussion will move on to look at the debates (and polemics) about the transition at the subnational level. Adopting the same epistemological method, the objective here is to examine how traditional spatial, top-down strategies have come under severe criticism and how as a result of this a major paradigm shift occurred in this area in the late 1970s.

Thus, it is hoped that the chapter will provide us with the theoretical discussion necessary to understand the central issues underlying the whole problematic of the book and will help us therefore to avoid the pitfall of analyzing our "case study" in a vacuum.

## THEORIES OF DEVELOPMENT

There are a number of different schools of thought concerning economic development in Third World countries—ranging from the conventional school, which advocates the importation by Third World countries of a private market economy, to the socialist school, which advocates a planned economy. Needless to say there are numerous variations of these two pure schools, and the debate within and between the schools has been rich in verbosity and polemics.[9] During the last 15 years a number of new schools of thought have emerged and challenged the orthodoxies. John Agnew has identified three major groups of theories of development:[10]

| | |
|---|---|
| 1. Modernization Theories | Stages of Growth<br>Dual Economy<br>Modernity<br>Institutional Reform<br>"Classic" Marxist |
| 2. World Political Economy Theories | Leninist<br>Development of Underdevelopment<br>World Systems<br>Multinational Corporation |
| 3. Ecopolitical Economy Theories | |

The most well known and the most tenacious, despite all the devastating criticism of their "theoretical adequacy" and "ideological-racist assumptions," are the modernization theories.[11] Their main concern is the problem of changing "traditional" societies (Third World countries) into "modern" societies in cultural, economic and political terms; in other words, how to "replicate the transition."[12] "They focus on national societies as the basic units of analysis and define development in terms of economic growth and "Westernization replicating the historical experience of Western societies."[13] The second group, world political economy theories, is concerned mainly with the "structure of economic and political relationships between 'dominant' and 'dominated' societies in the context of the global history of economic growth and political control."[14] The third group, ecopolitical economy theories, is the most recent one. It emerged during the late 1960s and expanded in the early 1970s with the work of people such as Schumacker, Seers, Sachs and his school in Paris, and Illich.[15] The central idea of this ecological-anthropological perspective is what Seers has called the "new meaning of development."[16] In other words, it is an approach that "involves a critical perspective on the purported benefits of development as usually defined and emphasizes the ecological and social/cultural disruption consequent to economic growth."[17]

## MODERNIZATION AND THE TRANSITION AT THE NATIONAL LEVEL: MODERNIZATION THEORIES

As we have seen, Agnew has suggested five different subgroups within the "modernization" theories group. In this section, I adopt an historical approach that is based on the distinction between what is called the "Marxist-Stalinist" school and the "bourgeois" school of modernization (which includes the dual economy, modernity, institutional reform, and stages of growth theories).[18] The main objectives are to present the general characteristics of the two schools, to analyze their ideological assumptions, and to show the extraordinary similarity in this respect between them.

### The Classic Marxist-Stalinist Version

Historically, although the orthodox Marxist version of modernization "is usually not characterized as such perhaps because of the company it is then forced to keep!"[19], one often-cited statement of Marx remains the central thesis of modernization theories: "The country that is more developed industrially only shows to the less developed the image of its future."[20]

Needless to say, this statement and many others in the writings of Marx and Engels on "colonialism and modernization"[21] have generated much debate: between anarchists in general, "Proudhoniens" in particular, and Marxists;[22] and among Marxists themselves—the orthodox and the neo-Marxists, most of whom represent the "voice from the periphery."[23] Even today despite some revaluation of the "Asiatic mode of production" during the sixties by, for example, orthodox French Marxists of the Stalinist

French Communist Party,[24] the debate is still very acrimonious between those who still believe in the "unilinearity of history" and even that imperialism is the "pioneer of capitalism,"[25] and those who accuse them of a "return to bourgeois ideology."[26]

The central idea behind Marx's statement and in his other few writings on non-European societies is that all these "barbarian," stagnant and static "nations of peasants" do not possess their own internal mechanisms of social change.[27] Since history involves the process of changing the environment by humans, where there is no change, there is no history, and humans remain pure natural beings. These "nations of peasants" therefore have no history at all, and the dialectics of historical development are not operative in them; therefore any change has to come from outside.[28] Why does Marx deny any history to these societies and go so far as to justify, as we will see, the "*mission civilisatrice*" of colonization? Avineri suggests one of the most interesting explanations for this:

> Since Oriental society does not develop internally, it cannot evolve toward capitalism through the dialectics of internal change; and since Marx postulates the ultimate victory of socialism on the prior universalization of capitalism, he necessarily arrives at the position of having to endorse European colonial expansion as a brutal but necessary step toward the victory of socialism. Just as the horrors of industrialization are dialectically necessary for the triumph of communism, so the horrors of colonialism are dialectically necessary for the World revolution of the proletariat since without them the countries of Asia (and presumably also Africa) will not be able to emancipate themselves from their stagnant backwardness.[29]

For the final victory of socialism therefore, the "impetus for change has to come from outside," even through colonialism. European bourgeois civilization is thus the external agent of change in non-European societies. Furthermore, the "more direct the European control of any backward society, the greater the chances for the overhauling of its structure and its ultimate incorporation into bourgeois, and hence into Socialist, society."[30] Marx's justification of colonialism, as Engels' too,[31] despite his moral indignation at its horrors, is a consequence of the Eurocentrism of his philosophy of history. He proposes, first, to have "a philosophy of history universal in its applicability," that is to say the sequences of historical changes in terms of the mode of production he found in European, especially English, history and on which he has built his theory of change must be universal. He also proposes that the capitalist mode of production is a necessary step to the socialist one, which will then spread throughout the world. The "unchanging nature of non-European society is thus a drag on the progress of history—and a serious threat to socialism."[32] Here are the reasons, then, why Marx denies any history to non-European societies: they represent the tangible proof of the nonuniversitality of, first, his conception of history, and second, his model of "socialism."

> Since Marx's socialism is a dialectical outcome of the *Aufhenbung*, transcendence, of European bourgeois civilization, he sees little reason to look for autochthonous roots for socialism in non-European society. "Chinese Communism" or "African Socialism" have no place in the universalistic scheme of Marx's socialist theory and make little sense within his philosophy of history.[33]

Far from using "village communism" as a paradigm for future communist society, Marx did the contrary. Instead of asking himself "is it absolutely necessary to go through the stage of capitalist development? Is it possible to profit from the survival of village communities?"[34], questions which might have led him to reconsider the universality of his theory, Marx looks down on this "village communism" and qualifies it as an "Oriental Despotism." For scientific purposes, Marx was forced, in order to keep his model intact, to justify the ultimate necessity for colonialism. Marx was not a colonialist or especially a racist. Even Avineri does not accuse him of this.[35] Marx's problem was that in his confrontation with non-European societies, with which he was not at all familiar,[36] his model was seriously challenged by autochthonous socialism, which suggests very clearly after all, that the capitalist stage is not everywhere a requisite step in the process of transition toward socialism and that "socialism" could be different from place to place. Instead of analyzing this possibility Marx was not only forced to deny any history to these societies, but went further and justifies colonialism as being "good" for them.

It is this dogmatic grip that paralyzed Marx and especially the Stalinists and that constitutes the contradiction of classic Marxism in regard to the problem of the transition from one mode of production to another. It argues that even in socialist countries, change came about as a result of influences from outside.[37] This was and still is the dilemma of orthodox Marxists who use the "mode of production" analysis as the fundamental base for their theory of social change. Even in Third World countries themselves, orthodox Marxists still believe in the "positive" role of national bourgeoisies in a supposed transition from feudalism to capitalism, and after, to socialism. And this is despite the reevaluation of the "Asiatic mode of production" that has given to Marxism "its flexibility, its ability to benefit from contact with reality. In particular, it has well and truly helped to demolish the concept of the unilinearity of history."[38]

This first contradiction of orthodox Marxism is deeply rooted in another more fundamental contradiction. To look at the possibility of other forms of transition from one mode of production to another is by implication to reopen the more fundamental issue of the possibility of many forms of socialism. This is an issue on which Marxists were always challenged by anarchists in general and by the "Proudhoniens" in particular.[39] For classic Marxists the key issue is the form of transition from one mode of production to another, or in other words, the path leading to socialism everywhere in the world. As this socialism has to be the same everywhere the nature of the transition therefore has to be the same everywhere. Here is the contradiction of dogmatic Marxism, which ironically makes this theory of social change absolutely similar to that of the "bourgeois" school. We have to keep in mind, however, the fundamental differences between the two schools. For Marxists the issue is the transition first toward capitalism and second to socialism. Using other categories, especially "traditional" and "modern," bourgeois theories are concerned with the form of the transition from a "non-modern/non-capitalist" stage to a "modern-western/capitalist" stage. There is no place here for socialism. Bourgeois theories, as we will see, were developed precisely to counter the attraction that Marxism has for Third World countries in spite of the adverse effects of its dogmatism.[40]

Bourgeois Modernization Theories

Nowhere do the bourgeois modernization theories find a clearer expression than in a report published by the United Nations Expert Group in 1951. This well-known report, entitled "Measure for the Economic Development of Underdeveloped Countries," represented

> ...the first comprehensive, non-technical account of the paradigm that would reign virtually unchallenged down to the end of the 1960s. Even today it is still widely used as a framework for discussion of development policy.[41]

The U.N. experts had been given the task of preparing a "success model" of development. The first thing to note is that this report established the now-common distinction between "developed" and "underdeveloped" countries. As Friedmann and Weaver have noted, this may be taken as an indicator of the experts' own alienation from their own national societies. Some of the experts who had been called on by the United Nations come from such Third World countries as Chile, India, Lebanon and Jamaica.[42] The U.N. experts identified the "success model" of economic development as the only way to go for the former colonies if they were to achieve the high standards of living of the Western World: they must reproduce the recent economic history of the already industrialized countries. Four basic conditions were identified:[43]

1. National economies must be open to international trade. In other words, they must supply developed countries with raw materials and

specialized foodstuffs, and accept foreign capital and technical assistance as a means for accelerating progress towards "modernization."

2. Modernization could only occur through a process of accelerated industrialization. Although agriculture had to be modernized in order to withdraw "excess labor" and to increase agricultural productivity, little hope was held out for activating agriculture as a leading sector. Industrialization has to be urban and the modernization of agriculture is the only way "to free" excess labor from rural areas to be employed in the cities.

3. A high rate of capital formation through both domestic savings and foreign exchange earnings for the importation of capital equipments and producer goods is necessary. A rate of saving of 12 percent was considered minimum. The State should encourage those with the highest propensity to save and invest. In other words, the "rational entrepreneurs."

4. Finally, a rational process for central resource allocation was regarded as an essential tool for successful economic development. National economic planning and preparation of formal planning documents were the preconditions of receiving foreign aid.

Each of these four conditions was seen as necessary for "development." The experts, in addition, state that

> ...rapid economic progress is impossible without painful readjustments. Ancient philosophies have to be scrapped; old social institutions have to disintegrate; bonds of caste, creed and race have to be burst; and large numbers of persons who cannot keep up with progress have to have their expectations of a comfortable life frustrated. Very few communities are willing to pay the full price of economic progress.[44]

All the other bourgeois modernization theories were based on the assumption of this necessary and universal economic culture: a "Schumpetarian" rhetoric based on three dichotomies: development-underdevelopment; agriculture-industry; tradition-modernity, all linked by the transition process of "modernization."[45] These other theories are described hereafter.

1. The Dual Economy Approach. One of the most widespread bourgeois views of underdevelopment is that of the dual economy.[46] This approach—whose main pioneer is perhaps W.A. Lewis,[47] one of the authors of the U.N. report mentioned above[48]—is based on the view that the major problem of Third World countries is the existence of two economic sectors. According to this theory these two sectors exist independently but side by side.[49] The major problem identified then is the lack of interaction between the two sectors. The whole idea is to build a model based on the conditions required to interrelate the two sectors and to cope with this dualistic situation, or what was elegantly called the "internal structural" problem of Third World economies. Many different approaches

and models were developed.[50] One assumption common to them, however, is that the conversion of the traditional sector—which was always identified as agriculture—is seen as the main avenue for the improvement of agricultural productivity,[51] which required two conditions. First, a transfer of labor (surplus) from the agricultural sector to the more productive industrial sector;[52] And, second, technological change, "a full rationalization" and decrease in rates of population growth are seen as the conditions which permit this process.[53]

This school has been severely criticized for its theoretical and ideological bias towards an idealized "Western" model of development. Sachs, for example, notes:

> Models of growth were altered to take into account the unlimited supply of unskilled labor. The pioneering writings of Lewis have had considerable repercussions in this area. The trouble is that they ignore the historical and institutional aspects of the establishment and functioning of dualist Third World economies and that they use a neo-classical apparatus which is ill-fitted to grasp the complexity of peasant economies in transition and of imperfect markets: is it possible to speak, in the Third World, of the homogeneity and the perfect mobility of labor, the substitutability of factors, and their value in terms of marginal and extramarginal productivity?[54]

He then makes a political point in his criticism of the dual economy theory.

> Originally, the dualist model had a colonialist aim; it was respectable to insist on the irrationality of economic behavior in the traditional sector, justifying the need for a trusteeship of the modern sector, established by the mother country....although its colonialist interpretation is discredited today, the idea of two sectors juxtaposed continues to be widely accepted, particularly in certain neo-classical models which present development as the progressive siphoning out of people from the traditional sector into the modern sector created by industrialization.[55]

But the most devastating criticism came from Amin and Frank.[56] It was argued that not only are the concepts used irrelevant (as noted by Sachs) but the dualistic approach assumes that the two sectors exist *side by side*, while in fact they are strongly related, and that strong relation is based on the exploitation of the traditional sector by the modern one. The dualist approach is not concerned with the nature or the characteristics of this exploitation. It is concerned with the "extinction" of the traditional sector. Unfortunately, many Third World economists and policy makers, especially during the sixties, were strong proponents of the dual economy approach, one of the most destructive theories of modernization.[57]

2. Modernity and Institutional Reform. These two theories of modernization are, as noted by Agnew, "largely the province of sociologists and political scientists who focus on ideological and institutional components of development."[58] The obstinate tendency of bourgeois economists to isolate the economic sphere, to construct models that completely exclude the institutional and social framework and to ignore noneconomic factors[59] was a lacuna that modernity and institutional reform theories were invented to correct. In this respect, the role of these theories is of capital importance to dual economy theories and in a sense "close the circle" of bourgeois modernization theories. Their contribution is perhaps by far the most important, in the sense that their main concern is to build the ideological framework within which nineteenth-century liberal theories could rediscover the historical and "scientific" foundations that Marxism had destroyed. The literature on these theories is vast. My concern here is to underline their basic assumptions, the link with the dual economy approach, and the ideological context within which they emerged in the early sixties.

The main concern of the two theories is change within the cultural and political spheres. Their common assumption is that these changes are important to economic development. Changes in attitudes, motivations, ideas, ways of life are the basic conditions for development: or, in other words, "westernization." These changes cannot occur without "social mobilization" and "cultural assimilation." The problem then is to build the institutional and political framework within which a leading group, an elite, acts as a force conducive to a gradual and continual process of social change.

Modernity theories see industrialization and urbanization as the interdependent variables upon which depend two other variables: the transformation of the "social structure" and the "culture" of the society.[60] A modern economy is seen as an industrial economy based upon a high degree of technology. This modern economy requires the creation of market structures that allow the unrestricted flow of the factors of production to industry: labor, capital, and technology. Urbanization in this scheme is then seen as the condition for the modernization of the economy. Migration to the cities is necessary to destroy peasant communities and free workers needed by the modern economy. Related to this urbanization process is the necessary destruction of old social structures. Modernity theories endorse at this point the assumptions of the dual economy theories and build in their own assumptions. This industrialization-urbanization tandem requires new behaviors, new perceptions and values, i.e., the "modernization of man."[61] A new type of person is required: one who is motivated and has the skills to operate efficiently and effectively in a factory.[62] Here again we are in the domain of the "Schumpetarian" and the "Protestant Spirit" rhetoric, on which is based the concept of "n-achievement," which is reduced by its own author to "a desire to do well, not so much for the sake of social recognition or prestige, but to attain an inner feeling of personal accomplishment."[63]

Institutional reform theories, however, focus on ways to create the framework within which this "new man" can be made. As modernity has to occur whatever the price or resistance, the process has to be imposed from above. For theorists of institutional reform, therefore, the central issue is the capacity of Third World elites to mobilize the masses and to build the political and the administrative structures that guarantee the political ability to bring about change. All the attention of these theorists is devoted to this issue: the ability of one "hegemonic" group to impose a gradual but continual change.[64] And here again the clear assumption is that these elites have to follow Western models of political organization, education, police forces, and armies based on Western models.[65] There is, however, an exception of capital importance. It is assumed that as the changes have to be imposed from above, ethical considerations vis-à-vis the issue of the power and its distribution are avoided. The power has to be concentrated in few hands. The emphasis here is not on the *form* of government but on the *degree* of government.[66]

While Marx denies any history for the "nations of peasants," bourgeois modernity theorists deny for them any motivation, skills or efficiency. All these values are "missing" in peasant societies, and thus have to be imposed from above. Institutional reform theorists, on their part, exclude the possibility of these societies creating by themselves new forms of political organization. Basing their models of social change upon the experience of Europe in general and Great Britain in particular,[67] Western writers have embraced the principle of unilinear change and have, as have classic Marxist theorists, universalized "modernization/westernization" as an end in itself. The "end of history" has already been achieved by "those whose history has produced the grammar of development" as Mennasemay stated.[68]

This "self-confidence of ethnocentric achievement"[69] or this "looking-glass self"[70] conception of development and social change, however, needed to "clean-up" the language of the colonial period in order to give a more neutral impression over its previous racist and ethnocentric terminology. Thus, terms such as "civilization" were replaced by "modernity"; "barbarism," and "primitive" were replaced by "traditional."[71]

These semantic substitutions have to be placed in the ideological context within which bourgeois modernization theories were developed in the early sixties: the context of the Cold War. This period was one during which the Third World became an important consideration in the competition between the Soviet Union and the United States and its allies; and according to Sauvy, even the raison d'être of the Cold War.[72]

Because Marxism and the Soviet Union provided a model that had a great deal of attraction for the newly independent nations and nationalism in general, bourgeois theorists were charged to clean up the language and to provide a new ideological framework capable of countering the spread of "communism."

> The idea of modernization is primarily an American idea, developed by American social scientists in the period after the Second World War and reaching the height of its popularity in the middle years of the 1960s.
>
> ...While the imperial societies of Western Europe were confronted with reconstruction at home and decolonization abroad, the United States emerged from the Second World War at the height of its industrial and military strength. It also emerged from the War with a peculiar conception of world politics as a struggle between Good and Evil; if Hitler was the embodiment of evil during the War, then Stalin and Mao became its embodiment in the postwar era. Spurred on by this belief, by the encouragement of its European allies, and by its expanding economic interests abroad, the United States assumed leadership of the "forces of freedom," involving itself not only in the international but also the domestic affairs of scores of nations in its efforts to save the world from the menace of the communist conspiracy and to secure a stable world order in terms favorable to its own political and economic interests. [73]

It is in this context that the "non-communist manifesto" of Rostow, who was working at that period with the Kennedy Administration, has to be placed.

3. Rostow's Non-Communist Manifesto. There was needed in bourgeois modernization theories, as mentioned above, an ideological framework within which nineteenth-century liberal theories could rediscover the historical and "scientific" foundations that Marx had destroyed. In order to fill the gap bourgeois theorists needed a doctrine or a general theory of history that could compete with historical materialism.

This was done by Walt Rostow, who "set himself up as a latter-day anti-Marx."[74] The basic idea of Rostow was that he too is a "materialist."[75] Rostow claimed that all societies can be located at some point along an historical process that is common to all of them. There are according to Rostow five stages of growth: "the traditional society," "the transition or precondition stage," "the take-off," "the drive to maturity," and "the stage of high mass consumption."[76] In this process, at some time everybody has an equal chance to develop. Needless to say, Rostow's "historical materialism" has been severely criticized by many orthodox Marxists, of course,[77] by neo-Marxists,[78] and even by non-Marxists such as Sachs:

> ...Walt Rostow's work on stages of development (whose ephemeral success derives above all from its being intended

> as an anti-communist manifesto and from the good-natured optimism of the doctrine of "take-off"), instead of analyzing in depth the experience of the countries of the Third World and, where possible, deducing theoretical lessons from it, straightway proposes a dogmatic and universal model of stages of development.[79]

But it is Frank who has delivered the most devastating critique when he examines the "empirical validity," "theoretical adequacy," and "policy effectiveness" of Rostow's work and the whole array of bourgeois modernization theories in his "Sociology of Development and Underdevelopment of Sociology":

> Rostow's stages and thesis are incorrect primarily because they do not correspond at all to the past or present reality of the underdeveloped countries whose development they are supposed to guide. It is explicit in Rostow, as it is implicit in Hoselitz, that underdevelopment is the original stage of what are supposedly traditional societies—that there were no stages prior to the present stage of underdevelopment. It is further explicit in Rostow that the now developed societies were once underdeveloped. But all this is quite contrary to fact. This entire approach to economic development and culture change attributes a history to the developed countries but denies all history to the underdeveloped ones. The countries that are today underdeveloped evidently have had a history no less than have the developed ones.[80]

Moreover, Frank adds

> Indeed, the economic and political expansion of Europe since the fifteenth century has come to incorporate the new underdeveloped countries into a single stream of world history, which has given rise simultaneously to the present development of some countries and the present underdevelopment of others. However, in their attempt to construct theory and policy for the underdeveloped countries, Rostow and others have examined the developed countries as if they had developed in isolation from this stream of world history. It stands to reason that any serious attempt to construct theory and policy for the development of the now underdeveloped countries has to be based on the examination of the experience of the underdeveloped countries themselves—that is, on the study of their history and of the world historical process which has made these countries underdeveloped.[81]

Frank was in fact directing his criticism at all bourgeois modernization theorists, who as he put it, "...associate particularism, ascription, and diffuseness in underdevelopment with the extended family, the primitive tribe, the folk community, the traditional sector of a dual society, and with the underdeveloped countries and part of the world in general," but who never make the connection with the "developed part of the world nor with the contemporary dominant social organization in the world as a whole."[82]

More recently, Samir Amin, a long-time colleague of Frank, has admirably summarized this "bourgeois vision" of development.

> This Bourgeois vision reduces social reality to economic, quantitative, global and simple measurements; the specificities of the local classes and their insertion in the global system are obliterated; one "industry" is as good as another since they bring in profits, one form of exchange is as good as another since those who exchange both apparently gain by so doing. Bourgeois' thoughts claim to Universalism leads it to reject that which is beyond the limits of the analysis of its "reality," which itself is reduced to mere economics, the political factor, the national factor, and so on. Within this frame of thought, there is no room for imperialism; it is a universal political fact ('the strong dominate'). The doctrinaire even claim that imperialism is a vestige of the past, in contradiction with the 'spirit of capitalism'! The refusal of peoples to submit to the requirements of 'development' is, therefore, always a conservative reaction of backward peoples who reject the progress being offered to them. A hint of racism comes to the surface here and there.[83]

I would like, at this point, to emphasize that what is particularly interesting in Frank's critique is that to him Rostow's theory "attributes a history to the developed countries but denies all history to the underdeveloped ones." This is a very important point, since one can see an interesting parallel between Frank's critique of Rostow's theory and those addressed to the "Marxist-Stalinist" version of modernization.[84] However, one question must be asked here: should we put Rostow at the same level as Marx? Sachs, again, who is not a Marxist, notes with humor:

> In order better to compete with historical materialism, Rostow set out to show he too is a materialist and does not hesitate to state that history is abstract. But in the process, all the richness of the dialectical relations between the base and the superstructure, the means and the relations of production disappears from his work. There remains only a mechanistic materialism, interspersed with references to the

> social preconditions of development and promising to the elites of the Third World a path of development which is historically necessary and almost painless, without conflict and without revolution.[85]

Now I would like to present a comparative approach to the two development plans mentioned in the introduction, which I believe illustrates very well the continuation of the debate between these two schools of thought about development and about the whole and fundamental question of transition, my main concern here.

The Lagos Plan

The philosophy on which the strategy of the Lagos Plan is based could be summarized by two principles: national and collective self-reliance, and self-sustaining development; in other words, the solidarity between African countries and the protection of their economies from external dependence. The Lagos Plan was designed to restructure and to diversify the economy of Africa on the basis of these twin principles. It is, therefore, an approach that stresses a development "from within." A necessary condition for another fundamental objective of the Plan is the creation of an African Common Market by the year 2000.

According to A. Bujra, the Lagos Plan is the result of

> ...a long intensive process of discussions and preparations by African scholars, experts and government officials, principally through the umbrella of the OAU and the ECA (U.N. Economic Commission for Africa). The Plan contains the fundamental ideas and sentiments concerning the future economic development of Africa as perceived by Africans.[86]

How it comes that despite all the political and the ideological divergences, the Lagos Plan was adopted unanimously by African governments? It is difficult to answer this question with certainty. What one may suggest is that there is obviously a general agreement among African governments, scholars, and experts on the causes of the dramatic situation in which the African continent finds itself today.

> ...in the 20 years from 1960 to 1980 the average annual rate of growth continent-wide has been no more than 4.8 percent, a figure which hides divergent realities ranging from 7 percent growth rate for the oil exporting countries, down to 2.9 percent for the least developed countries. Yet, if the world economic forecast for the next decade is to be believed, the overall poor performance of the African

> economy over the past 20 years may even be a golden age compared with future growth rate.[87]

Therefore, the Lagos Plan was adopted, after this "intensive process of discussions and preparations" by African governments, mainly

> Against the background of two decades of stagnation in output; worsening of balance of payments brought about by deteriorating terms of trade; increasing payments for the import of high-level skills, capital goods, spare parts and equipment, raw material inputs, marketing, shipping and insurance services, widespread unemployment and mass poverty; *and a painful realization that past policies are not viable and sustainable* if the objectives of self-reliance, eradication of mass poverty, reduction of widespread unemployment, equitable distribution of the benefits of development and economic growth, sovereignty over natural resources and equitable participation in international decision-making process are to be pursued and achieved.[88]

What were these "past policies?" The Executive Secretary of the U.N. Economic Commission for Africa, Dr. Adedej, the "catalyst" behind the Lagos Plan, puts it very bluntly indeed:

> The African economy today is the most open and the most exposed in the world, overly dependent on external trade and other external stimuli, foreign technology, and foreign expertise. The very strategies of development the African governments have been pursuing since independence *have come from outside, derived as they were from theories of economic development that were developed during the colonial and neo-colonial periods* to rationalise the colonial pattern of production in Africa. Not unexpectedly, these foreign theories of development and growth reinforce the economic dependence of Africa...The cumulative results is that, today, neither high rates, growth or diversification, nor an increasing measure of self-reliance and self-sustainment has been achieved in the African economy.[89]

Here are, briefly summarized, the profound causes of the African drama as analyzed by African scholars and governments and the main characteristics of the philosophy of the Lagos Plan for the future economic development of Africa. This general consensus of gloom and distrust within African governments and academic milieux vis-à-vis these "foreign theories" is very interesting to note. This is a big shift from the strong optimism of the 1960s concerning economic development.

The World Bank Report

The authors of the World Bank report, well known now as the "Berg Report," recognize that Africa is facing a "dim economic prospect" in the 1980s. They also acknowledge the existence of the Lagos Plan and even claim to build on it. In his introduction to the report, the president of the World Bank writes:

> The report accepts the long-term objectives of African Development as expressed by the Heads of State of the Organization of African Unity in the Lagos Plan of Action. It emphasizes that if these objectives for the year 2000 are to be achieved, actions must be taken to reverse the stagnation and possible decline of per capita incomes which are projected for the 1980s.[90]

But according to the authors of the report:

> This report deals with short-to-medium-term responses to Africa's current economies' difficulties. It focuses on how growth can be accelerated and how the resources to achieve the longer-term objectives set by the African Governments can be generated, *with the support of the international community*.[91]

It is very important to stress that the authors of the Bank report give the impression here that the Lagos Plan is only a long-term strategy of which the main objective is to create an African Common Market by the year 2000. Also, while the Lagos Plan advocates a "self-sustaining development," the World Bank report focuses on how growth can be accelerated and longer-term objectives can be achieved with the support of the international community.[92]

But the major differences between the two documents are the diagnosis of the World Bank and the strategy based on it. They are diametrically opposed to those of the Lagos Plan.

> The internal "structural" problems and the external factors impeding African economic growth have been exacerbated by *domestic policy inadequacies*, of which three are critical. First trade and exchange-rate policies have overprotected industry, held back agriculture, and absorbed much administrative capacity. Second, *too little attention has been paid to administrative constraints in mobilizing and managing resources for development; given the widespread weakness of planning, decision-making and management capacities, public sectors frequently become overextended.*

> Third, there has been a consistent bias against agriculture in price, tax, and exchange-rate policies.[93]

Thus, while the Lagos Plan and African governments see external factors as having played a major role in producing the actual situation, the World Bank report gives internal factors a greater role, if not *the* major role. Based on this diagnosis, the authors of the World Bank report propose an "agriculture-based and export-oriented development strategy."

> The agriculture-based and export-oriented development strategy suggested for the 1980s is an essential beginning to a process of long-term transformation, a prelude to industrialization. It is not a permanent course for any country, but one that in Africa generates resources more quickly than any alternative and benefits more people. Without these resources, the foundations of future development cannot be established.[94]

This agriculture-based and export-oriented strategy, in addition, claim the authors of the report,

> ...will help generate the resources Africa needs to consolidate its political and administrative forces, educate and improve the health of its people, and find out what will work and what will not. It will bring forth human talent now neglected and uncover physical resources not yet imagined. And it will open the way to a future whose shape we cannot yet see.[95]

We have here then two strategies diametrically opposed. We have on the one hand the agriculture-based and export-oriented strategy of the World Bank and on the other the internally oriented and intersector-based (diversification) strategy of the Lagos Plan. As was expected, the World Bank "prescriptions" were rejected and extremely criticized by African governments as well as by African scholars. First, the "OAU Report of the Secretary-General on the World Bank Report," published in March 1982, stated:

> ...the proposed outward-looking, external-oriented concept of development proposed for our countries in the IBRD report is indeed a suggestion that we continue to do what we have been doing all these years. The only difference is that we lose the independence to set our goals, adopt our strategy and determine our policies. Added to this is the glaning arrogant paternalism in the report with no concern shown for

> the need to increase the capacity of our countries to do in the near future what outsiders are doing for them now.[96]

A month later, the African ministers responsible for economic development and planning assembled in Tripoli declared:

> We declare that the strategy recommended in the World Bank report, which emphasizes export orientation in general and primary commodity export in particular, regards industrialization and economic cooperation and integration in Africa as longer-term issues and completely disregards external factors as being major constraints on Africa's development and economic growth, and which adopts approaches, concepts and objectives which are divergent from those of the Lagos Plan of Action and the Final Act of Lagos is in fundamental contradiction with the political, economic and social aspirations of Africa.[97]

Among the great number of African scholars and researchers,[98] Amin has expressed in the most virulent terms the dangers for African countries that constitute the World Bank strategy.

> If words have any meaning at all this is an outward-oriented and not a self-reliant strategy, a policy of adapting to the requirements of transnationalization, a strategy which means renouncing any intention of constructing a diversified national and regional economy which, through its own internal dynamics and autonomy, would be capable as a partner in an interdependent world system rather than being a mere excrescence of the Transnationals.[99]

Timothy M. Shaw has summarized in a very clear and pertinent way the real issues around this debate:

> Suffice to say that the two sides disagree fundamentally on the causes of and solutions for the current crisis. Ironically, the Plan blames external dependence and advocates internal self-reliance whereas the Agenda blames internal deficiencies and advocates external exchange. The former also prefers industry over agriculture; the later encourages private rather than State enterprise. *The OAU asserts that "modernization" can never produce development; the Bank argues that "trickle-down" just requires more time, care and input.*[100]

Here we are after 30 years of debate and polemic around this central issue: how Third World countries, after millions of deaths in their struggles for independence (one million in Algeria) must cope with their economic problems and rebuild their countries after the "pillage" of their economies during the long colonial night.

As we can see, the debates are not nearly finished on the question of the transition at the national level. But, even if I understand the relevance and the importance of Lipietz's question: "Marx or Rostow?"[101] (of course it is not Marx at all but Stalin vs. Rostow), I need to ask another question that seems to me much more relevant that Lipietz's. I would like to ask rather than "Marx or Rostow?", "Marx or Proudhon?". But I would go even further, whatever my "Prouhonism," along with DeViney and Crowley and Mennasemay to state that "the way out of this dilemma" contained in Lipietz's question "is to turn to the Third World itself."[102]

The World Bank plan, to the contrary, follows the universalistic logic of the modernization theories—in this case a bourgeois one, but it could just as well have been, as this section has tried to illustrate, the Marxist-Stalinist one. In other words, modernization theories, or as the Executive Secretary for the U.N. Economic Commission for Africa, Dr. Adedej, has bluntly put it, "...these foreign theories of development...," whether they come from Moscow or Washington, D.C., have nothing to offer toward the solution of the profound crisis in which Africa finds itself today. The solution has to come from *Africa* and *Africans themselves*. And this is precisely the fundamental objective of the Lagos Plan for African development. In this regard, I cannot think of a better conclusion for this section than Hermassi's remark, more relevant than ever in his *The Third World Reassessed*, that

> It is no longer possible to claim with any plausibility that the industrial societies hold up to the Third World the image of its own future; the future of the Third World remains to be invented and in this endeavor, the need for an imaginative social science is as compelling as ever. What is in part expected of it is neither to simply layout the failings of non-Western cultures nor to merely decry the overwhelming constraints of the world capitalist system, but to show how, despite inner flaws and outer assaults, Third World people are still capable of making their own history.[103]

## MODERNIZATION AND THE TRANSITION AT THE SUB-NATIONAL LEVEL: THE GROWTH POLE APPROACH

The previous section dealt with the "question of transition" at the national level. Theories of development, modernization theories in particular, the debate about them and their application in the Third World in general and Africa in particular have been discussed from this perspective. A continuation of the previous one, this section is concerned now with the subnational level. In other words, its main focus is the "question of transition" at the regional level.

Since it has provided the dominant framework for debate about regional development and planning for so many years, this section is focused on François Perroux's "growth pole theory." First I will present an historical review of the context within which the growth pole approach emerged as a response to the dissatisfaction with traditional spatial theories and a review of the main features of Perroux's theory, in order to show the extraordinary similarity of its basic tenets with those of modernization theories.

Then, I will summarize major critiques of the growth pole approach, especially critiques of its transfer in developing countries.

## The Emergence of the School

There is no theory of regional development and planning more popular than François Perroux's growth pole theory. Until the early 1970s it was the basic, and unchallenged, paradigm used for regional development strategies throughout the world.[104] Its use in regional development and planning for less prosperous regions in both developed and developing countries as well as the deluge of writings, seminars, and conferences on the subject reflect very well the popularity of the theory during the past three decades.

There are two main suggestions, made by different scholars, that explain the appeal of the theory.[105] First is the suggestion that the general dissatisfaction during the late 1950s with traditional spatial theories, such as those of Von Thünen, Lösch, and Isard, created the need for concepts and theories "more relevant to immediate policy problems" and that have "more greater prospective relevance as policy guides."[106] L. Rodwin has expressed this general dissatisfaction with traditional spatial theories in the following terms:

> Turning to the spatial theorists is a disappointing experience since the assistance furnished by them on this topic is relatively meager whereas one might have expected them to be the most helpful. To begin with, the traditional approach of location theory, with few exceptions, has been largely from the point of view of equilibrium theory with extensions to take account of transportation and trade variables. This aspect of location theory is, therefore, subject to all the strictures of the growth economists about equilibrium theory and comparative advantage....[107]

Although this dissatisfaction with traditional spatial theories in particular, and liberal economic growth theory in general, was not limited to France, it is the French regional planning school, with the contributions of French regional economists such as professors François Perroux, Jacques Boudeville, Joseph Lajugie, G. D. de Bernis and others, that made the most important break with traditional spatial theories.[108]

This break and the French contribution have to be understood within the context of post-World War II, when France was facing, as was the rest of Europe, the problem of "reconstruction" and especially the problem of regional disparities. It was in this context that professor Jean-François Gravier, a geographer, published in 1947 the first edition of his famous book: *Paris et le Désert Français* (Paris and the French Desert).[109] This book has been responsible in large measure for arousing French public opinion about the danger of the concentration of French economic, political, and cultural life in the Paris region at the expense of the rest of the country.[110] With the increasing concern, then, of French politicians and French planners with (1) the congestion of Paris and (2) the problem of regional disparities, the need for a more "applicable" theory emerged that could provide "guides for action."[111]

The second suggestion that was made to explain the success of Perroux's growth pole theory is, as noted by D.F. Darwent, its:

> ...powerful intuitive and emotive appeal which has been exploited by French economists to the neglect of informative, descriptive or analytical content. It has become a magic label and, in the 1950s a guarantee of publication when used at the head of a paper.[112]

This "intuitive and emotive appeal," due mainly to the simplicity of the theory,[113] has permitted the theory to enjoy "the privilege of all mythic catchwords" until the point that "when the concept is used in planning, the failures of the policies centered upon it are normally attributed to the ways and means by which it has been implemented, never to the adequacy of the concept itself."[114]

## The Main Features of Perroux's Theory

The concept of "growth pole" (*pôle de croissance*) in its original formulation can be traced back to the work of the late and prestigious French political economist François Perroux. Although Albert Hirschman and Gunnar Myrdal were working on the same ideas, e.g., the "polarization" processes in the process of economic growth and their consequences (especially Myrdal),[115] it is Perroux who first provided the conceptualization of the mechanisms by which polarization occurs in the process of economic growth.

Where Perroux's work differs from others is that Perroux's first concern was not the spatial dimension of growth, but rather its manifestation through forward and backward linkages within industrial sectors. In his early definition of the theory Perroux was not concerned with space in a geographical sense, in other words the "geographical milieu"[116] or certain classical notions of space as defined by geographical or political divisions.

In an early article Perroux defines his conception of space.[117] Influenced certainly by the consequences of Second World War upon European countries, he rejected classical notions of space, which he considered as "banal." Rather he concentrates on the notion of "economic" space or "abstract" space. He created a typology of economic spaces that he used later as a base for his growth pole theory. For Perroux there are three types of economic space: (1) economic space as defined by a plan; (2) economic space as a field of forces; and (3) economic space as a homogeneous aggregate. On the basis of this typology, in a second article a few years later—and the most widely cited reference in the literature—Perroux elaborated his theory.[118] The second type of space in the typology mentioned above will be central to the theory. As a field of forces, this second type of economic space is defined as: "centers (poles or foci) from which centrifugal forces emanate and to which centripetal forces are attracted. Each center being a center of attraction and repulsion has its proper field, which is set in the field of all other centers." Here a "pole" or a "foci" is typically thought of as "*industries motrices*" "propulsive industries," or the "*firmes motrices*," "propulsive enterprises." These industries have to have a higher growth rate than other industries. Moreover, the propulsive enterprises have to be large and innovative and have to exert an important influence on the activities of suppliers and clients in order to stimulate strong forward and backward inter- as well as intra-industrial linkages, a sine qua non condition for the whole system to grow. An aggregation of this type of propulsive enterprises constitutes a "*pôle de croissance*," which is then seen as a "generator of growth" for one given region.[119]

Here are very briefly the basic features of Perroux's theory, which contains four key elements: (1) the dependency of a growth pole upon one or several dynamic industries; (2) the large size and innovative capacities of the firms in these industries; (3) the importance of inter- and intra-industrial linkages that these large firms exert upon dependent or impelled firms in order to lead the growth of the whole system; and (4) finally, and deeply rooted in the third condition, the concept of "dominance."

From this highly descriptive and narrative theory, Perroux drew his model from his study of the Ruhr region in Germany and the region of Lyons in France,[120] a colleague of Perroux, Jacques Boudeville, has tried to operationalize the concept. Boudeville adopts Perroux's concept but changes his definition of economic space from a pure "abstract" space into a "geographic" space.[121] And the pole as defined by Perroux became "an urban centre in geographical space with its associated hinterland."[122] The efforts of Boudeville and some of his French and Belgian colleagues and students, in attempting to transform the growth pole concept into a spatial theory of development, have reinforced the belief that growth poles could be created where a region is retarded. Although Perroux himself never stated such policy conclusions, this simplistic idea was so attractive that "there is probably not a major retarded region anywhere in the world where some planners or politicians have not proposed the creation or strengthening of one or more 'pôles de croissance' as a solution to its economic and social problems."[123]

Here are then, the general context within which emerged the growth pole approach and the main features of Perroux's theory. All the debates and polemics during the last three decades or so about the question of the transition at the subnational level originated, in my view, from this simplistic and naive idea that Boudeville and his colleagues have helped to popularize by their efforts "to operationalize" the abstract concept of Perroux ( G. D. de Bernis in Algeria, Boudeville himself in Brazil and France, to mention just a few ). By doing that, however, they have helped, ironically, to put on the surface all the anomalies and biases that were deeply rooted in the theory itself.

## The Fall of the Growth Pole Approach

This leads us now to look at the major criticism addressed to the theory from both a practical and political-ideological point of view, especially criticism from scholars and planners concerned with the application of the approach in developing countries.

To begin with and as we have seen through the summary of the basic features of the theory, the growth pole approach was criticized for its obvious "urban bias."[124]

Second and related to this is the double "industrial bias"; first is the industrial bias in general. As we have seen, the theory of Perroux is concerned with industrial growth and the mechanisms of that growth. The role of agriculture is simply ignored. Second is the explicit bias in favor of large capital-intensive industries and firms, considered as the main engine of growth and development. As for agriculture, the role of small and labor-intensive industries is deliberately ignored. As we have seen in the theory, in order to be innovative, to be "propulsive" (*effets d'entrainement*), industries and firms have to be large. Since small industries are considered by definition as "traditional" and not innovative, the study of their "propulsive" role is simply neglected.

These are, among others, the two major criticisms of the approach: namely the "urban" and the "industrial" biases. For retarded rural regions, especially in Third World countries, this will be one of the major practical problems with the use of the approach as a major instrument of regional development policy [125]. The simplicity of the theory and the attempt of

French economist to transform it into a spatial theory of development have reinforced the "universal" character of the approach. As noted by Higgins it was believed that anywhere in the world where a region is retarded the creation of one or more "pôle de croissance" was seen as the miraculous solution.[126] This supposed "universal" character of the approach was criticized by many authors. V. Nichols, for example, was the first to observe that the approach is inappropriate for all types of regions, such as agricultural regions (most of all lagging regions in developing countries) or regions in decline that are unattractive to modern industries.[127]

Another key criticism was addressed to the central argument of the theory. The evidence from past growth pole strategies suggests that the overall result of these strategies has been an increase in, rather than the reduction of, disparities and that "spread effects from the growth centers were usually smaller than expected, or less than backwash effects."[128] In his analytical paper on the "propulsive effect of growth poles," Nichols argues that:

> The conclusion that might be drawn from this for growth pole policies is that, although it is probably advisable to concentrate investment in that town in a region which has the strongest linkages, there are also advantages to be gained from injecting capital into lower order centers, or even the agricultural base, because increases in incomes in these places will generate strong income multipliers in higher order centers but not the other way round.[129]

M. Moseley's conclusions from his study of the spatial impact of Rennes in France are absolutely similar. He argues that: 'trickle down' cannot be relied on. If 'some growth' is required throughout an urban hierarchy, then there is a case of neglecting the larger settlements to which some 'trickle up' might normally be expected.[130]

Based on these previous criticisms another key criticism has been raised, mainly by regional planners who are concerned with the problems of applying the theory in developing countries. Questions have been raised as to whether the approach can be transferred even with some modifications, as suggested some time ago by for example Richardson and Richardson,[131] to developing countries. As a theory of urban-industrial development, derived from the experiences of two industrialized countries (France and Germany), the growth pole approach relies heavily on the existence of well-articulated urban systems for the supposed spread of development. But as such, and as other theories of spatial development, the growth pole approach "could not be applied because the existing spatial patterns of most developing countries are substantially different from those in North America and Europe," observe Rondinelli and Ruddle.[132] These spatial patterns in developing countries are a reflection of their colonial experience.[133]

In line with this important criticism, some other authors pointed out that as a normative theory, the growth pole approach is an "ahistorical diffusion model,"[134] based implicitly on the "Rostowian" premise that developing countries are simply in a transitory stage of development progressing toward what the developed countries are today, ignoring, therefore, that developing countries have not only their specific spatial organizations but moreover their specific socioeconomic conditions and history marked by this recent colonial experience.[135]

Related to this type of criticism, further political and ideological questions have been strongly expressed as to whether the growth pole approach does not serve to reinforce in fact, class exploitation and the dominance at the national level of the 'periphery' by the 'center.'[136] Although some authors have argued that "the concept of development poles and growth centers as instruments of policy is politically and ideologically neutral"[137] the idea of "dominance" in the theory has led some authors such as Luis Corragio to denounce the approach as "an apology for capitalist imperialism" or, as in the case of Mihailovich, as "an apology for private enterprise."[138] Basic to this argument is the idea that a large firm does not need to be located in the region in order to exert a dominant role in its economy, to extract large profits from its activities in that region and to invest them in another region or even outside the country itself.[139]

These criticisms have directed the attention of some authors to another weakness of the approach. The strong emphasis on the economic process has led to the neglect of social and political factors. It was argued that as a traditional top-down regional strategy the growth pole approach is neglecting the institutional aspects, *the distribution of the political power*, used as a tool for spatial domination and the preservation of existing socioeconomic structures.[140]

A final criticism of a sociopolitical nature is based on the fact that as a 'place prosperity approach,' rather than a 'people prosperity approach,' the growth pole approach considers the problem of lagging regions mainly as a 'spatial' rather than a 'social' phenomenon.[141] This criticism is in line with that of the French economist, Matteaccioti, who has criticized Perroux for his neglect of the "geographical milieu."[142]

Here are then the major criticisms of the growth pole approach in general and of its transfer to developing countries in particular. All of them expressed the disenchantment with the approach as an instrument of regional development policy. All these criticisms had, by the early 1970s, transformed the idea of growth poles from an idea in 'good currency' during the 1960s to "almost a dirty word."[143] It is in response to this failure that new alternatives for regional development in developing countries have emerged by the end of the 1970s. It is to these that I should return now.

# REGIONAL DISPARITY AND ALTERNATIVE APPROACHES OF REGIONAL DEVELOPMENT AND PLANNING IN DEVELOPING COUNTRIES

The previous two sections have dealt with the "question of transition" and the debate about it during the last thirty years or so. They were therefore concerned with ideas and theories of the past. This section now, is concerned with ideas and theories of the present and, most important, of the future.

As it was stated in the introduction, with the disenchantment with modernization theories in general and with growth pole theory in particular, there emerged, during the late 1960s and early 1970s, growing evidence for the need for new alternatives for promoting economic development and spatial equity.

The objective of this section is to survey very briefly some of the major new theories of regional development and planning in the Third World that appeared during the last decade as a response to the failure of the older center-down paradigm of modernization theories at the national level and that of growth pole theory at the subnational level.

## The Agropolitan Development Approach

One of the most popular—and controversial—alternative approaches proposed as a response to the failure of the growth pole approach is the "agropolitan approach," as is reflected in the most recent literature on the subject in the English-speaking world.[144] Introduced first by John Friedmann,[145] it was published in a more extensive form in 1978,[146] and elaborated further since.[147]

As we have seen, critiques of the growth pole approach, especially those concerned with its transfer to developing countries, were based on both practical and political considerations. As a strategy of "accelerated rural development" designated originally for rural areas in Asia,[148] the approach is an attempt to deal with both kinds of problems, especially the political ones. In this respect, the approach is in complete opposition with the growth pole approach.

In order to understand this fundamental opposition, it is important to understand, I think, the whole philosophy upon which the agropolitan development approach is based. To begin with is the rejection of the old paradigm of development, the unmodified pursuit of which would be "suicidal."[149] This rejection is, of course, concerned with the spatial as well as the nonspatial dimensions of development. Second is the adoption of the basic philosophy of the emerging new paradigm of development, which is "no longer economic growth but social development, with focus on specific human needs."[150] Also, according to the new paradigm, priority attention must be given to rural development; the planning for this rural development "must be decentralized, participatory and deeply immersed in the particulars of local settings." This planning, therefore, "will have to be based on qualitative judgments as much as on quantitative techniques, and its style will have to be transactive."[151]

Based on these premises, J. Friedmann and M. Douglas's objective "is to propose a spatial policy for the emerging paradigm."[152] After a survey of past development strategies in several Asian countries and an analysis of their failure, Friedmann and Douglas propose a new approach, of which the major features can be summarized as follows:

—Contrary to the growth pole approach, and this is one of the most important features of the agropolitan approach, basic needs are given an absolute priority. Related to this, and although the diversification of the rural economy through the development of rural industries is required,[153] the development of agriculture is central to the strategy.

—These two socioeconomic objectives are related to a third objective: the stabilization of the rural population and the reduction therefore of rural-to-urban migrations. In order to do so, an attempt is made to transform the countryside by introducing and adapting elements of urbanism to rural areas. This can be done by redirecting investments in urban centers to these rural settings transforming them in "agropolises" or "cities-in-the-field."

—The spatial framework of the strategy is organized upon these "agropolises" or villages. Above the village, there is the central territorial unit of the agropolitan approach: the "agropolitan districts." The agropolitan districts are constituted as a collection of adjacent villages and are centered on an existing market town. Above the agropolitan districts there are the multidistrict regions, which constitute the national territory. The population of each agropolitan district varies according to local conditions from 50,000 to 150,000 people and at the multidistrict region level from 0.5 million to 5 million people.[154]

—Finally and most important of all, each agropolitan district is treated as a "single, integrated, and self-governing unit" which has "sufficient autonomy and economic resources to plan and carry out its own development."[155] Thus, self-sufficiency and self-government are considered the keys for the success of the agropolitan development approach. These two basic requirements are needed to protect the districts from any form of external exploitation. Here again the approach is in complete opposition with the growth pole approach. Since disparities exist not only between core and periphery itself, a policy of "selective territorial closures" is needed. This policy is defined as

> ...a policy of enlightened self-reliance at relevant levels of territorial integration: district, region and nation. This condition flies straight in the face of the ideology of free trade and comparative advantage and the attempts of transnational enterprises to organize a functionally integrated world economy under its tutelage...It means to rely less on

> outside aid and investment, to involve the masses in development, to initiate a conscious process of social learning, to diversify production, and to pool resources. It means to say 'we' and to assert a territorial interest.[156]

This policy of "selective territorial closure," however, does not mean that the approach advocates a pure policy of "autarky." Friedmann is very clear about that: "'Closure' does not mean, 'autarky,' but would help protect weak, peripheral regions against their domination and ruthless exploitation by more powerful core region interests."[157] In other words, this does not mean that the agropolitan district

> ...has complete autonomy over its own affairs, something close, say to political sovereignty. It is not, after all, a closed social formation, even though a large and perhaps a major part of its basic needs are furnished from its own production....The idea is not to create miniaturized agropolitan states (*the classical anarchist solution*) but a robust, humanly adequate, interdependent, and articulate political community—a social formation that gives full scope to individual and collective powers.[158]

In this scheme of development, "which is rooted in the household economy, the village, and the agropolitan district," the role of central government is defined as follows:

> ...central government must act to inspire, to empower, to guide, to facilitate, to promote, to assist and to support. It must not plan, command, administer, or implement projects of its own unless in support of the entire effort and therefore beyond local capacity.[159]

Here are very briefly, what seem to me the major features of the agropolitan development approach, which as a strategy of rural and regional development has its roots in a "federalist" political philosophy. It is interesting to note in this respect that in arguing that "in agropolitan development the age-old conflict between town and countryside can be transcended," Friedmann and Douglas in a footnote state:

> This is not as crazy as it sounds. Under a capitalist framework, it has already been achieved in countries such as Switzerland and Germany, where the contrast between rural and urban has virtually disappeared. Rural, or rather "agropolitan" life there has become simply another "lifestyle."[160]

The two countries given as examples both have a federalist political system. But Friedmann is aware of the problems that could face the approach in countries with "Jacobin," very centralized administrative and political systems, such as almost all former French protectorates and colonies. In countries with this type of administrative and political systems, the success of the strategy will depend on the good will of central governments as Friedmann observes:

> Those who look for simple answers will be disappointed. Though necessary, the agropolitan framework does not, by itself, ensure results for accelerated rural development. A framework provides the context within which development occurs; it is not itself that development. The framework, of course, should be facilitative, and it should direct the stream of development activities in the desired direction. But how well it does its work will depend on other circumstances, not least on the commitment of the central government. Action must be locally based and motivated, but the state must prepare the right environment for action.[161]

In another paper, Friedmann expresses, however, a much more skeptical, even pessimistic view:

> Unfortunately, political approaches to development are not particularly welcome. Because they assume a different distribution of power, they challenge the existing structures. And since they are merely the writings of scholars, politicians can safely ignore them.[162]

<u>Decentralization and the Transformational Approach</u>

The second major new approach I would like to review is Dennis Rondinelli and Kenneth Ruddle's regional development strategy.[163] In line with the "development from below" school, Rondinelli and Ruddle, as a response not only to the failure of the growth pole approach but to the whole traditional economic and spatial strategies of the past, propose a strategy that advocates economic and spatial integration from below. Rejecting the assumptions of conventional economic theory, they express the central argument upon which their strategy is based:

> For us, the essence of development is expansion of participation in economic activities through the creation of social and economic systems that draw larger numbers of people into processes of production, exchange, and consumption, that involve greater numbers in entrepreneurship and employment, that increase levels of

> income for the poorest group and reduce disparities between rich and poor so that a larger majority of people can obtain basic goods, save and invest, and gain access to services necessary to enrich the quality of their lives. Development is a process of expanding the productive capacity of public and private organizations, large and small firms, rural and urban regions of a country at a steady pace.[164]

Based on this central idea, the strategy calls for local participation and a "deliberate policy of economic intervention and spatial planning of investment" in order to reduce social and spatial disparities.[165] What characterizes first, Rondinelli and Ruddle's regional development approach, is that, as noted by Friedmann, "The authors go further than almost anyone in advocating a regional approach to rural development."[166]

And indeed, chapter after chapter, Rondinelli and Ruddle provide in a very detailed manner all the social, economic and political-institutional components of their approach. Here is a brief summary of some of them:

—The socioeconomic components include: the rationalization of marketing structures; the development and improvement of agricultural credit and financial institutions in general; the development of basic physical infrastructure; the development of community services; the development of rural industrialization in combination with farming development; the use of appropriate technology; and the development of education and training.

—The political-institutional components are: the development of local organizational capacities and local support services; the development of local capacities of project planning and implementation through the creation of local implementing organizations and managerial and technical labor power; the existence of real political commitment to decentralization and local participation; finally and most important of all is the use of *regions* as the base for national development is seen as the sine qua non condition of the approach's success.

These are then, very briefly summarized, some of the major nonspatial components of the approach.[167]

But although rural development is the central component of the approach, it does not neglect urban development. Contrary to the growth pole approach an attempt is made here to integrate rural-urban development in a unique regional economic policy. That is why special attention is paid to all the linkages between economic activities, social, physical infrastructures, and rural-urban settlements at different levels. And the concept of "transformational development approach" is used here as the process of a gradual and continual economic and spatial integration of existing human communities and their productive activities.[168] Contrary to the growth pole approach as well as to the agropolitan approach, the approach of Rondinelli and Ruddle in avoiding the "urban-industrial" bias, does not fall in the "trap" of what can be called the "rural bias."[169] Rondinelli and Ruddle express this position in these terms:

> Large cities and rural communities both play crucial roles in the development process. The whole spectrum of human settlements—villages, market towns, intermediate cities, and metropolitan areas—must be strengthened and integrated into a mutually sustaining network of national production, distribution, and exchange centers. Basic structural imbalances are the primary obstacles to achieving growth with greater equity, and the dualism that now characterizes most developing societies must be radically reduced.[170]

So here, as a "bottom-up" approach and although special attention is given to lower order spatial units such as villages, market towns and small cities, their strategy does not neglect the developmental role of larger urban centers such as intermediate cities or regional centers.

Continuing his efforts, Rondinelli, in several other publications, focuses his attention on these intermediate cities, which play a crucial role in the spatial strategy he advocates with Ruddle.[171] It is in the frame of that strategy that Rondinelli develops further his research on the different factors and dynamics of the growth of these cities and the ways of strengthening their role in regional and national development. It is in that frame that their role has to be understood. In this respect, Rondinelli observes that

> Secondary city development strategies are also a reaction to the failure of growth pole policies that attempted during the 1950s and the 1960s to transplant modern, large-scale, export-oriented, capital-intensive industries in a few regional centers. Programs for strengthening the network of secondary cities seek instead to build on the existing economic base and reinforce the dynamics of development in intermediate urban centers.[172]

So, here, a regional policy based on an integrated rural-urban development and focusing more specifically on the crucial role of these intermediate spatial units of the spatial system, is not a simple replication of the growth pole approach. What Rondinelli advocates here, is a secondary city development strategy, which

> ...must go beyond creating a few urban "growth poles." Unless development policies seek to strengthen indigenous economic activities and to diversify them in appropriate ways, they will either have little impact or be perverse. Unless the economies of secondary cities are integrated with those of their regions, through appropriate linkages with small cities, towns, and rural villages, their growth may generate strong "backwash effects" that drain their hinterlands of resources.[173]

In brief, what Rondinelli advocates in the framework of the development strategy he has proposed with Ruddle[174] is a more balanced and integrated spatial development strategy, in which secondary cities and towns could play, through appropriate economic and spatial linkages, their development role. Writing about Africa, Rondinelli, after having analyzed the failure of past economic and spatial development policies in the continent, wrote:

> All of this suggests that widespread economic growth, a more balanced distribution of population, and more diffuse patterns of urbanization, are unlikely to be achieved by investing heavily in a single metropolitan area and expecting spread and trickle-down effects automatically to raise average levels of income and reduce high levels of poverty throughout the country. *If African governments want geographically widespread economic development and a more balanced distribution of population, they will have to invest in a more geographically dispersed manner.*[175]

## CONCLUSION: REGIONAL DISPARITY, THE NEW DEBATE AND THE TRANSITION'S DILEMMAS

As a response to the failure of modernization theories in general and growth pole theory in particular, new theories of economic and spatial development in Third World countries have emerged during the late 1970s. This section presented a brief review of some of them.

In this review, I have tried to show how some authors, who are in the forefront of the current debate about regional development and planning in the Third World, have tried to address the problems created by past and present economic and spatial development strategies. Despite their divergences, all of them, it is important to stress, agree on one basic fact: that past and present economic and spatial strategies must be radically changed if both social and spatial, as well as growth and development objectives are to be achieved.

Now, one may ask: why these two alternatives? Why has the focus been on so limited number of alternatives? The focus on only these two alternatives has two reasons: (1) these two alternative approaches are the only most comprehensive and most elaborated alternatives. They deal with economic, political and spatial problems in a holistic and integrated manner. All other propositions I can find in the literature, although very useful, are, however, partial, fragmented and deal with one or few aspects of the problem.[176] (2) As attested to by the literature of the last five or six years, the alternative approaches reviewed here have become, in the English-speaking world at least,[177] the base for the current debate—and even for controversies on regional development and planning in the world in general and in the Third World in particular.

I have no desire here to get into these controversies. But I have to discuss, even very briefly, this very important aspect of this new debate about the question of the transition and therefore some of the criticisms addressed to the alternative approaches reviewed above and state in few words my own position.

The criticism I mentioned came, interestingly, from both non-Marxist and Marxist (I would say "classic" Marxist) sides. The agropolitan strategy, for example, was dismissed as "Utopian" and "naive and superficial." Its main author was accused of liking "to dream and romanticize."[178] Marxists' critiques—and these are I believe the most serious and powerful critiques[179]—on the other hand dismissed the "new territorialism" for its "overly romantic and utopian presentation of regionalism, regional planning and the territoriality of social life, and for its obfuscating interpretation of the history of capitalist development, the role of the state, and the nature of territorial politics."[180]

Another author simply dismissed the two new approaches as "neo-populist."[181] Because, it is argued, they both failed to deal with class interests and because their objective, in focusing on <u>spatial</u> rather than <u>social</u> change, is to maintain the "status quo."[182]

This is simply unfair. As we have seen, the issue of power and its distribution, and the issue of participation and decentralization were the key elements in both approaches. Again, it is not my intention to get into these controversies. And the authors of the new approaches have in fact responded themselves to these critiques,[183] and they don't need me to respond for them. My answer is addressed to the heart of this new debate and would be, again, the same question: "Comrades, Marx or Proudhon?" In other words: "Comrades, do we need, when it comes to propose concrete solutions to regional problems in the Third World, to have the "green light" of the "Party Central Committee?"

For all those who are familiar with the debate that has and continue to oppose "Marx et Proudhon" and are still concerned about the forms of the transition towards a genuine and democratic socialism—a feasible socialism—the answers to these questions are of a vital importance. It is the only way out from the transition's dilemmas that continue to face so many Third World countries today.[184]

## NOTES

1. The first section of this chapter is a revised and expanded version of a paper published with John Agnew: "Modernization Theories, African Development Plans and the Question of Transition," in *Cultures et Developpement*, no. 1, 1985, pp. 71-96.

2. For more details, see for example: Roland Marx, *La Révolution Industrielle en Grande-Bretagne* (Paris: Armand Colin, 1970).

3. Ignacy Sachs, *The Discovery of the Third World* (Cambridge: MIT Press, 1976).

4. See for example: Carl E. Pletsch, "The Three Worlds or the Division of Social Scientific Labor, Circa 1950-1975," *Comparative Studies in Society and History*, no. 4 (1981), pp. 565-90; S.J. Patel, "The Age of the Third World," *Third World Quarterly*, no. 1 (1983), pp. 58-71; and Y. Lacoste, *La Géographie du Sous-Développement* (Paris: P.U.F., 1976).

5. See among others: S. Amin, "A Critique of the World Bank Report Entitled 'Accelerated Development in Sub-Saharan Africa,'" *Africa Development*, nos. 1-2 (1982), pp. 23-30; idem, "Expansion or Crisis of Capitalism?", *Third World Quarterly*, no. 2 (1983), pp. 360-80; Alain Lipietz, "Marx or Rostow?", *New Left Review*, no. 132 (1982), pp. 48-58; Timothy Shaw, "Debates about Africa's Future: The Brandt, World Bank and Lagos Plan Blueprints," *Third World Quarterly*, no. 2 (1983), pp. 330-44.

6. World Bank, *Accelerated Development in Sub-Saharan Africa: An Agenda for Action* (Washington, DC: World Bank, 1981).

7. For further discussion of the two documents, see among others, two special issues of *Africa Development*, nos. 1-2 and no. 3, 1982. *Africa Development* is the journal of the Council for the Development of Economic and Social Research in Africa (COSDERIA) located in Dakar; see also the special issues of *Rural Africana*, nos. 19-20, Spring-Fall 1984 and of the *African Studies Review*, no. 4, December 1984.

8. See note 4.

9. See Amin, op. cit.; Lipietz, op. cit.; Andre G. Frank, *Latin America: Underdevelopment or Revolution* (New York: Monthly Review Press, 1969); Dudley Seers, "The Meaning of Development," *International Development Review*, no. 4 (1969), pp. 2-6.

10. John Agnew, "Technology Transfer and Theories of Development: Conceptual Issues in the South Asian Context," *Journal of Asian and African Studies*, nos. 1-2 (1982), pp. 16-31.

11. On this particular criticism, the literature is vast. See for example: A. Portes, "Modernity and Development: A Critique," *Studies in Comparative International Development*, no. 3 (1973), pp. 247-79; D. Tipps, "Modernization Theory and the Comparative Study of Societies: A Critical Perspective," *Comparatives Studies in Society and History*, no. 2 (1973), pp. 199-226; A.R. de Souza and Ph. W. Porter, *The Underdevelopment and the Modernization of the Third World*, Commission of College Geography, Resource Papers, no. 28 (Washington, DC: Association of American Geographers, 1974); H. Brookfield, *Interdependent Development* (London: Methuen, 1975); A. Hoogvelt, *The Sociology of Developing Societies* (London: Macmillan, 1979); I. Roxborough, *Theories of Underdevelopment* (London: Macmillan, 1979); S. DeViney and J. Crowley, "Universality of Modernization: An Empirical Critique," *Studies in Comparative International Development*, no. 2 (1978), pp. 23-39.

12. Roxborough, op. cit.

13. Agnew, op. cit., p. 18.

14. Ibid.

15. Ignacy Sachs, "Ecodevelopment," *C.E.R.E.S.*, no. 48 (1974), pp. 8-12; E. Schumacker, *Small Is Beautiful* (New York: Harper and Row, 1973); I. Illich, *La Convivialité* (Paris: Ed. du Seuil, 1973); idem, *Libérer l'Avenir* (Paris: Ed. du Seuil, 1971); D. Seers, op. cit.; idem, "The New Meaning of Development," *International Development Review*, no. 3 (1977), pp. 2-7; idem, "What Are We Trying to Measure?", in *Measuring Development*, ed. N. Basta (London: CASC, 1972), pp. 21-36.

16. Seers, "New Meaning of Development."

17. Agnew, op. cit., p. 18.

18. A. Asamoa, "On Bourgeois Development Theory: A Critique of Behrendt," *Africa Development*, no. 3 (1982), pp. 87-108.

19. Agnew, op. cit., p. 19.

20. K. Marx, *Capital*, vol. 1 (New York: International Publishers, 1967), pp. 8-9.

21. See. S. Avineri, *Karl Marx on Colonialism and Modernization* (New York: Anchors Books, 1969).

22. See for example: G. Gurvitch, *Proudhon, sa Vie, son Oeuvre* (Paris, P.U.F., 1965); idem, "Proudhon et Marx," *Cahiers Internationaux de Sociologie*, janvier-juin 1966, pp. 7-17; J. Langlois, *Défense et Actualité de Proudhon* (Paris: Payet, 1976); *La Rue* (Revue Culturelle et Littéraire d'Expression Anarchiste) "L'Autogestion," no. 29, 1981 (Dossier).

23. Brookfield, op. cit.

24. See for example: J. Chesnaux, "Le Mode de Production Asiatique. Quelques Perspectives de Recherche," *La Pensée*, no. 114 (1964), pp. 35-55; C. Parrain, "Le Mode de Production Asiatique: Une Etape Nouvelle dans une Discussion Fondamentale," *La Pensée*, no. 114

(1964), pp. 3-7; J. Suret-Canale, "Les Sociétés Traditionnelles en Afrique Tropicale et le Concept du Mode de Production Asiatique," *La Pensée*, no. 117 (1964), pp. 21-47.

25. B. Warren, *Imperialism: Pioneer of Capitalism* (London: New Left Books, 1980).

26. Lipietz, op. cit.; Amin, "Expansion or Crisis of Capitalism?", p. 361; Hoogvelt, op. cit., pp. 78-88.

27. Avineri, op. cit., p. 3.

28. Ibid., pp. 9-11.

29. Ibid., p. 12.

30. Ibid., p. 18.

31. On this particular point Engels, quoted by Avineri, says: "The conquest of Algeria an all important and fortunate fact for the progress of civilization" (Avineri, op. cit., p. 13).

32. Ibid., p. 19.

33. Ibid., p. 26.

34. Sachs, *Discovery of the Third World*, p. 134.

35. Avineri, op. cit.

36. Parrain, op. cit; see also: Umberto Melotti, Marx and the Third World (Atlantic Highlands, N.J., Humanities Press, 1977).

37. Roxborough, op. cit., pp. 19-25.

38. Sachs, *Discovery of the Third World*, p. 149.

39. Langlois, op. cit.; Gurvitch, "Proudhon et Marx"; *La Rue*, op. cit.

40. Sachs, *Discovery of the Third World.*

41. John Friedmann and Clyde Weaver, *Territory and Function: The Evolution of Regional Planning* (Los Angeles: University of California Press, 1979), p. 108.

42. Ibid.

43. Clyde Weaver, "Development Theory and the Regional Question: A Critique of Spatial Planning and Its Detractors," in *Development from Above or Below? The Dialectics of Regional Planning in Developing Countries* eds., W. Stöhr and D.R.F. Taylor (New York: Wiley, 1981), pp. 73-105.

44. Quoted from Friedmann and Weaver, op. cit., p. 112.

45. Brookfield, op. cit., p. 53.

46. De Souza and Porter, op. cit., p. 19.

47. W.A. Lewis, "Economic Development with Unlimited Supplies of Labor," *Manchester School of Economic and Social Studies*, no. 2 (1954), pp. 139-91.

48. Friedmann and Weaver, op. cit., p. 112.

49. De Souza and Porter, op. cit., p. 19.

50. See Brookfield, op. cit., pp. 54-76.

51. See for example: D.W. Jorgenson, "The Development of a Dual Economy," *Economic Journal*, no. 71 (1961), pp. 309-34.

52. Lewis, op. cit.
53. Jorgenson, op. cit.
54. Sachs, *Discovery of the Third World*, p. 142.
55. Ibid., pp. 137-38.
56. S. Amin, *Croissance et Développement* (Douala: Institut Panafricain pour le Développement, 1971); Frank, op. cit.
57. See for example: E. Moudoud, *Modernisation, Centralisation et Destruction de l'Economie Rurale: L'Expérience des Cooperatives en Tunisie, 1962-1969*, U.B.C. Planning Papers, no. 7, School of Community and Regional Planning, Vancouver, University of British Columbia, 1983.
58. Agnew, op. cit., p. 19.
59. Sachs, *Discovery of the Third World.*
60. DeViney and Crowley, op. cit.
61. See for example: A. Inkeles, "The Modernization of Man," in *Urbanism in World Perspective: A Reader*, ed. S. Fara (New York: T.Y. Crowell, 1968), pp. 360-69; A. Inkeles and D.H. Smith, *Becoming Modern* (Cambridge, MA: Harvard University Press, 1974).
62. DeViney and Crowley, op. cit.
63. Quoted from DeViney and Crowley, op. cit., p. 26.
64. Tipps, op. cit., pp. 200-201.
65. De Souza and Porter, op. cit., p. 10; Brookfield, op. cit., p. 80.
66. Roxborough, op. cit., p. 113.
67. Brookfield, op. cit.
68. M. Mennasemay, "Political Theory, Political Science and African Development," *Canadian Journal of African Studies*, no. 2 (1982), p. 225.
69. Tipps, op. cit., p. 206.
70. DeViney and Crowley, op. cit., p. 36.
71. See Tipps, op. cit.; and Pletsch, op. cit.
72. Pletsch, op. cit.; see also DeViney and Crowley, op. cit., p. 37.
73. Tipps, op. cit., pp. 208-9
74. Brookfield, op. cit., p. 37.
75. Sachs, *Discovery of the Third World.*
76. W. Rostow, *The Stages of Economic Growth: A Non-Communist Manifesto* (Cambridge: Cambridge University Press, 1960).
77. See for example: J. Serinsky, *The Anti-Communist Manifesto of Mr. Rostow* (Washington, DC: U.S. Joint Publications Research Service, 1962).
78. Amin, *Croissance et Développement*; idem, "Critique of the World Bank Report"; idem, "Expansion or Crisis of Capitalism?"; and Frank, op. cit.
79. Sachs, *Discovery of the Third World*, p. 148.
80. Frank, op. cit., p. 40.

81. Ibid., p. 41. To illustrate his argument, Frank cites as an example the deindustrialization of India, the slave trade in Africa, and the destruction of the Inca and Aztecs civilizations in Latin America (Ibid., pp. 41-42). Other studies further illustrate Frank's argument and the literature on this particular point is vast. For the African case, see for example, Walter Rodney's, *How Europe Underdeveloped Africa* (Washington, DC: Howard University Press, 1982).

82. Frank, op. cit., pp. 33-34.

83. Amin, "Expansion.or Crisis of Capitalism?",.p. 361.

84. See Avineri, op cit.; and Sachs, *Discovery of the Third World.*

85. Sachs, *Discovery of the Third World*, pp. 148-49.

86. A. Bujra, "Editorial Note," *Africa Development*, nos. 1-2 (1982), p. 1.

87. Shaw, op. cit., p. 332.

88. C.O.S.D.E.R.I.A., "Accelerated Developments in Sub-Saharan Africa: An Assessment by the OAU, ECA and ADB Secretariats," *Africa Development*, no. 3 (1982), p. 110 (emphasis mine).

89. Quoted from Shaw, op. cit., p. 339 (emphasis mine).

90. World Bank, op. cit., p. v.

91. Ibid., p. 1 (emphasis mine).

92. That is to say, the international capital: Private capital and international financial institutions.

93. Ibid., p. 4 (emphasis mine).

94. Ibid., p. 6.

95. Ibid., p. 7.

96. Quoted from Shaw, op. cit., p. 341.

97. C.O.S.D.E.R.I.A., "Declaration of Tripoli on the World Bank Report Entitled 'Accelerated Development in Sub-Saharan Africa: An Agenda for Action,'" *Africa Development*, no. 3 (1982), p. 138.

98. See for example: A. Benachenou, "La Coopération Sud-Sud: Le Plan Lagos et l'Indépendence de l'Afrique," *Africa Development*, nos. 1-2 (1982), pp. 6-22; T. Mkandawire, "The Lagos Plan of Action and the World Bank on Food and Agriculture in Africa: A Comparison," *Africa Development*, nos. 1-2 (1982), pp. 166-77.

99. Amin, "Critique of the World Bank.Report," p. 24.

100. Shaw, op. cit., p. 341 (emphasis mine).

101. Lipietz, op. cit.

102. DeViney and Crowley, op. cit.; Mennasemay, op. cit.

103. E. Hermassi, *The Third World Reassessed.* (Berkeley: University of California, 1980), p. 209.

104. For a general discussion of this, see: E. Moudoud, "*The Rise and Fall of the Growth Pole Approach*," Discussion Paper, no. 89, Department of Geography, Syracuse University. November 1986

105. L. Rodwin, "Choosing Regions for development," *in Regional Development and Planning: A Reader,* eds. J. Friedmann and W. Alonso (Cambridge, MA: MIT Press, 1964), pp. 37-58; N. Hansen, *French Regional Planning* (Bloomington: Indiana University Press, 1968); D.F. Darwent, "Growth Poles and Growth Centers in Regional Planning: A Review," *Environment and Planning,* no. 1 (1969), pp. 5-31.

106. Hansen, op. cit., p. 104

107. Rodwin, op. cit., p. 45.

108. Hansen, op. cit., pp. 102-22.

109. J.F. Gravier, *Paris et le Désert Français: Decentralisation, Equipement, Population* (Paris: Le Portulan, 1947) (reprinted in 1972 as: *Paris et le Désert Français in 1972* [Paris: Flammarion]).

110. G.W. Ross and S.S. Cohen, "The Politics of French Regional Planning," in *Regional Policy: Readings in Theory and Applications,* eds. J. Friedmann and W. Alonso (Cambridge, MA: MIT Press, 1975), pp. 727-50; and A. Gilbert, ed., *Development Planning and Spatial Structure* (London: Wiley, 1976).

111. Hansen, op. cit.

112. Darwent, op. cit., p. 5.

113. K. Allen and M. MacLennan, *Regional Problems and Policies in Italy and France* (Beverly Hills: Sage, 1970), p. xv; and B. Higgins, "Development Poles: Do They Exist?" in *Growth Pole Strategy and Regional Development Policy: Asian Experiences and Alternative Approaches,* eds. F. Lo and K. Salih (Oxford: Pergamon Press, 1978), p. 229.

114. J.R. Lasuen, "On Growth Poles," *Urban Studies,* no. 2 (1969), p. 137.

115. G. Myrdal, *Economic Theory and Underdeveloped Regions* (Oxford: Duckworth, 1957); A.O. Hirschman, *The Strategy of Economic Development* (New Haven: Yale University Press, 1958).

116. See for example, the analysis of A. Matteacioti; *Diversité Régionale et Coherence Nationale: L'Exemple des Régions Méditerranéenes* (Paris: Economica, 1981), pp. 6-7.

117. F. Perroux, "Economic Space: Theory and Applications," *Quarterly Journal of Economics,* no. 64 (1950), pp. 89-104.

118. F. Perroux, "Note sur la Notion de 'Pôle de Croissance,'" *Economie Appliqueé,* nos. 1-2 (1955), pp. 307-20; also in idem, *L'Economie du XXe Siècle* (Paris: P.U.F., 1964).

119. Higgins, op. cit., p. 229.

120. See Matteaciotti, op. cit.; and M. Monsted, "François Perroux's Theory of 'Growth Pole' and 'Development Pole': A Critique," *Antipode,* no. 2 (1974), pp. 106-14.

121. R. J. Boudeville, Problems of Regional Economic Planning (Edinburgh: Edinburgh University Press, 1966); and idem, Les Espaces Economiques (Paris: P.U.F., 1961).

122. M. Darkoh, "Growth Poles and Growth Centers with Special Reference to Developing Countries—A Critique," *Journal of Tropical Geography*, no. 44 (1977), pp. 12-22.

123. Higgins, op. cit., p. 229.

124. See for example: D. Rondinelli and K. Ruddle, *Urbanization and Rural Development: A Spatial Policy for Equitable Growth* (New York: Praeger, 1978); J. Friedmann and C. Weaver, *Territory and Function; The Evolution of Regional Planning* (Los Angeles: University of California Press, 1979); and J. Friedmann, *Urban Bias in Regional Development Policy*, School of Architecture and Urban Planning, UCLA Working Paper, C.U. 29, 1981.

125. For a detailed discussion of this particular issue, see. E. Moudoud: "The Rise and Fall of the Growth Pole Approach...," op. cit.,

126. Higgins, op. cit., p. 229.

127. V. Nichols, "Growth Poles: An Evaluation of their Propulsive Effects," *Environment and Planning*, no. 1 (1969), p. 194.

128. Ibid.; see also Friedmann and Weaver, op. cit., E. Moudoud, op. cit., Darkoh, op. cit.,

129. Nichols, op. cit., p. 199.

130. M. J. Moseley, "The Impact of Growth Centers in Rural Regions," Regional Studies, No. 7 (1973) pp. 57-94; H.W. Richardson and H. Richardson, "The Relevance of Growth Center Strategies to Latin America," Economic Geography, No. 51 (1975) pp. 163-78

131. Richardson and Richardson, op. cit., p. 169.

132 Rondinelli and Ruddle, op. cit., p. 15.

133 Ibid., pp. 15-16.

134. See Monsted, op. cit.

135. Darkoh, op. cit., p. 18; see also J. L. Corragio, "Polarization, Development and Integration," A. Kuklinski (ed) Regional Development and Planning: International Perspectives (Leyden Sijthoff, 1975) pp. 353-74 (see especially pp. 361-66)

136. See among others: Monsted, op. cit.; Friedmann and Weaver, op. cit.; Corragio, op. cit.; and P. Kongstadt, "Growth Poles and Urbanization: A Critique of Perroux and Friedmann," *Antipode*, no. 2 (1974), pp. 114-22.

137. Higgins, op. cit., p. 234.

138. Quoted from Higgins, op. cit., p. 234.

139. See Corragio, op. cit.; this argument has been widely developed and documented by Marxist economists. See for example: Alain Lipietz, *Le Capital et son Espace* (Paris: Maspero, 1977); Stuart Holland, *Capital Versus the Regions* (London: Macmillan, 1976); and idem, *The Regional*

*Problem* (New York: St. Martin's Press, 1976). See also: Fu. Cheu Lo and Kamal Salih, "Growth Poles, Agropolitan Development, and Polarization Reversal: The Debate and Search for Alternatives," in W. Stohr and D.R.F. Taylor (eds.) Development from Above or Below? (New York: Wiley, 1981) pp. 123-152; Y. Durieu, L'impossible Regionalisation Capitaliste: Temoignages de Fos et du Languedoc (Paris: Ed. Anthropos, 1973); M. Conroy, "Rejection of Growth Center Strategy in Latin America Regional Development Planning," Land Economics, No. 4 (1973), pp. 371-80; M. Santos, "Underdevelopment, Growth Poles and Social Justice," Civilizations, Nos. 1-2 (1975), pp. 18-30;

140. See for example: Corragio, op. cit., p. 371; Darkoh, op. cit., Santos, op. cit.,

141. Darkoh, op. cit., p. 18.

142. Matteaccioti, op. cit., pp. 6-7.

143. H.W. Richardson, "Growth Centers, Rural Development and National Urban Policy: A Defense," International Regional Science Review, no. 2 (1978), pp. 163-178

144. See for further details: A. Gilbert and J. Gugler, *Cities, Poverty and Development. Urbanization in the Third World* (Oxford: Oxford University Press, 1982); Ch. Gore, *Regions in Question: Space, Development Theory and Regional Planning* (London and New York: Methuen, 1984); E.W. Soja, "Regions in Context: Spatiality, Periodicity, and the Historical Geography of the Regional Question," *Society and Space*, no. 2 (1985), pp. 175-90; and idem, "Territorial Idealism and the Political Economy of Regional Development," *City and Region: Journal of Spatial Studies*, no. 6 (1983), pp. 55-73.

145. J. Friedmann, "A Spatial Framework for Rural Development: Problems of Organization and Implementation," *Economie Appliquée*, nos. 2-3 (1975), pp. 519-44.

146. J. Friedmann and M. Douglas, "Agropolitan Development: Towards a New Strategy for Regional Planning in Asia," in *Growth Pole Strategy and Regional Development Policy: Asian Experience and Alternative Approaches*, eds. F. Lo and K. Salih (Oxford: Pergamon Press, 1978), pp. 163-92.

147. J. Friedmann and C. Weaver, *Territory and Function: The Evolution of Regional Planning* (Los Angeles: University of California Press, 1979); J. Friedmann, "Basic Needs, Agropolitan Development, and Planning from Below," *World Development*, no. 6 (1979), pp. 607-13; idem, "The Active Community: Toward a Political-Territorial Framework for Rural Development in Asia," *Economic Development and Cultural Change*, no. 2 (1981), pp. 235-61; idem, *Urban Bias in Regional Development Policy*, op. cit.; idem, "Regional Planning for Rural Mobilization in Africa," *Rural Africana*, nos. 12-13 (1982), pp. 3-20; and

idem "Political and Technical Moments in Development: Agropolitan Development Revisited," *Society and Space*, no. 2 (1985), pp. 155-67.

148. And subsequently for Africa (Friedmann, "Urban Bias") and all agrarian societies of the Third World (Friedmann, "Political and Technical Moments in Development").

149. J. Friedmann and M. Douglas, op. cit., p. 164.

150. Ibid.

151. Ibid.

152. Ibid.

153. See Friedmann, "Active Community," p. 242.

154. Ibid., p. 252; and Friedmann and Douglas, op. cit., p. 185.

155. Ibid.

156. Friedmann and Weaver, op. cit., p. 195.

157. Friedmann, "Urban Bias," p. 18.

158. Friedmann, "Basic needs," p. 610.

159. Friedmann, "Active Community," p. 267.

160. Friedmann and Douglas, op. cit., p. 183.

161. Friedmann, "Active Community," p. 260.

162.. Friedmann, "Urban Bias," p. 18.

163. D.A. Rondinelli and K. Ruddle, *Urbanization and Rural Development: A Spatial Policy for Equitable Growth* (New York: Praeger, 1978).

164. Ibid., p. v.

165. Ibid., p. 58.

166. Friedmann, "Urban Bias," p. 9.

167. For further details, see Rondinelli and Ruddle, op. cit., Chapters 4, 5 and 6.

168. Ibid., p. 159.

169. See Gilbert and Gugler, op. cit.

170. Rondinelli and Ruddle, op. cit., p. 52.

171. See: D. Rondinelli, "Intermediate Cities in Developing Countries: A Comparative Analysis of Their Demographic, Social and Economic Characteristics," *Third World Planning Review*, no. 4 (1982), pp. 357-86; idem, "The Dynamics of Growth of Secondary Cities in Developing Countries," *The Geographical Review*, no. 1 (1983), pp. 42-57; idem, *Secondary Cities in Developing Countries* (Beverly Hills, CA: Sage, 1983); idem, "Towns and Small Cities in Developing Countries," *The Geographical Review*, no. 4, (1983), pp. 379-95; idem, "Population Distribution and Economic Development in Africa: The Need for Urbanization Policies," *Population Research and Policy Review*, no. 2 (1985), pp. 173-96; and idem, "The Crisis of Urbanization in Asia: Finding Alternatives to Megapolitan Growth," *The Journal of Social, Political and Economic Studies*, no. 1 (1985), pp. 69-86.

172. Rondinelli, "Intermediate Cities," p. 1.

173. Rondinelli, "Secondary Cities," p. 14.
174. Rondinelli and Ruddle, op. cit.
175. Rondinelli, "Population Distribution," pp. 187-88 (emphasis in the text).
176. See for example the excellent paper by D.R.F. Taylor, *The Role and Functions of Lower Order Centers in Rural Development*, U.N. C.R.D., Working Papers, no.79, Nagoya, 1979; and his attempt to conceptualize his propositions in "Conceptualizing Development Space in Africa," *Geografiska Annales*, no. 63 (1980), pp. 87-93; see also his book (with W. Stöhr), *Development from Above or Below*.
177. Again, I would like to stress that I am aware of the work of other researchers in other parts of the world: Europe, Latin America, Africa and Asia. It is, however, beyond the scope of this book to review all the literature existing (in different languages) in the world. Secondly, despite all my efforts it is almost impossible to keep track of all published new work in at least the francophone world from the United States.
178. See Friedmann, "Political and technical Moments...," op. cit., p. 156.
179. See especially Soja, "Territorial Idealism...," and Idem, "Regions in Context...," op. cit..
180. Ibid, "Regions in Context...," p. 176
181. Ch. Gore, op. cit., see chap. 5, pp. 146-171.
182. Ibid.
183. See Friedmann, op. cit.; and Rondinelli, "Regions in Question: A Critical Review," Third World Planning Review, No. 3 (1985) pp. 263-68.
184. For further discussion on this particular aspect of this issue, see: C. Weaver, "Romance of the Roses: A Discourse on the Path to Religional Reconstruction," Society and Space, no. 2 (1985), pp. 239-58; B. Voyenne, *Le Federalisme de P.J. Proudhon* (Paris: Presses D'Europe, 1973); and idem, *Histoire de l'Idee Federaliste: Les Lignees Proudhoniennes* (Paris: Presses d'Europe, 1981); Pierre Kropotkine, *L'Etat: Son Role dans l'Histoire* (Paris: Publico, 1983); and Federation Anarchiste de Paris, Centralisme and Federalisme (Paris: Publications de la Federation Anarchiste, 1983). H. Lefebvre, La Proclamation de la Commune (Paris: Gallimard, 1965) see especially, pp. 149-154; R. Williams, "Towards Many Socialisms," Socialist Review, no. 85 (1986) pp. 45-65; see also references in fn. 21.

# PART TWO
# REGIONAL DISPARITY AND THE QUESTION OF TRANSITION IN TUNISIA

---

La rupture de l'indépendance nationale délivre d'un pouvoir et simultanément en constitue un autre qui n'est pas seulement une substitution, mais qui réaménage toute la commande politique. En refusant cette responsabilité qui pourtant objectivement est la sienne, l'homme politique national cherche constamment à se disculper de ses échecs posterieurs à la libération.

Hélé Béji,
*Désenchantement National. Essai sur la décolonisation.*
(Maspero, Paris 1982, p. 18)

The purpose of this second part is to address the first objective of the study, which is to answer the two questions of the research: (1) Why didn't the overall good economic performance of Tunisia during the last 30 years benefit all regions of the country, and (2) why have past regional development policies failed?

To this end, the next chapter will present first, an overview of Tunisia achievement; and second, it will provide a descriptive analysis of the nature and the magnitude of current regional disparities. Chapter 4 will retrace the historical roots of these disparities. The focus here will be on the policies that "created" them during the colonial period . Finally, Chapter 5 will continue with the documentation and analysis of the policies that have, after independence, and until 1982, the date of the launching of the Sixth Tunisian Five Year Plan (1982-86), attempted to eliminate or to reduce them.

# 3
# GROWTH, DEVELOPMENT, REGIONAL DISPARITY AND THE TUNISIAN DILEMMA

## INTRODUCTION

It was stated in the introduction to this study that Tunisia has been particularly successful among Third World countries in stimulating economic growth. It was also stated that social and regional disparities, however, remain crucial and have become, because of their aggravation, a serious threat to the unity and the stability of the country. Finally, it was argued that this aggravation reflected, in fact, the limits and impasses that past and present Tunisian development strategies themselves have reached.

The objective of this chapter is to explain all this. The first part will discuss Tunisia's economic performance. Here, the concern is about *what* was achieved and *how* it was achieved. The second part will then discuss regional disparities. Here, a descriptive statistical analysis is provided in order to see not only *what* was achieved but also and especially *where* it was achieved. It is hoped that this will give a clear picture of the nature and the magnitude of the regional problem today in Tunisia.

## GROWTH OR DEVELOPMENT? THE TUNISIAN DILEMMA

It is not my intention to get into a debate about this very sensitive issue, which is generating more and more polemics between the leaders of the Parti Socialiste Destourien (P.S.D.), in power for 30 years, and the leaders of the oppositions, who have accused them of having transformed the country, with their "neo-colonialist" development strategy, into a "fiscal heaven" and a "labor reservoir" for international capital and that the only thing they have achieved in 30 years is "growth without development."[1]

My only objective here is to look at the facts and to explain what is meant in this study by the "impasses and limits of past and present Tunisian development strategies." I believe that only facts can tell us what Tunisia's achievements are in terms of "growth" or in terms of "development." But before doing that, and for the clarity of the discussion, let me go back to the contention itself and start first with the concept of "growth without development."

## The Concept of "Growth without Development"

The expression was coined in the mid-1960s in what is called in the literature on development the "underdevelopment/dependency theory" (U.D.T.). Samir Amin, Giovanni Arrighi and Andre Gunder Frank are considered among those who have popularized the concept the most. But it was Amin who first developed it in his study on the "Development of Capitalism in Ivory Coast."[2] In this study, Amin defines the concept as follows:

> A growth generated and maintained from outside without the socio-economic structures being capable to allow an automatic passage to the ulterior phase, a phase of an autocentric and self-maintained dynamism.[3]

"Growth" and "development" are defined more specifically. "Growth" is defined as this "banal" phenomenon of the increase of the product per capita and whatever the fundamental structures are that accompany this increase. On the contrary "development" is defined as this "radical structural change" that conditions growth, but a growth within an autocentric structure: a structure, Amin continues, "shaped in function of the requirements of the construction of an autocentric society."[4] For Amin, this is by no means to imply the refusal of contacts or exchanges with the external world. It simply means the refusal to submit the very conditions of internal development to external conditions.

From this basic definition, the concept integrates further new elements. While Amin's definition of "growth" was quite clear, his definition of "development" is very restrictive. What is, for example, an "autocentric structure" and what are the "requirements of the construction of an autocentric society?" And furthermore what is "development" itself? Thus a more precise definition of development is needed.

This very delicate task was very successfully tackled, I believe, a few years later by the late Dudley Seers in his famous article, a classic in the literature on development, "The Meaning of Development," published in 1969.[5]

In line with Amin's central argument, Seers denounces the deliberate assimilation of "development with economic development and economic development with economic growth."[6] The fundamental questions to ask about a country's development, Seers says, are not about economic growth or increases of per capita incomes alone. The questions to ask, Seers says, are:

> What has been happening to poverty? What has been happening to unemployment? What has been happening to inequality? If all three of these have declined from high levels, then, beyond a doubt this has been a period of development for the country concerned. If one or two of

> these central problems have been growing worse, especially if all three have, it would be strange to call the result "development," even if per capita income has doubled.[7]

In addition to these basic elements, and although added in a footnote, Seers adds some other conditions. These are what he calls "human requirements," such as education, freedom of speech and "citizenship of a nation that is truly independent both politically and economically."[8]

Eight years later, regretting that he did not pay sufficient attention to these last elements, Seers develops further his definition of development in his "The New Meaning of Development," a more political version of the "Meaning of Development" published in 1977. In addition to the decline of poverty, unemployment and inequality, Seers introduced the notion of "self-reliance."

> The time is indeed ripe for another critical look at the meaning of development. One could—even more easily than in 1969—defend the view that the word 'development' is too tarnished to be usable. The political and institutional reasons for retaining it still apply, however, and once more the way forward is to redefine it rather than reject it completely. The essential element to add—as being widely recognised—is *self-reliance*.[9]

But what did Seers mean by self-reliance? Is he speaking of *autarchy*? Here again, as for Samir Amin, self-reliance does not mean autarchy. What Seers meant by self-reliance follows:

> Of course an emphasis on reducing dependence does not necessarily mean aiming at autarchy. How far it is desirable, or even possible to go in that direction, depends on a country's size, location and natural resources; on its cultural homogeneity and the depths of its tradition; on the extent to which its economy needs imported inputs to satisfy consumption patterns which have to be taken—at least in the short term—as political minima. The key to a development strategy of the type suggested is not to break all links, which would almost anywhere be socially damaging and politically unworkable, but to adopt a selective approach to external influences of all types.[10]

We can see here the similarities between Seers's definition of development and self-reliance with that of Samir Amin. We have to note, however, that Seers's definition of development is clearer and more focused on the "content" of development itself.

Here are, then, the origins and the evolution of the "growth without development" concept. I admit this is a very brief review. My objective here was simply to retrace the origins of the concept and to show how and why "growth" and "development" were defined in a contrasting, if not in an opposite manner.

Let me now refer back to Tunisia to see, according to the definition we have just seen of the concept, if the contention that Tunisia has achieved "growth without development" is true? To begin with, let us take Tunisian growth achievements.

## Tunisian Growth Achievements

As was stated in the introduction, by most conventional measures Tunisia has been particularly successful among Third World countries in stimulating economic growth. From less than US$100 in 1956, year of the independence of the country, the GNP per capita has passed US$1,400 (1,420) in 1981, with an annual average rate of growth of 4.8 percent between 1960 and 1980.[11] Moreover, from an export-oriented colonial economy based on one or two primary products (agriculture and mining products) during the 1950s, the Tunisian economy has been transformed during the last three decades to a more diversified and plurisectoral economy as shown by: (1) the sectoral evolution of the structure of the GDP (Gross Domestic Product) between 1960 and 1980 (table 3.1); (2) the evolution of the labor force distribution by economic sector (table 3.2); and (3) the sectoral distribution of Tunisian exports in general (table 3.3).

Now, what one may conclude from all this data? I think that even if we cannot speak of a "miracle" à la Ivory Coast or à la Taiwan, for example, the Tunisian overall economic performance is, to paraphrase a report of the World Bank, "excellent."[12] Inflation, in addition, has been kept relatively low in comparison with other Third World countries. The average annual rate of inflation has been 3.6% for the decade 1960-70 and only 7.7% during the decade 1970-80. This last indicator has led recently one observer to qualify Tunisia as one of the "best students" among Third World countries, of the IMF and the World Bank![13]

These are then, very briefly, the Tunisian achievements in terms of growth. Now, what about development? How has this "excellent" economic performance been translated—to go back to our earlier discussion of the concept of development according to Samir Amin and Dudley Seers—in terms of: (1) the reduction of poverty and inequality; (2) reduction of unemployment and underemployment; (3) political and social participation; and (4) finally, self-reliance?

Table 3.1

STRUCTURE AND GROWTH OF PRODUCTION BY SECTOR 1960-1980

**(1) Sectoral Composition of GDP (in %)**

| GDP- Millions of US$ | | Agriculture | | Industry | | Manufacturing | | Services | |
|---|---|---|---|---|---|---|---|---|---|
| 1960 | 1980 | 1960 | 1980 | 1960 | 1980 | 1960 | 1980 | 1960 | 1980 |
| 770 | 7,300 | 24 | 17 | 18 | 35 | 8 | 13 | 58 | 48 |

**(2) Average Annual Growth Rate of Production (in %)**

| GDP | | Agriculture | | Industry | | Manufacturing | | Services | |
|---|---|---|---|---|---|---|---|---|---|
| 1960-70 | 1970-80 | 1960-70 | 1970-80 | 1960-70 | 1970-80 | 1960-70 | 1970-80 | 1960-70 | 1970-80 |
| 4.7 | 7.5 | 2.0 | 4.9 | 8.2 | 9.0 | 7.8 | 11.2 | 4.5 | 7.8 |

Source: World Bank, *World Development Report, 1982*, pp. 113, 114.

Table 3.2

EVOLUTION OF THE LABOR FORCE DISTRIBUTION BY SECTOR 1960-1980 (in %)

| Population 1980 | Urban Pop. as % of Total Pop. | | Agriculture | | Industry | | Services | |
|---|---|---|---|---|---|---|---|---|
| | 1960 | 1980 | 1960 | 1980 | 1960 | 1980 | 1960 | 1980 |
| 6.5 million | 36 | 52 | 56 | 34 | 18 | 33 | 26 | 33 |

Source: World Bank, *World Development Report, 1982*, p. 147.

Table 3.3

DISTRIBUTION OF EXPORTS BY SECTOR
1964-1980 (in %)

| | 1964 | 1980 |
|---|---|---|
| Primary Products: | | |
| Food | 59 | 4 |
| Minerals | 22 | 3 |
| Oil, Gas | 0 | 53 |
| Semi-Processed Goods: | 17 | 17 |
| Finished Goods: | | |
| Machinery & Capital Goods | 0 | 2 |
| Consumer Goods | 2 | 19 |

Source: Banque Centrale de Tunisie, *Statistique Financières*, 1981, p. 66.

Tunisian Development Achievements

1. Poverty and Inequality. I think that the best and most honest way to look at this very controversial issue is to first let Tunisian policy makers themselves speak about it.

In a very important document, a comprehensive background document for the third decade of development and the Sixth Development Plan (1982-86), published in November 1980, Tunisian central planners admitted very frankly the persistence of poverty and the existence of great distributional inequalities within Tunisian society:

> We must have the honesty to say that there is in 1980 unacceptable social inequalities for us: the richest 20 percent of the population dispose alone of 50 percent of the national income, whereas the poorest 20 percent of the population dispose of only 5 percent.[14]

Also, continue the authors of the document, while "absolute poverty" has diminished substantially during the last two decades, 22.5 percent of the Tunisian population (about one million) lived in "absolute poverty" in 1980[15] (absolute poverty here is officially defined as having an annual income of less than 100 TD in 1980 prices; the Tunisian Dinar is at present around US$1.60).In a study by the World Bank published the same year as the important document by the Ministry of Planning, we can read in respect to poverty the following:

> While absolute poverty is diminishing rapidly, there is little cause for complacency. Absolute poverty as defined in this report, remains a problem affecting one out of six people in Tunisia. Rapid overall growth did not create sufficient opportunities for everyone.[16]

Table 3.4

EVOLUTION OF "ABSOLUTE POVERTY" BETWEEN 1961 AND 1980

| Year | Population in Poverty in % | Variation | Poverty Line |
|---|---|---|---|
| 1961 | 73 | - | 50 TD (1961 prices) |
| 1971 | 42 | -31 | - |
| 1980 | 22.5 | -19.5 | 100 TD (1980 prices) |

Source: Republique Tunisienne/Ministère du Plan and des Finances, *Notes d'Orientation*, p. 2; and idem, *VIème Plan de Développement Economique et Social (1982-86)*, p. 3.

Furthermore, add the authors of the study,

> While rapid economic growth in Tunisia during 1967-75 on average was reflected in rapidly increasing standards of living, distributional inequalities worsened, with the top 5 percent of the population accumulating shares of the expenses of everybody else.[17]

I think that the least one may say here is that this is a very severe statement from the World Bank on one of its "best students." But beyond that, what one may conclude from this evidence? One may conclude from this that the lower strata of the Tunisian population, the "have nots," cannot see what "growth" could mean for them.

2. Unemployment and Underemployment. Let us now look at another important area: unemployment and underemployment. What has been happening here? This is another very controversial issue between Tunisian policy makers and the opposition. The controversy is of course about *data*. The official rate of unemployment was 11 percent in 1981.[18] The opposition says it was at least 30 percent.[19] But, and in any case, it is obvious that the Tunisian government is trying to hide the real magnitude of this real cancer that is undermining the foundations of the Tunisian society. Because of this controversy about the data, I will use neither government statistics nor those of the opposition. I have used the data of the World Bank, an institution that no one I believe would suspect of an hostile attitude towards the Tunisian government!

In the same study of the Bank I just mentioned, we can read the following about the unemployment problem in Tunisia:

> One of the most striking characteristics of the Tunisian economy is widespread unemployment and underemployment. This is probably the most important social and political problem facing the Tunisian authorities today. In 1978 some 16 percent of the labor force, i.e. a quarter million people, were unemployed. Considering the underemployed, especially in agriculture and services, the effective overall unemployment rate is closer to 30 percent. Also, there are enormous differences in rural and urban unemployment and generally among *regions*.[20]

I must add here that the World Bank study does not take into account the estimated 400,000 Tunisian workers abroad.[21] Without this "safety valve" (which is no longer available) the unemployment situation would have been worse. Whatever the rate, a question must be asked here: why, in a time of rapid economic growth, has the unemployment situation been deteriorating since 1969 (from 10 percent in 1969 the unemployment rate jumped to 13 percent in 1973 and to 16 percent in 1978 and probably more in 1980)?

According to another Bank study (a report on the Sixth Development Plan [1982-86] published in March 1983), two main factors seem to account for this:

> Persistently high unemployment at a time of rapid economic growth and high investments reflect government policies, which led to excessively capital intensive investments and a sharp increase in the average cost per job created. First and foremost, Government agreed to a rapid increase in labor costs during the 1970s. At the same time, capital investments remained relatively cheap because of low interests rates and low tariffs on capital good imports; incentive laws stimulated investments rather than

> employment; highly subsidized energy prices policies discouraged labor intensive exports and labor intensive agriculture.[22]

And the economists of the Bank add:

> While social considerations understandably militated in favor of substantial wage and salary increases, such increases clearly tended to discourage employment. The question has to be asked, therefore, whether in a situation of high structural employment and underemployment more consideration should not be given to expand employment rather than to increase the incomes of those who already have a job.[23]

Whether we disagree with this proposition, which seems to me politically unfeasible, or not, what may one conclude from this analysis? First and most important is that by low tariffs on capital good imports the government was subsidizing employment abroad and creating unemployment at home! Secondly and equally important, as the excellent analysis of the Bank's report indicates, the deliberate bias in favor of capital intensive sectors and projects explains the incapacity of the Tunisian economy, in spite of the thousands of Tunisian workers abroad, to absorb the continual increase of labor. It is therefore this anti-employment bias of government policies that is responsible for the high structural unemployment and underemployment and their aggravation. Thus, it is clear that the unemployment cancer has nothing to do, or little at least, with the so-called "demographic pressures," as the "Malthusianist" official approach would suggest.

3. Citizenship and Political Participation. Now let us look at a third important area: citizenship and political participation. What has been happening in this area? I am afraid that here too, as with the unemployment problem, we have a very negative picture.

For more than two decades now, Tunisia has been, and still is, one of the most centralized countries in francophone Africa. It is beyond the scope of this study to get into a detailed analysis of all the factors that have contributed to the excessive centralization of the Tunisian political and administrative system. I will therefore be very brief.

The first important factor is an external one: the heritage of the centralist, jacobin, French colonial past. This has been very well documented in the literature on Tunisia as well as on all francophone Africa.[24] Suffice therefore to mention it.

But, and along with John Nellis, I don't think that after 30 years of political independence we can continue to blame the centralization "syndrome" on this French heritage alone.[25] On the contrary, I believe that this is caused by strictly internal factors. As in other African countries and "in spite of considerable lip service...to decentralization" the tendency in Tunisia has been "to strengthen the inherited administrative traditions rather than to restrict or to dismantle them."[26] These internal factors to which I will limit my brief survey, are of two kinds: the first is an ideological and political one; the second is what Nellis calls "the self-interest of the dominant elites."[27]

The ideological and political factor is related to, and deeply rooted in, the conception of development itself of the Tunisian leaders. This conception of development, based on an obsession with "organic unity," or I would rather say on a "hegemonic" conception of "national unity," considered political participation, or what I would also call "political rights," as a luxury that the country cannot offered in the early stages of "development" and "nation building." Political divisions that could emerge from the exercise of these political rights must be avoided at any price. In order to win the "battle of development" all forces must unite and stick together behind those who have already won the "battle for independence."[28]

In this scheme, State control over the society and the economy, based on and totally supported by a single-party political system, was seen as the sina qua non condition for political stability and development. Based on these premises, centralization was therefore justified and presented as an absolute necessity.

The second factor I mentioned and that Nellis has called the "self-interest of the elite," is very well documented and I will not get here into a detailed discussion of this very sensitive issue![29] Two examples suffice to illustrate what is meant by this: the use of centralization as a means of self-enrichment (in other words corruption); the use of centralization by the elites, in the absence of strong judicial and real counterpower mechanisms, to perpetuate their dominance. As noted by Nellis, the justification of centralization "masks much elite behavior aimed at self-enrichment and perpetuation of their position of power. Centralization facilitates these aims."[30]

Here are then, very briefly, what I consider the major internal factors for the highly centralized political and administrative Tunisian system. And they explain why, for example, the subnational government system is so weak in spite of nearly 30 years of independence now. A few words about the system to illustrate this.

Tunisia is divided into twenty *gouvernorats*, each headed by a centrally appointed *gouverneur* (akin to the French *préfet*). Each gouvernorat is subdivided into *délégations*, headed by a *délégué* (akin to the French *sous-préfet*). These officials are also central appointees. The délégations, in turn, are divided into *secteurs*, which are directed by the *omdahs*, nonremovable leaders elected from the local cells of the party. In addition all these administrative divisions are matched by parallel party units of the sole official party until 1980, the Parti Socialiste Destourien (P.S.D.) (see figure 3.1). At the gouvernorat level the structure is completed with a supposedly consultative and representative assembly: the *conseil de gouvernorat*. Now, what is the function of this top-down structure? As noted by many observers their only function "has been and largely remains that of sending information to the center and applying locally the directives passed down from on high," writes Nellis.[31] This is a clearly an antidemocratic subnational government structure.

Under increasing pressures, however, some efforts to decentralize it have been undertaken, especially since 1975, when an important decentralization reform was announced with fanfare! But as of 1979, an assessment of the reform by two Tunisian scholars has shown that very little was accomplished and that the centralist and centralizing habits remain unchanged.[32] The two authors of the assessment conclude their study by arguing that the 1975 reform was simply a "political myth," used by the leadership, they say, "to offset criticism of their centralized single-party rule" and by a regime that "cannot or does not want to reconsider fundamentally its own norm and political behavior." Their conclusion is supported by the fact that "all sectors of social activity" as of 1979, four years after the reform, "are regulated by the center in their least detail."[33]

This analysis was confirmed in 1980 by the important document of the Ministry of Planning mentioned earlier, in which Tunisian central planners themselves admitted that:

> There is presently, and everyone can see it everyday and everywhere, a true bottling-up in the country brought about by centralization....The present paralysis stems from the fact that everything or almost everything comes out of Tunis, and every attempt to loosen the congestion of the capital...clashes with great difficulties...all means are concentrated in Tunis, especially the power, men and financial resources.[34]

Speaking about the inefficiency of the Tunisian administration, the authors of the *Note d'Orientation*, add:

> ...in the eyes of the citizenry, the administration has become synonymous with heaviness (lourdeur), with red-tape indeed and in certain cases with inefficiency. Its anonymous, impersonal and sometimes inhuman character adds to the politically dangerous phenomenon of its rejection by the country.[35]

In another document published by the same ministry in 1983, it is stated that one of the objectives of the Sixth Development Plan is

> to give to the regions essential rights and powers in the field of administration and management, and an economic orientation in order to re-link the administration and the

> administered, and to develop *at last* in the latter a sentiment of *participation* in the taking of decisions and the effort of development.[36]

I note in this passage a key word: "to develop *at last* in the administered, a sentiment of participation." This is a clear confession of what has been happening in the area of "citizenship and political participation" in Tunisia during the last 30 years. So, here too the conclusion is obvious, the picture is very negative.

4. Self-Reliance. Now, what has been happening to self-reliance? (i.e., "economic independence," and I don't mean by this "autarchy").

In the early 1960s, self-reliance was one of the most important goals of Tunisian socialist development. Two of the four fundamental objectives of the first ten-year plan (1962-71) were: *decolonization* of the economy and the society, and *self-development*, so that by the year 1973, investment could come from internal sources and not depend on foreign assistance.[37] But after the disastrous failure of the socialist experiment, especially the cooperative system,[38] these objectives and the whole socialist option were abandoned in 1969 and a new development strategy, based on a liberal economic policy, was put into effect in the early 1970s. This new economic strategy, based on a dogmatic philosophy of laisser-faire, has stressed instead the need for foreign private capital and the privatization of major sectors of the economy, especially agriculture, industry and tourism.

In the farming sector, the cooperative system was dismantled and replaced by private ownership. And even public land was sold or rented to the private sector. In the industrial sector, large and direct public investments were abandoned and two special laws were created in 1972 and 1974 in order to attract private foreign capital.

Here is what an American political scientist, John Pierre Entelis, has said, about this new economic policy in general and about these two laws in particular:

> This and subsequent liberal laws have virtually abdicated a portion of Tunisian sovereignty in the eager pursuit of foreign capital. Stressing the availability of cheap labor and the absence of social conflict, Tunisian authorities have voluntarily shifted Tunisia into the ranks of those Third World countries where development is carried out by, and for the benefit of foreign investors....

FIGURE 3.1 - LOCAL POLITICAL/ADMINISTRATIVE STRUCTURE

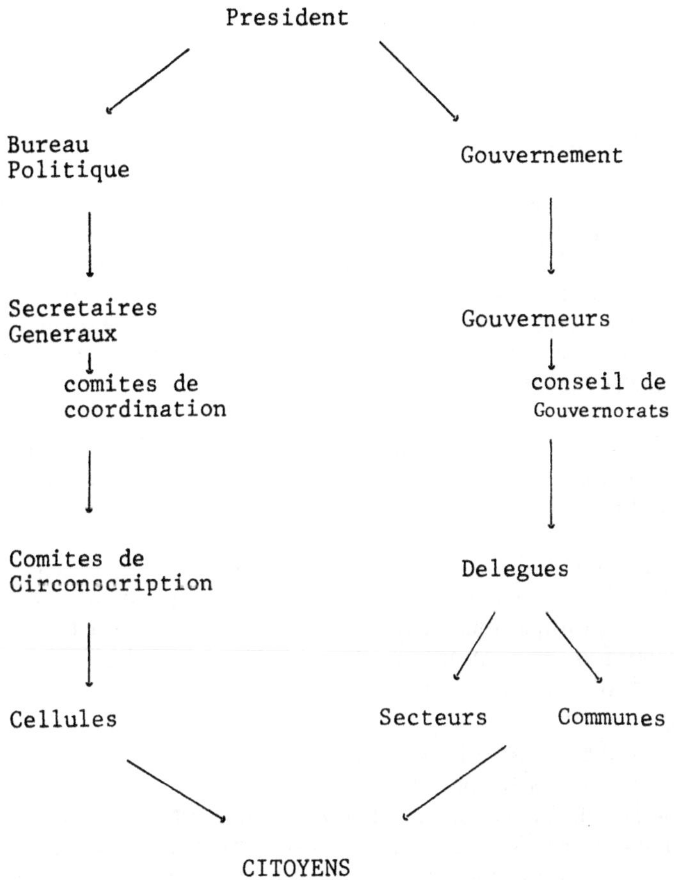


Source: Adapted from: P.F. Godinec - <u>Les Systemes Politiques Africains</u>. L.G.D.J., Paris 1978, p. 171.

In fact, he adds:

> ...the 1972 law will provide Tunisia with very few benefits since there will be no government revenues, no significant training and development of management expertise since the law allows the free entry of alien staff, no creation of local sources of capital since profits are repatriated, and few employment opportunities for skilled or semi-skilled workers since only jobs for unskilled labor will be created, a category of people for which there is already an abundant supply.

And he concludes:

> What will inevitably happen, of course, is that rather than emigrating, as some 15,000 Tunisians annually do, to become the proletariat of industrial Europe, the Government is encouraging the bringing of foreign industry to these unemployed Tunisians, who will thus become an indigenous proletariat, while the profits flow out of the country unchecked.[39]

Entelis put his finger here, and summarizes admirably, I think, the whole and damaging consequences of the political and economic philosophy in respect to self-reliance, of the Tunisian development strategy during the 1970s.

But, and although very crucial, this is only one aspect of the "dependent" and "extroverted" character of this new strategy. Its dependence is further illustrated when we look more closely to the structure of Tunisian foreign earnings and their origins. In 1981 for example, 68 percent of all foreign earnings came from only four sources: oil (33 percent), tourism (16 percent), textile (10 percent) and remittances from Tunisian workers abroad (9 percent).[40] If we also look at the geographical destination of Tunisian foreign trade, we find that more than 65 percent of this trade is with the European Economic Community (E.E.C.), where, in addition, more than 80 percent of Tunisian workers are in spite of the slow-down in emigration since 1973. Now that oil reserves are declining; earnings from tourism are sharply down as Europe, the main market for Tunisian tourist industry, is deeply locked in recession and structural unemployment; and that in addition and as a consequence of this, migration is shut off, Tunisian economic dependence is more apparent than ever. Even traditional agricultural products, such as olive oil, wine and citrus are threatened by new comers in the European Common Market, such as Spain, Greece and Portugal.

We can see here what future the Tunisian economy is facing. And I did not even mention the "debt bomb," which is relatively low in comparison with other Third World countries, but which has, however, jumped from $US600 million in 1971 to $US5 billion in 1981 and was estimated at $US12 billion in 1984.[41]

So, here too, the picture seems to be very negative. Of course one may argue that many of the international political and economic trends are beyond the control of a small country like Tunisia.[42] This is partly true of course. But frankly I do not believe, at least totally, in the explicit fatalist argument in this thesis, nor in the "conspiracy theory" implicit in almost all the writings of the "dependency school."

As we have seen, in respect to the unemployment problem for example, Tunisian authorities are the only ones to blame. They have had complete control over the policies they have implemented, which were, as the economists of the World Bank have correctly pointed out, deliberately anti-employment policies.

The point I am making here is that the good results of the Tunisian economy during the last three decades, especially during the 1970s, were not due, as certain models of development would suggest, to the "modernization" or the "maturity" of the economy but they were rather due to the extroverted character of the Tunisian development strategy, which was conceived, not in function, to paraphrase Amin or Seers, of the "requirements of an autocentric development," but in function of the needs and the demands of Western European economies. When these demands are no longer available the Tunisian economy finds itself in an impasse. In spite, therefore, of its achievement in terms of growth, it is still very vulnerable and very open to external economic forces, as it was at independence 32 years ago.

Missing from the discussion above are inequalities that I would like to return now. Because of their importance, for they constitute now a serious threat to the unity and the stability of the country and are therefore for this reason the focus of this study, they are to be discussed in a different section: these are regional disparities.

## REGIONAL DISPARITIES: THE NATURE AND THE MAGNITUDE OF THE PROBLEM

The objective of this section in discussing regional disparities is to look not at *what* was achieved and *how*, but at *where* it was achieved. Therefore, the discussion now focuses on inequalities from a spatial perspective, the regional one, and moves from a national to a subnational level.

One of the most striking characteristics of Tunisia today in this respect is the division of the country into two different countries. On one hand there is the *littoral*, which constitutes—with its cities, industries, infrastructures, ports, airports, fancy hotels, cultural activities especially in the summer (festival of this, festival of that...) and the thousands of tourists who each summer bring with them a certain "joie de vivre"—a country on its own. And I must add, even in the winter, the littoral always seems to be in another century, in another world; a world that doesn't belong to Tunisia. With or without tourists, the people of this other country seem happy despite all the problems. Of course there are "slums" and poor in the littoral. But Rome is just two hours away. Paris, London are not much more. And even the "Big Apple," or Los Angeles are no longer the "impossible dream." For the "entrepreneur," for the "smart"—with the help of "Allah" and the benediction of the government—everything is possible. And only those "fatalists," "traditionalists," would refuse the society of progress and wealth.

Looking with "hate" and frustration to this "promised land" are the people of the *other* Tunisia: the one that Dali Jazy has called "le Pays réel," or what Souhayr Belhassen has called the "forgotten country."[43] This country is the *interior*. There are no tourists in the summer here (nor in the winter), few industries, no dynamic and prosperous cities except in the memory of the people who still remember the glorious past of Kairouan, or as attested by Roman and Arab ruins of numerous other cities. No infrastructure exists either; in the winter most parts of the interior are isolated from the rest of the country. There is no money to spend (it doesn't stay in the region; see Chapter 6). Agricultural, rural, poor (despite its huge resources) and young, this other country seems a part of another world, belonging to the past—a past that no one in the littoral wants to remember. Why look behind? It is for the lagging to look forward, to the future, to the "*terre promise*," to the sea, to Rome, Paris and London, and one day perhaps to Los Angeles!

Beyond this "impressionistic" vision, there is a cruel truth that no *data* (I mean statistical) will ever describe. And this very simple truth can be best seen in the eyes of everybody in the interior, especially the youth.[44] One of them expressed it to me in the most simple words. On my way back to Kairouan from Kasserine on August 21, 1981, I was sitting in the bus beside a group of young workers. They were going back to their work after a short visit to their families in a village near Kasserine. When they knew who I was and why I was in Kasserine (because for them I was obviously a guy from the littoral...) they opened their hearts and began to talk freely. At the end, one of them in few words summarized the whole drama of the interior: "you see," said he, "how our region can develop, if *they* continue to send us teachers, engineers, experts, etc., and *we* are forced in order to survive, to leave our children, our village, our region and migrate to the littoral to build *their* houses, to clean *their* streets and to serve *their* tourists." I think that in this young fellow's statement there is all the explanation of the anger and even the hate that the people of the interior feel about those of the littoral. I couldn't begin this section without even mentioning what I saw, what I heard; especially since I promise to the young fellow that "yes, I will write it in *my book* ."

Now is this "impressionistic" vision or "témoignage" based on any evidence, any facts? To answer this question, let us now look at the *data*. And to begin with let us see, first what official documents can tell us.

In the *Note d'Orientation*, the important document of the Ministry of Planning quoted earlier,[45] we can read in respect to regional disparities the following:

> The socialist option of Tunisia requires from us to have a qualitative evaluation which translates the impact of development upon the different regions of the country. The ascertainment (*constatation*) that we must do, as cruel as it may be, is that the country is divided with regard to infrastructure and living standards *into two parts*:
>
> —The coastal regions which possess an infrastructure far beyond the national average and where the economic activities, in industry, commerce, administration or tourism is concentrated.
>
> —The regions of the south and the west where infrastructure is insufficient and where the economic activity is, with few exceptions, reduced to agriculture and petty trade. For a large part of their needs, these regions depend totally if not on the capital, on large coast cities.[46]

The *Note d'Orientation* was published in 1980. Two years later, in another not less important document, the *VIth Five Year Plan 1982-1986*, published in June 1982, a more precise statement is made in these terms:

> Whatever the indicator one can choose (per capita private consumption, the proportion of poor families, the unemployment rate, water or electricity consumption, the illiteracy rate, health facilities per capita, km of road/km$^2$) one can observe that the Western and the Southern regions of the country are behind the coastal regions and below the national average.[47]

And indeed, as reflected by the geographic distribution of the population and the economic activity, this is the least one may say. In what follows, we will look at all these indicators, and a few others mentioned by the VIth Plan. All the data used, except when indicated otherwise, are for 1980-81.

<u>The Population Distribution and Population Density</u>

To begin with, let us take the geographic distribution of the Tunisian population. In 1980 for example, the ten gouvernorats of the littoral, from

Bizerte to Mednine (figure 3.2), had a population of 4,111,000—64.7 percent of the total population—although they occupy only 27 percent of the country's total area (table 3.5). The average population density in this zone is 98.3 persons/km$^2$, against 41.2 persons/km$^2$ in the whole country.

The region of the North-East alone (where Tunis, the capital, is located) has 33.6 percent of the total population and a density of 179.3 persons/km$^2$. This is four times the population density of the whole country and nearly nine times that of the whole interior.

The Economic Activity Distribution

Moreover and in addition to this population concentration, the littoral zone has the most important economic activities of the country. In 1980-81 for example, 67 percent of all employment in the country (and this does not include defense, construction and public works and the Ministry of Interior employment) was concentrated there; 81.9 percent of all employment in the nonagricultural sector; 87.6 percent of all employment in the private sector and 75.6 percent of all employment in the public sector (this includes administration and public enterprises) (tables 3.6 and 3.7).

And as if this was not enough, the littoral zone also concentrates 83 percent of all employment in industry (83 percent in manufacturing industries) and 94 percent of all employment (permanent jobs) and 93 percent of capacity (number of beds) in the touristic sector (tables 3.8 and 3.9).

In addition, the littoral zone has a non-negligible share of the agricultural sector. It produces about 95 percent of the citrus fruit and the vineyard (grapes) of the country, and more than two-thirds of the olive trees. It also produces a large part of the irrigated market-garden-cultivation (vegetables) and even some cereals and livestock.[48]

This concentration of population and economic activities is based on a relatively well-integrated urban network. The littoral zone alone has 79 percent of the total urban population of the country. And while the national rate of urbanization is, as of 1980-81, 52.2 percent, in the littoral it is 57 percent (tables 3.10 and 3.11).

In 1981, five cities in the littoral alone contained 51.4 percent of the total urban population of the country. All five cities are city-ports and the largest in the country. In addition to Tunis, population 1,123,000 (32 percent of the total urban population), there are: Sfax: 303,000 (8 percent); Sousse: 210,000 (6 percent); Bizerte: 92,500 (2.7 percent); and finally the city-port of the South-East, Gabes: 90,000 (2.7 percent).[49]

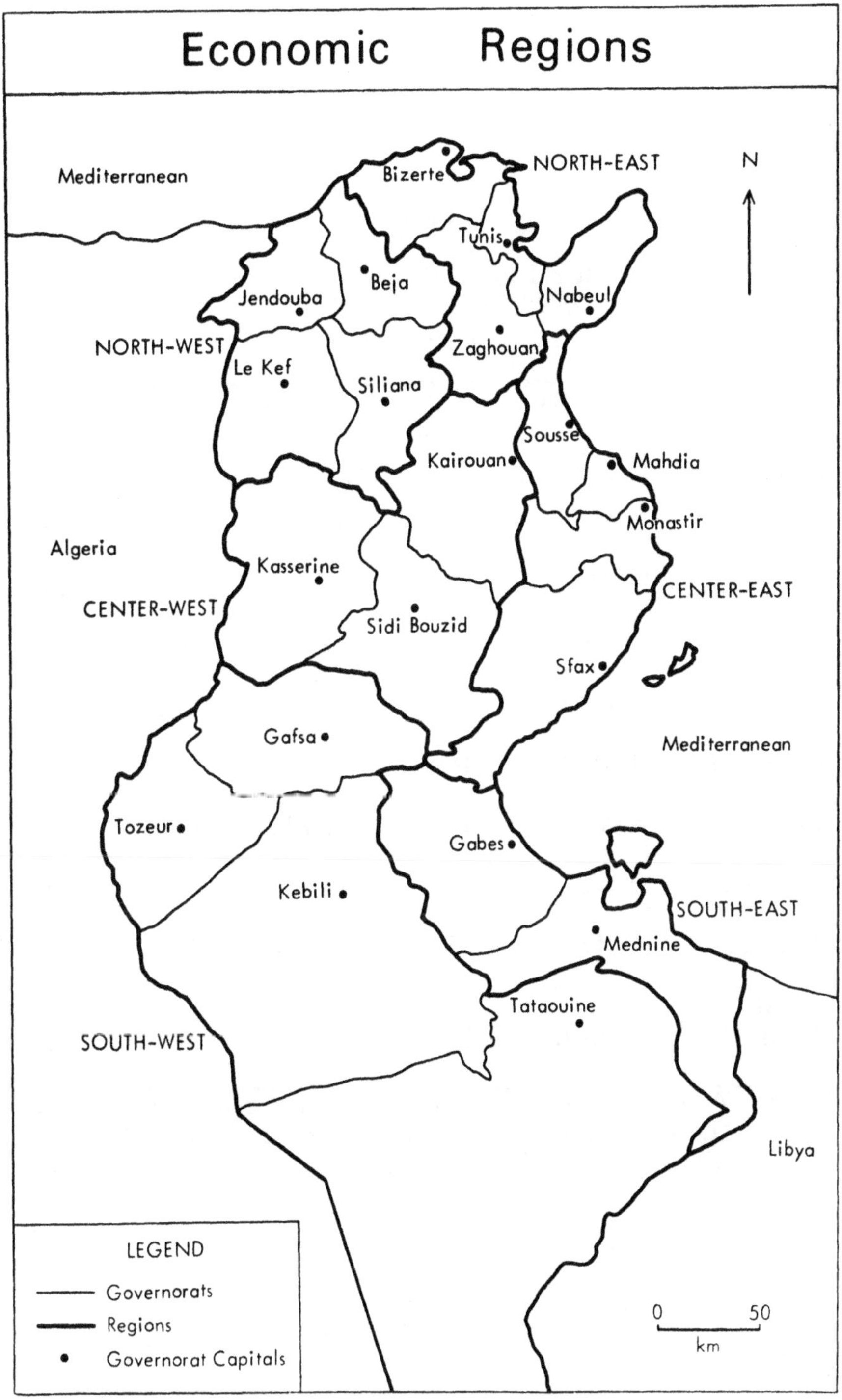
Economic Regions
Mediterranean
NORTH-EAST
N
Bizerte
Tunis
Beja
Jendouba
Nabeul
NORTH-WEST
Zaghouan
Le Kef
Siliana
Sousse
Kairouan
Mahdia
Monastir
Algeria
Kasserine
CENTER-EAST
CENTER-WEST
Sidi Bouzid
Sfax
Gafsa
Mediterranean
Tozeur
Gabes
Kebili
SOUTH-EAST
Mednine
Tataouine
SOUTH-WEST
Libya
LEGEND
Governorats
Regions
Governorat Capitals
0 50
km

Table 3.5

POPULATION DISTRIBUTION AND POPULATION DENSITY BY REGION IN 1980
(in thousands)

| Regions | Population | % of Total Pop. | Surface $km^2$ | % of Total Surface | Density $km^2$ |
|---|---|---|---|---|---|
| North-East | 2,135.0 | 33.6 | 11,906 | 7.7 | 179.3 |
| Center-East | 1,342.0 | 21.0 | 14,151 | 9.2 | 94.8 |
| South-East | 634.0 | 10.1 | 15,763 | 10.1 | 40.2 |
| LITTORAL | 4,111.0 | 64.7 | 41,820 | 27.0 | 98.3 |
| North-West | 1,068.0 | 16.8 | 16,256 | 10.4 | 65.6 |
| Center-West | 915.0 | 14.2 | 21,772 | 14.3 | 42.0 |
| South-West | 275.0 | 4.3 | 74,682 | 48.3 | 36.8 |
| INTERIOR | 2,258.0 | 35.3 | 112,710 | 73.0 | 20.0 |
| TOTAL TUNISIA | 6,369.0 | 100 | 154,530 | 100 | 41.2 |

Source: Adapted from: Direction de l'Aménagement du Territoire (D.A.T.), *Schéma National et Schémas Régionaux d'Aménagement du Territoire*, vol. 2, 1983, p. 10.

Table 3.6

EMPLOYMENT DISTRIBUTION BY ECONOMIC SECTOR AND BY REGION IN 1980 (in thousands)

| Regions | Agri-culture | % | Industrial/ Service[a] | % | Total | % | Population in % |
|---|---|---|---|---|---|---|---|
| North-East | 121.8 | 21.1 | 341.4 | 51.6 | 463.2 | 37.4 | 33.6 |
| Center-East | 116.3 | 20.2 | 149.2 | 22.5 | 265.5 | 21.4 | 21.0 |
| South-East | 50.5 | 8.8 | 52.0 | 7.8 | 102.5 | 8.3 | 10.1 |
| LITTORAL | 288.6 | 50.1 | 542.6 | 81.9 | 831.2 | 67.1 | 64.7 |
| North-West | 119.7 | 20.8 | 54.5 | 8.2 | 174.2 | 14.1 | 16.6 |
| Center-West | 152.4 | 26.4 | 34.8 | 5.3 | 187.2 | 15.1 | 14.3 |
| South-West | 15.6 | 2.7 | 30.2 | 4.6 | 45.8 | 3.7 | 4.3 |
| INTERIOR | 287.7 | 49.9 | 119.5 | 18.1 | 407.2 | 32.9 | 35.2 |
| TOTAL TUNISIA | 576.3 | 100 | 662.1 | 100 | 1,238.4 | 100 | 100 |

Source: Adapted from D.A.T. *Schéma National*, vol. 3, 1983, pp. 85-87.

[a] This includes all employment in public and private sectors, except: construction and public works and Ministries of Defense and Interior.

Table 3.7

DISTRIBUTION OF EMPLOYMENT IN
PUBLIC AND PRIVATE SECTORS IN 1980
(INDUSTRY/SERVICES)
(in thousands)

| Regions | Public[a] | % | Private | % | Total[b] | % | Population in % |
|---|---|---|---|---|---|---|---|
| North-East | 156.1 | 49.2 | 185.2 | 53.6 | 341.4 | 51.6 | 33.6 |
| Center-East | 57.3 | 18.2 | 91.9 | 26.6 | 149.2 | 22.5 | 21.0 |
| South-East | 26.2 | 8.2 | 25.8 | 7.4 | 52.0 | 7.8 | 10.1 |
| LITTORAL | 239.6 | 75.6 | 302.9 | 87.6 | 542.6 | 81.9 | 64.7 |
| North-West | 34.9 | 11.0 | 19.6 | 5.9 | 54.5 | 8.2 | 16.6 |
| Center-West | 19.7 | 6.3 | 15.1 | 4.4 | 34.8 | 5.3 | 14.3 |
| South-West | 22.7 | 7.1 | 7.5 | 2.1 | 30.2 | 4.6 | 4.3 |
| INTERIOR | 77.3 | 24.4 | 42.2 | 12.4 | 119.5 | 18.1 | 35.2 |
| TOTAL TUNISIA | 316.9 | 100 | 345.1 | 100 | 662.1 | 100 | 100 |

Source: Adapted from D.A.T., *Schéma National*, vol. 3, 1983, pp. 61 and 84-87

[a] Includes administration and public enterprises.

[b] Does not include construction and public works, ministries of defense and interior.

Table 3.8

EMPLOYMENT IN INDUSTRY
BY REGION IN 1980

| Regions | Nonmanufacturing Industries | | Manufacturing Industries | | Total | |
|---|---|---|---|---|---|---|
| | Number | % of Total | Number | % of Total | Number | % of Total |
| North-East | 15,959 | 40.4 | 72,770 | 61.9 | 88,729 | 5.98 |
| Center East | 2,903 | 7.3 | 31,963 | 27.2 | 34,866 | 18.9 |
| South-East | 2,270 | 5.7 | 4,453 | 3.8 | 6,723 | 4.3 |
| LITTORAL | 21,132 | 53.4 | 109,186 | 92.9 | 130,318 | 83.0 |
| North-West | 5,035 | 12.9 | 5,746 | 5.0 | 10,781 | 6.6 |
| Center-West | 346 | 0.9 | 2,448 | 2.0 | 2,794 | 1.8 |
| South-West | 12,985 | 32.8 | 108 | 0.1 | 13,093 | 8.3 |
| INTERIOR | 18,366 | 46.4 | 8,302 | 7.1 | 26,668 | 17.0 |
| TOTAL TUNISIA | 39,498 | 100 | 117,488 | 100 | 156,986 | 100 |

Source: D.A.T., *Schéma National*, vol. 2, 1983, pp. 209 and 215.

Figure 3.3

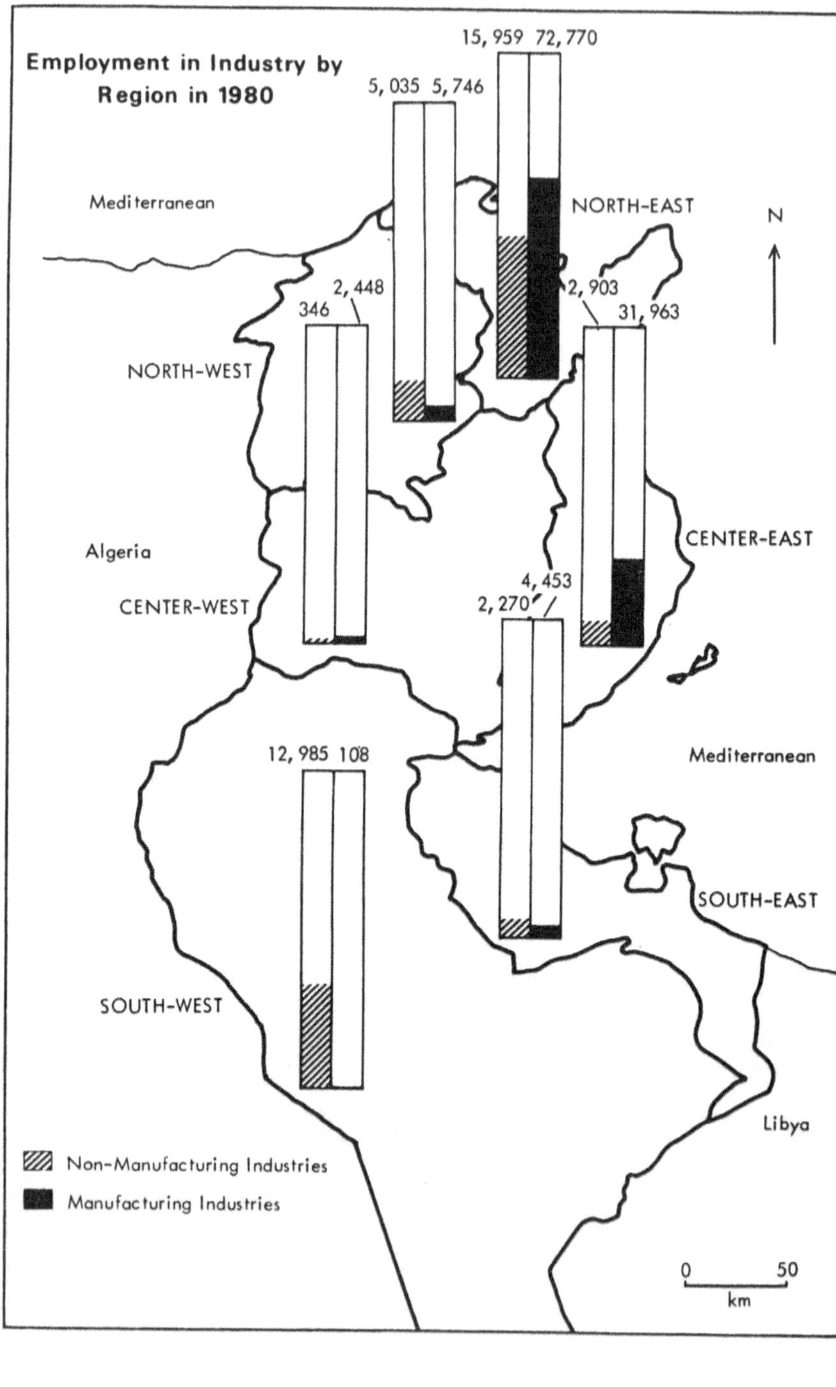

Employment in Industry by Region in 1980
15,959 72,770
5,035 5,746
Mediterranean
NORTH-EAST
N
2,448
346
2,903
31,963
NORTH-WEST
Algeria
CENTER-EAST
4,453
2,270
CENTER-WEST
12,985 108
Mediterranean
SOUTH-EAST
SOUTH-WEST
Libya
Non-Manufacturing Industries
Manufacturing Industries
0 50
km

Table 3.9

EMPLOYMENT IN TOURISM AND TOURIST CAPACITY BY REGION IN 1980

| Regions | Number[a] | % of Total | Capacity (# of beds) | % of Total |
|---|---|---|---|---|
| North-East | 12,050 | 48 | 34,730 | 44.0 |
| Center-East | 7,600 | 30 | 24,460 | 31.0 |
| South-East | 3,900 | 16 | 14,500 | 18.0 |
| LITTORAL | 23,550 | 94 | 73,690 | 93.0 |
| North-West | 500 | 2.0 | 1,760 | 2.2 |
| Center-West | 150 | 0.8 | 790 | 0.9 |
| South-West | 700 | 3.2 | 3,020 | 3.8 |
| INTERIOR | 1,350 | 6.0 | 5,570 | 7.0 |
| TOTAL TUNISIA | 24,900 | 100 | 79,260 | 100 |

Source: D.A.T., *Schéma National*, vol. 1, 1983, p. 86; and vol. 2, 1983, p. 242.

[a] Permanent Jobs (estimate).

Figure 3.4

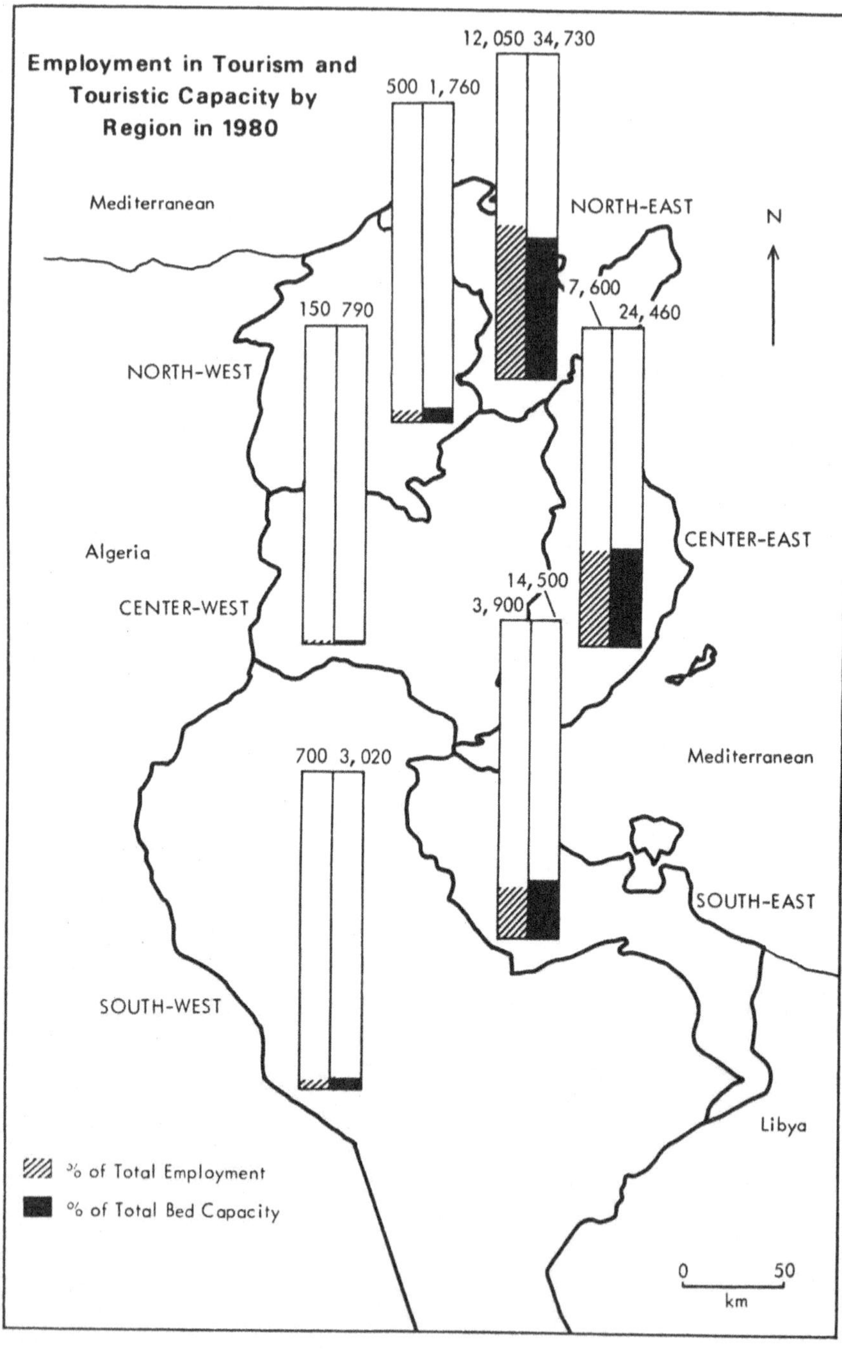
Employment in Tourism and Touristic Capacity by Region in 1980
12,050 34,730
500 1,760
Mediterranean
NORTH-EAST
N
7,600
150 790
24,460
NORTH-WEST
CENTER-EAST
Algeria
14,500
3,900
CENTER-WEST
700 3,020
Mediterranean
SOUTH-EAST
SOUTH-WEST
Libya
% of Total Employment
% of Total Bed Capacity
0 50
km

Table 3.10

POPULATION BY MILIEU AND REGION
IN 1980

| Regions | Urban | | Rural | |
|---|---|---|---|---|
| | Pop. | % of Total Urban Pop. | Pop. | % of Total Rural Pop. |
| North-East | 1,530,300 | 46 | 604,800 | 19 |
| Center-East | 844,200 | 25 | 497,400 | 16 |
| South-East | 272,100 | 8 | 235,700 | 8 |
| LITTORAL | 2,646,600 | 79 | 1,337,900 | 43 |
| North-West | 269,700 | 8 | 798,200 | 27 |
| Center-West | 197,000 | 6 | 718,400 | 24 |
| South-West | 211,800 | 7 | 198,400 | 6 |
| INTERIOR | 678,500 | 21 | 1,706,000 | 57 |
| TOTAL TUNISIA | 3,325,100 | 100 | 3,043,900 | 100 |

Source: Adapted from D.A.T., *Schéma National*, vol. 2, 1983, p. 10

Table 3.11

RATE OF URBANIZATION BY REGION
IN 1980

| Regions | Total Pop. | Urban (in %) | Rural (in %) | |
|---|---|---|---|---|
| North-East | 2,135,000 | 72.0 | 28.0 | 100 |
| Center-East | 1,342,000 | 63.0 | 37.0 | 100 |
| South-East | 634,000 | 50.0 | 50.0 | 100 |
| LITTORAL | 4,111,000 | 57.0 | 43.0 | 100 |
| North-West | 1,068,000 | 25.0 | 75.0 | 100 |
| Center-West | 915,000 | 21.0 | 79.0 | 100 |
| South-West | 275,000 | 56.0 | 44.0 | 100 |
| INTERIOR | 2,258,000 | 43.0 | 57.0 | 100 |
| TOTAL TUNISIA | 6,369,000 | 52.2 | 47.8 | 100 |

Source: Adapted from D.A.T., *Schéma National*, vol. 2, 1983, p. 10.

In addition to these five cities, there are a number of other smaller cities and towns (50-10,000) that constitute a solid base for the littoral urban network and that are, in addition, well interconnected by commercial linkages. Fifty-four out of 80 cities of this category in the whole country are located in the littoral zone (table 3.12).

This urban network is, in addition, sustained by a dense and modern physical infrastructure: communications, transportation, roads and highways, airports and ports, electrical power and production; in brief the quasi-totality of the country's physical infrastructure (table 3.13).

By contrast, the interior since independence in 1956 continues to be isolated, rural, and heavily dependent on agriculture. In the North-West and the Center-West, for example, the rural population represented in 1980-81, 75 percent and 79 percent respectively. And the economy of the region, which is comprised by 11 gouvernorats from Jendouba and Béjà in the north to Tataouine and Kebili in the south (figure 3.1), is very disarticulated and its base is very weak despite the huge mineral resources the region has. For example, while the percentage of the labor force in agriculture is 39 percent at the national level and 32 percent in the littoral, it is as high as 56 percent in the interior (table 3.14).

And without the employment in the public sector or especially the creation of some industries during the 1960s, the economic situation of the region would be worse, or as an official report has put it, "explosive."[50] But even with these jobs, unemployment is high and the percentage of those living in absolute poverty is twice that of the littoral (table 3.15).

And all this explains why, therefore, income estimated on the base of per capita private consumption is far below the national average and is 40 percent less than the littoral (table 3.15). The poverty of the interior is further illustrated when we look at the gap between the two regions in the distribution of social services and public infrastructure: education, health and sanitation, and housing, (table 3.16).

In addition to all this, the "rurality" of the interior is also illustrated when we look at its urban system. Contrary to the littoral, the urban network here is weak and disarticulated, reflective of the economy of the region. Only 9 cities have a population of over 20,000. The largest, Kairouan, and capital of the country for nearly seven centuries and second city until the turn of the century, has 70,000. The second, Gafsa, the mining city of the South-West has only 53,000. And out of a total of 80 small cities (50-10,000) the interior has only 26 (table 3.12). Moreover all these "large" cities are capitals of their gouvernorats (table 3.17 and figure 3.5). In other words, and without the jobs in administration and public services (the presence of which is due mainly because of this status of gouvernorat's capital), these cities would not have the size they have and perhaps would not even survive (table 3.17).

In brief, here are then the nature and magnitude of today's regional disparities in Tunisia. And indeed as we can see, the authors of the *Note d'Orientation* are absolutely right. We have here two different countries. One that has really benefitted from the overall economic good performance of the last quarter of a century, and another one that still is lagging far behind and still has its rural, poor, nondiversified, export-oriented economy, as was Tunisia at independence in 1956.

## CONCLUSION

Now what may one conclude from all this? Based on all the evidence we have from the comparison of Tunisia's achievements in terms of "growth" and "development," and if we accept Amin and Seers's definition of development (and of course I accept it, because I believe that it is the only definition in which development has any meaning), the conclusion I think is very clear. Yes, unfortunately, Tunisia has achieved "growth without development." Unfortunately, I said, because I believe that it would be marvelous if we can have both. In other words, and I would like to stress this, the issue here is not being against "growth" per se, but not to confuse growth, this "banal" phenomenon, to use Amin's terminology, with "development." And this is all what this chapter meant by the "Tunisian Dilemma."

**Table 3.12 Distribution of Cities by Size and by Region in 1980**

| REGIONS | CITY SIZE +200.000 | | 200-100.000 | | 100-50.000 | | 50-20.000 | | 20-10.000 | | < 10.000 | | TOTAL | |
|---|---|---|---|---|---|---|---|---|---|---|---|---|---|---|
| | Nb. | Pop. | Nb. | Pop. | Nb. | Pop. | Nb. | Pop. | Nb. | Pop. | Nb. | Pop. | Nb. | Pop. |
| North-East | 1 | 665.000 | - | - | 5 | 333.500 | 14 | 409.600 | 13 | 161.900 | 25 | 113.300 | 58 | 1,683.300 |
| Center-East | 1 | 233.000 | - | - | 1 | 95.500 | 10 | 294.500 | 13 | 182.900 | 32 | 126.100 | 57 | 932.000 |
| South-East | - | - | - | - | 2 | 179.000 | 2 | 58.900 | 2 | 25.000 | 17 | 56.500 | 23 | 319.400 |
| LITTORAL | 2 | 898.000 | - | - | 8 | 608.000 | 26 | 763.000 | 28 | 369.800 | 74 | 295.900 | 138 | 2,934.700 |
| North-West | - | - | - | - | - | - | 3 | 107.500 | 8 | 93.600 | 27 | 108.000 | 38 | 308.100 |
| Center-West | - | - | - | - | 1 | 70.600 | 1 | 32.300 | 4 | 48.400 | 16 | 43.600 | 22 | 134.900 |
| South-West | - | - | - | - | 1 | 53.000 | 3 | 77.500 | 7 | 97.100 | 24 | 61.500 | 35 | 289.100 |
| INTERIOR | - | - | - | - | 2 | 123.600 | 7 | 217.300 | 19. | 238.100 | 67 | 213.100 | 95 | 792.100 |
| TOTAL TUNISIA | 2 | 898.000 | - | - | 10 | 731.600 | 33. | 980.300 | 47 | 607.900 | 141 | 509.000 | 233 | 3,726.800 |

Source: Adapted from: D.A.T., Schéma National, op. cit., Vol. 3, 1983, p. 104.

Table 3.13

INFRASTRUCTURE INDICATORS BY REGIONS IN 1981-82

| Regions | % of km Paved Roads per km$^2$ (1981) | Infrastructure Rate of Motorization Vehicle/1000 inhab. (1982) | Telephone Density Lines per 1000 inhab. (1981) |
|---|---|---|---|
| North-East | 0.199 | 42.05 | 24.80 |
| Center-East | 0.164 | 23.05 | 15.80 |
| South-East | 0.015 | 24.75 | 11.95 |
| LITTORAL | 0.125 | 31.00 | 19.00 |
| North-West | 0.109 | 14.47 | 6.70 |
| Center-West | 0.047 | 11.06 | 5.33 |
| South-West | 0.024 | 22.22 | 13.05 |
| INTERIOR | 0.060 | 15.91 | 7.65 |
| TOTAL TUNISIA | 0.095 | 31.40 | 20.60 |

Source: Adapted from D.A.T., *Schéma National*, vol. 3, 1983, p. 14.

Table 3.14

LABOR FORCE BY ECONOMIC SECTORS AND REGIONS IN 1980[a] (in %)

| Regions | Agriculture | Industry | Services | |
|---|---|---|---|---|
| North-East | 27.4 | 31.2 | 41.4 | 100 |
| Center-East | 31.2 | 35.6 | 33.2 | 100 |
| South-East | 39.0 | 29.9 | 31.1 | 100 |
| LITTORAL | 32.5 | 32.2 | 35.3 | 100 |
| North-West | 53.5 | 26.4 | 20.1 | 100 |
| Center-West | 61.3 | 24.2 | 14.5 | 100 |
| South-West | 53.2 | 25.0 | 21.8 | 100 |
| INTERIOR | 56.0 | 25.2 | 18.8 | 100 |
| TOTAL TUNISIA | 39.4 | 30.2 | 30.4 | 100 |

Source: Institut National des Statistiques, *Enquête Population-Emploi 1980* (Tunis: I.N.S., 1982), pp. 116-17.

[a] Based on Colin Clark's classification, the I.N.S. classification includes in the agricultural (or primary) sector: agriculture, forestry, hunting, fishing and extractive industry; in industry: manufacturing, chemical and mechanical industries, electricity, gas and water, construction and public works; in services: transport and communications, commerce and banking, insurance, public (administrative and public enterprises) and private services.

Table 3.15

HOUSEHOLD CASH CONSUMPTION, POPULATION IN "ABSOLUTE POVERTY" AND UNEMPLOYMENT RATE BY REGIONS IN 1980

| Regions | Household Cash Consumption[a] Urban-Rural-Total | Population in Poverty (%)[b] | Rate of Unemployment[c] |
|---|---|---|---|
| North-East | 380 - 183 - 324 | 8.8 | 10.3 |
| Center-East | 303 - 164 - 255 | 12.9 | 10.6 |
| South-East | 283 - 191 - 237 | 10.0 | 10.0 |
| LITTORAL | 322 - 179 - 272 | 9.9 | 10.4 |
| North-West | 262 - 138 - 169 | 17.6 | 20.5 |
| Center-West | 284 - 132 - 166 | 19.7 | 6.7 |
| South-West | 239 - 182 - 217 | 10.9 | 12.5 |
| INTERIOR | 261 - 146 - 184 | 18.3 | 13.7 |
| TOTAL TUNISIA | 332 - 157 - 248 | 12.9 | 12.6 |

Source: Adapted from D.A.T., *Schéma National*, vol. 3, 1983, p. 14; and Commissariat Général au Développement Régional (C.G.D.R.), *Les Aspects Régionaux du VIème Plan* (Tunis, 1982), p. 4.

[a] Per capita/year in Tunisian Dinar. The TD is currently at about US$1.20.

[b] The definition here is different from that of the VIth Plan (see table 5.4); here it is population having an annual income (per person) of less than 120 TD in urban areas and less than 60 TD in rural areas in 1980 prices.

[c] Population between 18-59 of age. One observation here about the unemployment rate of the Center-West region. The 6.7 percentage rate is, as the authors of the study of the D.A.T. put it, an "aberration" (*Schéma National*, vol. 3, 1983, p. 89). Without this obvious error in the National Survey *Enquête Population-Emploi 1980*, this rate would be much higher. For example, in 1975 the region has an unemployment rate of 18 percent. It is impossible therefore that the unemployment rate suddenly, in five years, fell to 6-7 percent.

Table 3.16

BASIC SOCIOECONOMIC INDICATORS
BY REGION IN 1980

| Regions | Education | | Health | |
|---|---|---|---|---|
| | Illiteracy Rate | % In Primary Education | Beds for 1,000 inhab. | Doctors for 1,000 inhab. |
| North-East | 39.0 | 39.6 | 1.7 | 2.1 |
| Center-East | 44.7 | 35.9 | 1.7 | 2.7 |
| South-East | 48.0 | 39.1 | 1.5 | 1.5 |
| LITTORAL | 43.9 | 38.2 | 1.9 | 2.5 |
| North-West | 58.4 | 31.4 | 1.5 | 1.3 |
| Center-West | 60.1 | 30.8 | 0.8 | 0.8 |
| South-West | 47.9 | 39.7 | 2.1 | 2.2 |
| INTERIOR | 55.4 | 33.9 | 1.2 | 1.3 |
| TOTAL TUNISIA | 47.5 | 37.3 | 2.1 | 2.8 |

*    *    *

| Regions | Housing | | |
|---|---|---|---|
| | % served by Water (1980) | % served by Urban Sewage (1980) | % with Electricity (1980) |
| North-East | 60.4 | 68.5 | 72.6 |
| Center-East | 48.9 | 35.4 | 63.2 |
| South-East | 32.9 | 15.0 | 51.7 |
| LITTORAL | 47.4 | 48.0 | 62.5 |
| North-West | 22.3 | 52.7 | 33.6 |
| Center-West | 14.9 | 23.6 | 20.6 |
| South-West | 42.4 | 9.6 | 60.1 |
| INTERIOR | 26.5 | 28.6 | 38.1 |
| TOTAL TUNISIA | 41.7 | 53.1 | 54.1 |

Source: Adapted from D.A.T., *Schéma National*, vol. 3, 1983, p. 14.

Figure 3.5

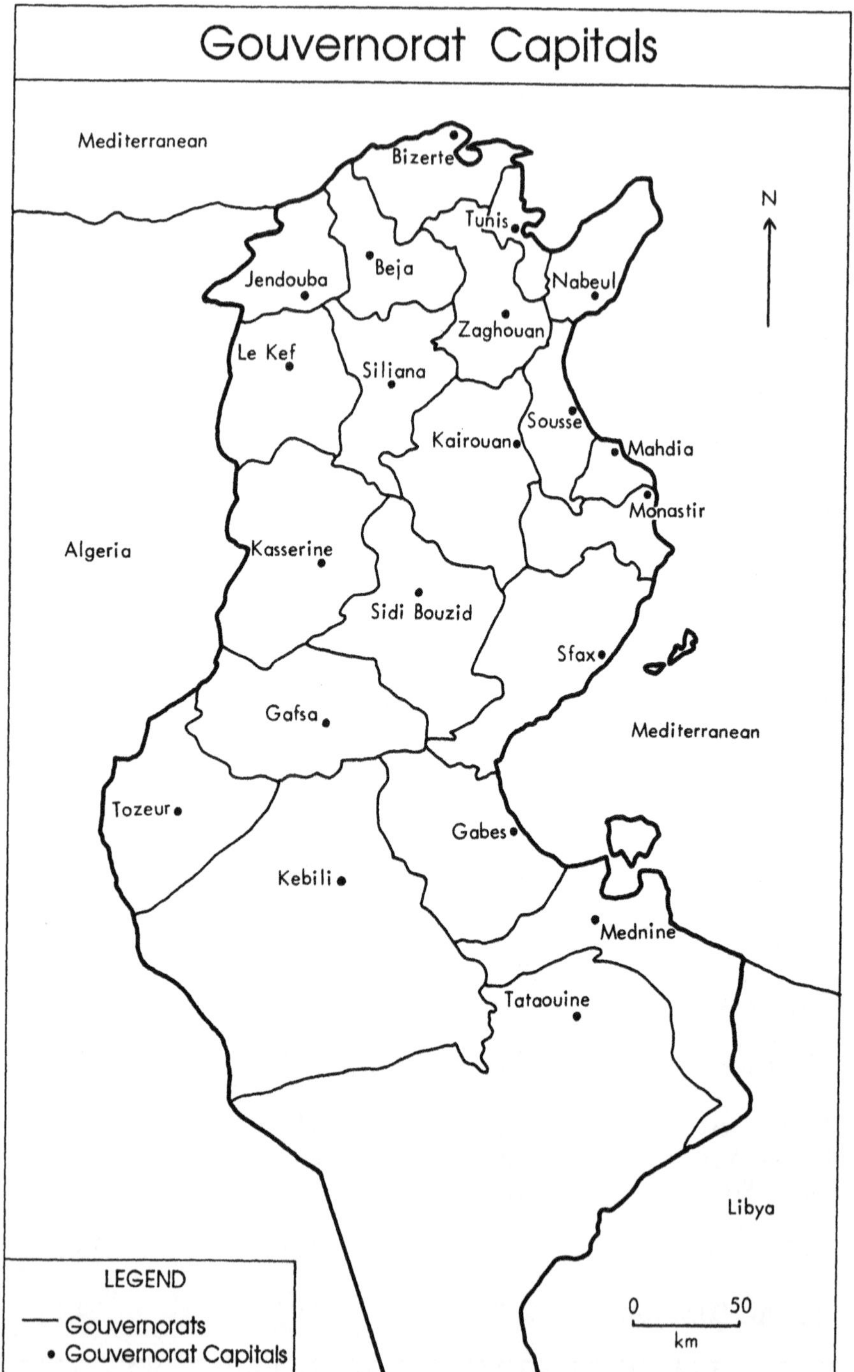
Gouvernorat Capitals
Mediterranean
Bizerte
Tunis
N
Beja
Jendouba
Nabeul
Zaghouan
Le Kef
Siliana
Sousse
Kairouan
Mahdia
Monastir
Algeria
Kasserine
Sidi Bouzid
Sfax
Gafsa
Mediterranean
Tozeur
Gabes
Kebili
Mednine
Tataouine
Libya
LEGEND
Gouvernorats
Gouvernorat Capitals
0
50
km

Table 3.17

EMPLOYMENT STRUCTURES IN THE GOUVERNORAT'S CAPITALS IN 1981-82

| Gouvernorat | Pop. 1981 (in 1,000s) | Total Employ. in 1982 | Empl. % inhab. | Employ. in 1982 (%) Adm. | Serv. | Ind. |
|---|---|---|---|---|---|---|
| 1. Tunis | 1,123.6 | 286,890 | 26 | 19.6 | 56.6 | 23.9 |
| 2. Sfax | 303.0 | 62,541 | 20 | 15.4 | 45.7 | 38.9 |
| 3. Soussa | 210.0 | 33,183 | 16 | 23.2 | 44.2 | 32.6 |
| 4. Bizerte | 92.5 | 12,554 | 14 | 28.8 | 46.4 | 24.8 |
| 5. Gabes | 90.0 | 15,306 | 18 | 22.1 | 50.0 | 27.1 |
| 6. Nabeul | 65.6 | 14,878 | 23 | 18.0 | 36.7 | 45.3 |
| 7. Mahdia | 37.5 | 4,308 | 12 | 44.6 | 36.6 | 18.8 |
| 8. Monastir | 35.7 | 9,933 | 28 | 29.1 | 41.0 | 29.9 |
| 9. Mednine | 23.4 | 5,535 | 24 | 33.5 | 55.5 | 11.0 |
| 10. Zaghouan | 9.0 | 3,270 | 36 | 52.7 | 30.2 | 17.1 |
| LITTORAL | 1,990.2 | 448,398 | 23 | 28.7 | 44.2 | 24.2 |
| 1. Kairouan | 70.6 | 9,769 | 14 | 27.9 | 51.1 | 21.0 |
| 2. Gafsa | 53.0 | 7,737 | 15 | 39.2 | 48.7 | 12.1 |
| 3. Béjà | 47.5 | 8,631 | 18 | 31.1 | 45.2 | 23.7 |
| 4. Kasserine | 32.3 | 6,547 | 20 | 22.2 | 44.7 | 33.1 |
| 5. Le Kef | 32.3 | 7,294 | 22 | 38.5 | 43.8 | 17.7 |
| 6. Jendouba | 28.2 | 6,139 | 21 | 33.1 | 46.3 | 20.7 |
| 7. Tataouine | 22.5 | 2,585 | 11 | 30.3 | 51.0 | 18.7 |
| 8. Tozeur | 22.0 | 1,898 | 9 | 36.3 | 49.6 | 14.1 |
| 9. Sidi Bouzid | 16.0 | 3,551 | 22 | 42.4 | 44.9 | 12.7 |
| 10. Kebili | 13.0 | 1,406 | 10 | 40.0 | 48.6 | 11.4 |
| 11. Siliana | 10.5 | 2,785 | 26 | 40.7 | 37.1 | 22.2 |
| INTERIOR | 347.9 | 58,342 | 16 | 34.7 | 47.0 | 18.8 |

Source: Adapted from D.A.T., *Schéma National*, vol. 3, 1983, Annexe 111.

## NOTES

1. See among others: Abou Tarak, "Tunisie: La Satellisation," *Les Temps Modernes*, no. 375 bis (1977), pp. 95-112; M. Toumi, *Tunisie: Pouvoirs et Luttes* (Paris: Les Editions le Sycomore, 1978); H. Djait, "Tunisie: Dérive? ou Renouveau," *Jeune Afrique*, no. 1207 (1984), pp. 42-44, and no. 1208 (1984), pp. 32-33; and D. Jazy, "Le Mal Tunisien," *Jeune Afrique*, no. 1264 (1986), pp. 68-69.

See also the reply to these accusations in: Republic of Tunisia, Ministry of Plan and Finances (RT/MPF), *VIème Plan de Développement Economique et Social 1982-1986* (Tunis: Imprimerie Officielle, 1982), pp. 188-89.

2. S. Amin, *Le Développement du Capitalisme en Côte d'Ivoire* (Paris: Les Editions de Minuit, 1967).

3. Ibid., p. 281 (translation mine).

4. S. Amin, *Croissance et Développement* (Douala: Publications de l'Institut Panafricain de Développement, 1971), p. 15.

5. D. Seers, "The Meaning of Development," *International Development Review*, no. 4 (1969), pp. 2-6.

6. Ibid., p. 2.

7. Ibid., p. 3.

8. Ibid., p. 3.

9. D. Seers, "The New Meaning of Development," *International Development Review*, no. 3 (1977), p. 5 (emphasis mine).

10. Ibid., p. 6.

11. World Bank, *World Development Report 1983*, p. 149.

12. World Bank, *Tunisia: Country Economic Memorandum* (Washington, DC: World Bank, 1981), pp. ii.

13. Gabsi [pseud.],"Le Vent a Tourné en Tunisie," *Jeune Afrique*, no. 1295 (October 1985), p. 36.

14. RT/MPF, *Note d'Orientation pour la IIIème Décennie de Développement et le VIème Plan* (Tunis: MPF, 1980), p. 3.

15. Ibid., p. 3.

16. World Bank, *Tunisia: Social Aspects of Development* (Washington, DC: World Bank, 1980), p. ii; (the definition of the report does not differ much from that of the Tunisian government).

17. Ibid., p. 8.

18. RT/MPF, *VIème Plan*, p. 167.

19. Personal interview with an economist of the Union Générale des Travailleurs Tunisiens (U.G.T.T.), Tunis, October 1985.

20. World Bank, *Tunisia: Social Aspects*, pp. 5-6; one observation is necessary here. One may ask where the Bank got its data in the first place.

Did all the data of the World Bank come from the Bible or the Coran? I think that these questions are important since the data of the Bank came from government sources. The point here, however, is not where the Bank gets its data; the point is: can we trust the government data? If not, why? And how to overcome this problem? My view is simply to try to use the available data with very critical eyes when it seems suspect. And the least one may say about government data on unemployment and underemployment are more than suspect. They are manipulated. Here is what the authors of the study mentioned above wrote about this:

> ...the official figures only refer to the 18-59 years old age group. They thus leave out about 74 thousand people between 15-17 years old and 9 thousand of those of 60 and older, who are actively looking for work, i.e. are definitely members of the labor force. This means that some 6 percent of the labor force are not taken into account and a full third of those looking for work are not considered as being unemployed in official documents, even though the plight of these age groups is just as real as that of any other group. The official argument that the 15-17 year old belong in school and not in the labor force is not convincing (pp. 96-97).

For further discussion of this later point, see C. Bernard, ed., *La Politique de l'Emploi-Formation au Maghreb, 1970-1980* (Paris: Editions du Centre National de la Recherche Scientifique, 1982).

21. Economist Intelligence Unit, *Quarterly Economic Review of Libya, Tunisia and Malta. Annual Supplement 1982* (London: The Economist, 1982), p. 16.

22. World Bank, *Tunisia: Review of the VIth Development Plan 1982-1986*, vol. 1 (Washington, DC: World Bank, 1983), p. ii.

23. Ibid.

24. On Africa in general, see among others: P.F. Gonidec, *Les Systèmes Politiques Africains* (Paris: Librairie Générale de Droit et de Jurisprudence [L.G.D.J.], 1978); Revue Pouvoirs, *Pouvoirs Africains* (Dossier Special) *Pouvoirs*, no. 25 (1983); Th. Michalon, *Quel Etat pour l'Afrique* (Paris: Les Editions L'Harmaton, 1984). On Tunisia in particular, see among others: Ch. Micaud et al., *Tunisia: The Politics of Modernization* (New York: Praeger, 1964); M. Camau, "Le Discours Politique de Légitimité des Elites Tunisiennes," *Annuaire de l'Afrique du Nord*, vol. 10 (Paris: Editions du C.N.R.S., 1972), pp. 25-68; M. Sbih, *Les Institutions Administratives du Maghreb* (Paris: Hachette, 1977); J.P. Entelis, *Comparative Politics of North Africa* (Syracuse, NY: Syracuse University Press, 1980); W. Zartman et al., *Political Elites in Arab North Africa* (New

York: Longman, 1982); J. Nellis, "Decentralization in North Africa: Problems of Policy Implementation," in *Decentralization and Development: Policy Implementation in Developing Countries*, eds. G.S. Cheema and D. Rondinelli (Beverly Hills: Sage, 1983), pp. 127-82.

25. Nellis, op. cit., p. 135.

26. Ibid., p. 134.

27. Ibid., p. 138.

28. On this particular issue, see the excellent analysis of Camau, op. cit.; and those of J.P. Entelis, op. cit.; M. Toumi, op. cit.; see also H. Béji, *Désenchantement National. Essai sur le Décolonisation* (Paris: Maspero, 1982) (especially Chapter 5).

29. For further details see J. Nellis, op. cit.; see also several articles in *Jeune Afrique* about malversations of public funds and briberies; see for example: S. Belhassen, "Tunisie: Un Métro Nommé Scandale," no. 1306 (1986), pp. 43-46; and the articles of H. Djait and D. Jazy, cited in footnote one; see also the speech of Prime Minister Mohamed Mzali on the national budget for 1986, published by *L'Action*, December 10, 1985. A week later, in a speech before the central committee of the Parti Socialiste Destourien (PSD), President Habib Bourguiba himself, at the age of 83, declared that he is going to devote the rest of his life fighting the "cancer of corruption" (*L'Action*, 20 December 1985); and Françoise Chipaux, "Intrigue et Disgrâce au Palais de Carthage," *Le Monde*, January 20, 1986.

30. See Nellis, op. cit., pp. 138-39.

31. J. Nellis, "A Comparative Assessment of Algeria and Tunisia Economic Performance," *The Middle East Journal*, no. 3 (Summer 1983), p. 390.

32. Y. Ben Achour and F. Moussa, "Réformes, Election Municipales et Discours Décentralisateur en Tunisie," *Annuaire de l'Afrique du Nord*, vol. 16 (Paris: Editions du C.N.R.S, 1979), pp. 345-78.

33. Ibid., pp. 348-49; the English translation is from Nellis, "Decentralization in North Africa," p. 162.

34. RT/MPF, *Note d'Orientation*, p. 11; the English translation is from J. Nellis, *Decentralization, Regional Development and Local Public Finance in Tunisia*, Occasional Paper no. 79, Metropolitan Studies Program, Maxwell School, Syracuse University, Syracuse, NY, March 1984, p. 43.

35. Ibid., pp. 16-17 and English quotation, Ibid., p. 8.

36. RT/MPF, Commissariat Général au Développement Régional (C.G.D.R.), *Note sur la Décentralisation et le Développement Régional*, (Tunis: CGDR, 1983), p. 1; English quotation is from Nellis, *Decentralization, Regional Development*, p. 3.

37. The two other fundamental objectives were: *structural reforms* (la réforme des structures) and *human development* (la promotion de l'homme); see RT/Secretariat d'Etat au Plan et à l'Economie Nationale, Perspectives Décénnales de Développement 1962-1971 (Tunis: SEPE, 1962), pp. 37-40.

38. For a detailed discussion of this failure see E. Moudoud, *Modernisation, Centralisation et Destruction de l'Economie Rural: l'Expérience des Cooperatives Agricoles en Tunisie 1962-1969*, U.B.C. Planning Papers, no. 7, School of Community and Regional Planning, University of British Columbia, Vancouver, 1983.

39. Entelis, op. cit., p. 177.

40. RT/MPF, *VIème Plan*, p. 2.

41. See A. Adedej, "Foreign Debt and Prospects for Growth in Africa during the 1980s," *Journal of Modern African Studies*, no. 1 (1985), p. 54; and the Economist Intelligence Unit, *Quarterly Economic Review of Tunisia and Malta*, no. 3 (London: The Economist, 1985), p. 23.

42. This unacceptable view is held by many foreign observers of Tunisia. See for example: A. Findlay, "Tunisia: The Vicissitudes of Economic Development," in *North Africa: Contemporary Politics and Economic Development*, eds. R. Lawless and A. Findlay (London: Croom Helm / New York: St. Martin's Press, 1984), pp. 217-240 (see p. 217).

43. See D. Jazy, op. cit.; and S. Belhassen, "Kasserine ou le Sud Oublié," *Jeune Afrique Economie*, no. 61 (April 1985), pp. 97-106.

44. See the excellent article by J.B. Oakes, "Youth's Threat to Tunisia," the *New York Times*, April 13, 1984, p. A35; see also S. Belhassen, "Kasserine."

45. See footnote 14.

46. RT/MPF, *Note d'Orientation*, pp. 110-11 (translation and emphasis are mine).

47. RT/MPF, *Sixth Plan*, p. 185.

48. See H. Sethom and A. Kassab, *Les Régions Géographiques de la Tunisie*, (Tunis: Publication de l'Université de Tunis, 1981; and M. Fakhfakh et al., *Atlas de Tunisie* (Paris: Editions Jeune Afrique, 1979).

49. See République Tunisienne (RT), Ministère de l'Equipement (ME), Direction de l'Aménagement du Territoire (DAT), *Schéma National et Schémas Régionaux d'Aménagement du Territoire*, vol. 12, June 1984, p. 172.

50. *Rapport du Comité de Réflexion sur l'Aménagement du Territorie et de la Décentralisation Industrielle* (Tunis: D.A.T., 1979), p. 26.

# 4
# THE HISTORICAL ROOTS OF REGIONAL DISPARITY

## INTRODUCTION

One of the three major premises of this study is that regional underdevelopment has nothing to do with "mother nature," but can be *historically* explained. In other words, and to put it simply, it is not a *natural* but a *created* phenomenon. Based on this simple premise, this chapter attempts to provide (1) a thorough understanding of the "genesis" of regional disparities in Tunisia (described in the previous chapter) through the analysis of their historical origins; (2) an analysis of the fallacy that stipulates that the "causes" of regional underdevelopment lie in the underdeveloped regions themselves. It is frequently argued that if regions are poor, it is because they lack the resources necessary to create and sustain economic development. Sometimes it is even argued that they lack the "attributes necessary for development."[1]

Based on both "geographical determinism" and on "ahistorical" explanations, these fallacious views stipulate, therefore, that the main causes of regional underdevelopment are due strictly to "internal factors." External factors are completely ignored or at best minimized. This is a very important element to keep in mind, for we can see here the similarities between this perception of underdevelopment at the subnational level and that of modernization theories at the national one (see Chapter 2).

Now, and after having said that, it is not my intention at all here to remake the trial of French colonization in Tunisia. My concern is limited to the analysis of the transformations—in respect to regional disparities—imposed by the colonial economy upon the socioeconomic and spatial structures of precolonial Tunisia. These transformations and their impact will be examined through the analysis of:

1. the destruction of precolonial social formations and productive forces;

2. the destruction of the entire precolonial space economy.

But before doing that and in order to measure correctly the devastating impact of these transformations, we must have at least a brief idea of what was the situation in precolonial Tunisia in respect to: (1) the organization of the space economy of the country, and (2) the economic evolution and its relationship with the external world.

## PRECOLONIAL TUNISIA: AN HISTORICAL BACKGROUND

As many historians and geographers have shown, Tunisia is a very ancient urban country[2] (figure 4.1). But the urban development reached its highest moments with the "islamization" of Ifriqiya (Tunisia) during the sixth and the seventh centuries.[3] Since that period, especially after the founding of Kairouan in 690, and until the late eighteenth century, urban development based on strong and complementary relationships between agriculture-industry-trade was, on the internal level, one of the most important characteristics of the spatial-economic organization of the country.[4] On the external level this integrated spatial-economic organization was favored by a complex system of long-distance trade connecting Tunisia with the Middle East, Sub-Saharan Africa and the rest of North Africa.[5] According to Fernand Braudel, by the fourteenth century this triangular trade, based on a well-integrated system of land routes, has made of Tunisia and North Africa the "driving force of the entire Mediterranean."[6]

Another non less important characteristic of this spatial-economic structure is that it was, for centuries, based on an urban network of inland cities and towns. And it is important to note here that Kairouan, the capital for centuries, was an inland city, constituting by its strategic position in the urban system a kind of a "*passage obligé*" of the whole circulation system of Tunisia (figure 4.2). It is also interesting to note that during all of this period, "at least until the sea routes were as firmly under Arab control as the land routes," writes J. Abu-Lughod, former Roman cities on the coast declined.[7]

Now, the question to be asked is this: when, therefore, and most important how, this spatial economic organization began, slowly but irreversibly to disintegrate and to be based on an extroverted-coastal urban system.

### The Myth of the 'Hilali Invasion'

For a long time, until less than two decades ago, Tunisian and North African history in general has been dominated by colonialistic interpretations.[8] The dominant view of these interpretations was that the primary causes of the region's "colonization yesterday and its underdevelopment today"[9] were its "static" and "unchanging" character; its "fragmented" and "archaic" sociopolitical structures; its "retarded" economic and technological base; its "rural" and "nomadic" civilization; and (and this is the best of all!) plagued as it was by "cyclical" thus nondevelopment movements, its "congenital impotence to create anything"!![10]

This dominant but unscientific view has been of course discredited. The need to "decolonize" North African history has resulted, since the late 1960s, in a tremendous effort of research (inside as well as outside the region) aimed at providing an adequate understanding of North African past.[11] Due to this effort we began to have a better and more articulated understanding of the primary causes of the region's "colonization yesterday and its underdevelopment today," as well as of the historical turning point in its economic and spatial disintegration.

According to the colonialistic interpretation mentioned above, this historical turning point is located at the eleventh century with the second Arab invasion of North Africa, known as the "Hilali Invasion." This thesis claims that the economic decline and the destruction of urban life in Tunisia and in the whole region began at that period, when the "Beni Hilal," coming from Egypt, destroyed everything in their path, pushing back sedentary life in and around a few towns on the coast.[12] This "myth" as J. Poncet put it,[13] has been popularized for decades by what V. Berdoulay calls "*le mouvement colonial*" of the French School of Geography of the early part of the century.[14] It has, however, been discredited, too.[15] The economic decline of Tunisia and the disintegration of its space economy did not begin, it was argued, with the eleventh century. The Hilali invasion has been exaggerated. The Hilali did not destroy everything. At best, it was argued, the invasion was a crisis among many others the country had experienced through its long history. And although Tunisia and its capital, Kairouan, suffered serious injuries, they recovered during the next centuries.[16] Braudel, for example, in his well-documented study of the Mediterranean in the sixteenth century, and as if he was replying to the "Hilali" thesis, notes that:

> It is an error (sometimes committed by the most knowledgeable) to consider North Africa as a rural complex. In the fourteenth and fifteenth centuries towns grew up sometimes out of all proportion to the surrounding countryside. They looked not only towards the Mediterranean but also to the South, the lands of Black Africa, the Bled es Soudan.[17]

In other parts of the region, in Morocco, for example, Abu-Lughod notes that the eleventh century was "a time of city building...not of urban destruction."[18] Furthermore, and according to other sources, North Africa as a whole, but in Morocco and Tunisia in particular, have known an "urban renaissance" with the return of the Arabs from Spain during the fourteenth and sixteenth centuries.[19] The "Andalous" or "Moriscos," with their settlements in Tunisia, marked a new period of urban development on the coast as well as in the interior, especially in the North-West of the country.[20] Secondly, and most important, not only has Tunisia recovered from the "Hilali" invasion but has continued to prosper. So, long after the

Figure 4.1

## The Urbanization of Tunisia During The Roman Period

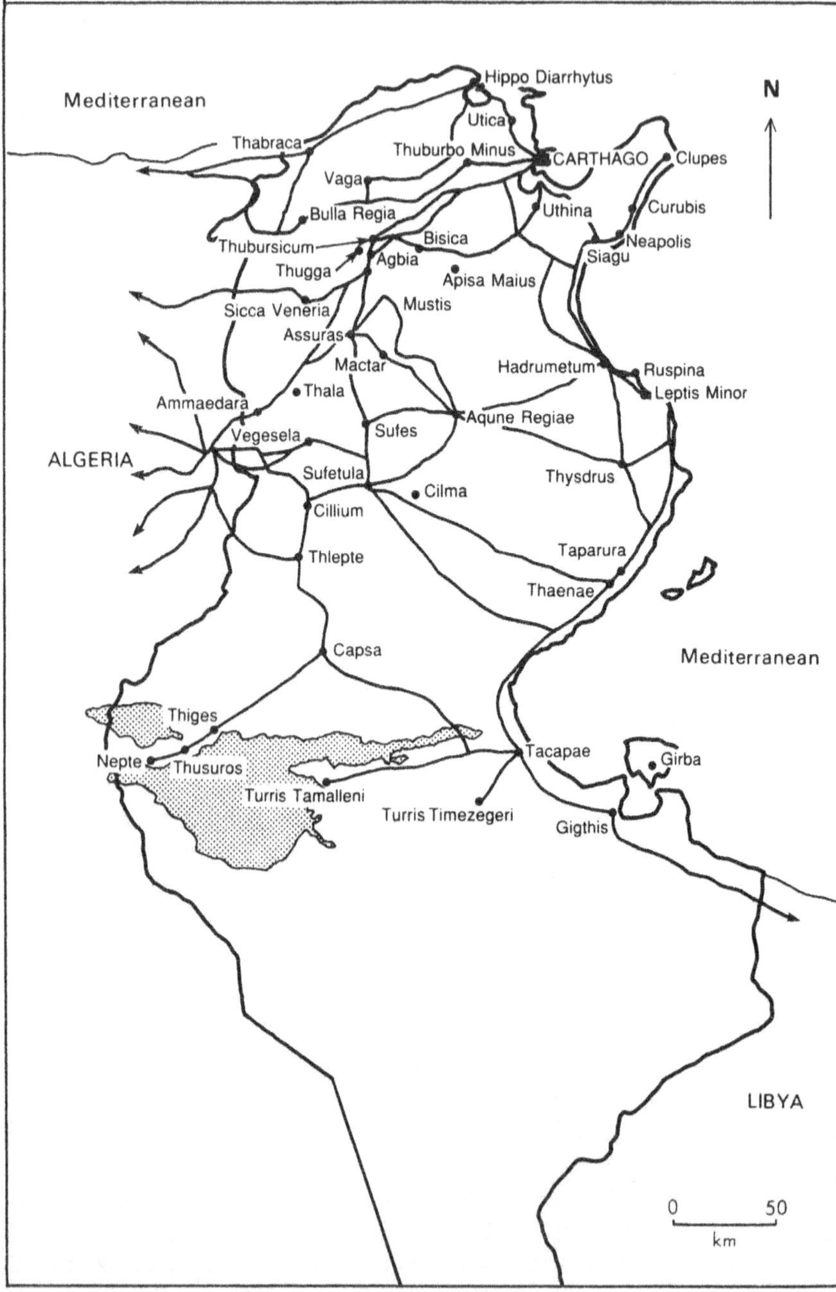


Source: Adapted from: British Government, Naval Intelligece Division. Tunisia. Geographical Handbook Series. Oxford: Oxford and Cambridge University Presses, 1945, p. 130.

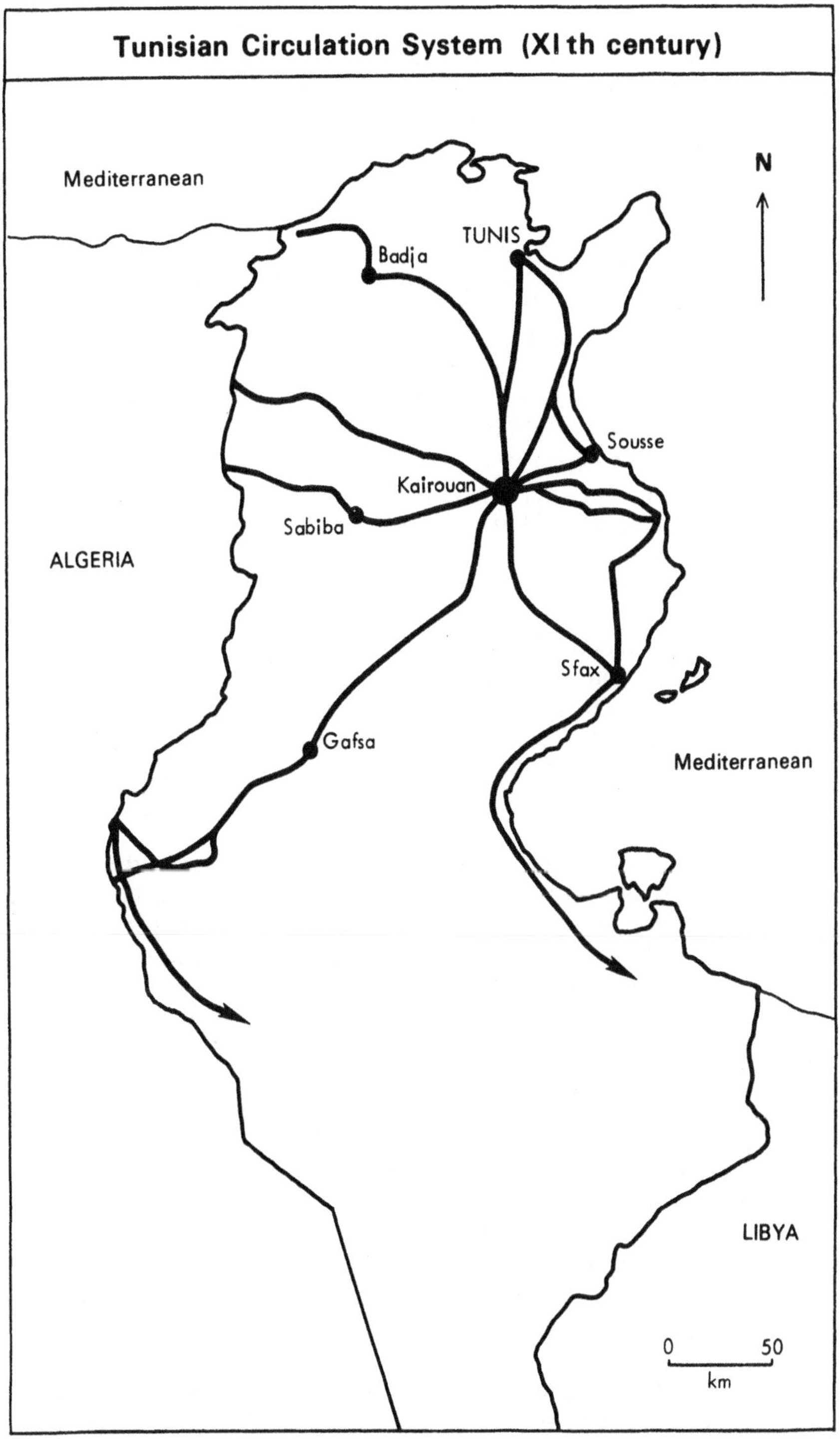


Source: Adapted from: C. Vanacker, "Geographie Economique de l'Afrique du Nord," Annales E.S.C., no. 3 1973, pp. 659-680 (Map 2).

invasion, the interior was not this land of "*nomades*" that the colonial French School of Geography has always described.

The early and significant historical turning point with respect to the destruction of the whole space economy of Tunisia began to appear far later than with the eleventh century. As Braudel has shown, it is with the first incursions of the Portuguese and the Spanish, around the middle of the fifteenth century, that the space economy and the economy itself of the whole country began to be slowly, but irreversibly, altered.[21]

It is with the slow but continuing economic decline of North Africa and the whole Arab world, consequence of the rising maritime power of Christian Europe in the Mediterranean, that the cities along the coast began to assume a dominant role. This decline was further accelerated when North Africa's traditional trans-Saharan trade was strangled with the penetration of West Africa by the Portuguese.[22] As noted by Abu-Lughod, however, even during this period of decline (the late fifteenth century) during which Tunisia and North Africa as a whole were facing an economic war on two fronts, inland cities continued to play an important role in the survival of the region:

> As the balance of power tipped in Europe's favor, small enclaves along the North African coasts were occupied militarily; in others the trade was increasingly "taken over" by foreign merchants. Whenever possible the Arabs pulled inland away from the coast in response to the incursions, trying to regroup or even to ignore them.[23]

As far as these first assaults have been contained in these coastal small enclaves, the three countries of the Maghreb have been able to maintain their economic base and the internally oriented space-economy sustaining it. It is not before the early nineteenth century as economic and military domination of North Africa was a fait accompli that a new space economy structure began to appear. And it is from that period—late eighteenth, early nineteenth centuries—that:

> ...the cities along the coasts again began to assume prominence. As in the days of imperial Rome, the North African economies became increasingly dependent upon a core region on the outside, a dependence that stimulated the ports into which manufactured goods were dumped and from which local resources were shipped out. But this time the core lay not in Rome but London and, even more, in Paris.[24]

This historical turning point was marked in Tunisia by the capture of Kairouan, after fierce resistance, by the French in 1881, year of the official colonization of Tunisia, as pointed out by Elisee Reclus:

> While all the cities of the Tunisian coast had been successively visited by foreign armies, Kairouan was captured for the first time in 1881 by the French.[25]

Beyond this being an historical-symbolic event, it marked the beginning of the end for the regions and cities of the interior as economic activities moved more and more toward the coast. This fundamental historical rupture will be further accelerated during the first decades of the colonial period (see below), which, with the colonial economy imposed upon the country, will in a few decades completely transform the whole organization of the Tunisian space economy and the respective role, in this organization, of the interior and the littoral: the interior—the core for centuries—became the periphery and the littoral, formerly the periphery, became the core.[26]

These are, then, the historical facts that explain the "rural" character of the interior. As we can see this has nothing to do with the myth of the "Hilali invasion" and especially with the dominant view of colonialistic interpretations of the history of Tunisia, which popularized the idea that, with the exception of a few urban centers on the coast, the rest of the country has always been "rural" and "archaic."

It is to the colonial period that I should now return, in order to examine further the historical roots of the "regional question."

## REGIONAL DISPARITY AND THE LEGACY OF FRENCH COLONIZATION

As it was briefly sketched, for centuries—especially from the founding of Kairouan—Tunisia developed a well-integrated space economy, the main characteristic of which was its base in an inland cities urban network. This space economy system was itself the result and reflection of the strategic economic position of Tunisia in a Mediterranean-African global economic system (world system?) linking together vast economic spaces.

By the sixteenth century, however, with the rising military and economic powers of Christian Europe and the slow but irreversible decline of the African-Arab world, the whole structure of the physical base of the economy, the spatial system, began to disintegrate. By the late eighteenth and early nineteenth centuries when European economic and military domination was a fait accompli, especially after the Conference of Berlin, an historical rupture marked a turning point not only in the economic and political evolution of Tunisia, but as well as in its spatial organization. This rupture will be further accelerated by the official colonization in 1881 and the economic policies that have been imposed on the country. In what follows, I will examine those policies that have had a direct and profound impact on the organization of the Tunisian space economy.

## The Destruction of Precolonial Social Formations and Productive Forces

The Destruction of the Urban Economy. The destruction of social formations and productive forces of precolonial Tunisia was not limited to rural areas as the vast amount of research on this issue and the quasi absence of studies on urban areas would suggest.[27] The destruction of precolonial social formations and productive forces in urban areas was as devastating as it was in rural areas (see below). The problem here is that no systematic studies have been undertaken in this area. The data available are still very fragmented and disparate.[28] It is, however, possible from this data to draw a clear picture of the devastating impact of, first, European and second, French economic and political domination during the eighteenth and the nineteenth centuries.

Despite the general economic decline in North Africa during the late eighteenth and early nineteenth centuries, Tunisia was not in a desperate situation or, we would say today, an "underdeveloped" country. Throughout that period, Tunisia, on the contrary, even experienced a long period of relative prosperity.[29] The base of this prosperity was, according to a Tunisian economist, "a certain global coherence of the internal socio-economic structures."[30] This coherence was itself the result of the "sectoral and regional complementarity of the economy."[31] But this coherence will be undermined by the first assaults by the European economies, especially during the first decades of the nineteenth century. They took several forms. But the most brutal one was the imposition by force of a number of commercial treaties, the objectives of which were to open the Tunisian protected market for European manufactured goods: first the treaty of 1824 and then, after the conquest of Alger in 1830, the treaty of the same year, which "has put an end to the Bey's monopoly over external trade..."[32] Here is what J. Ganiage, a French historian, wrote about the consequence for Tunisia of these commercial treaties in particular and what was called "the capitulation regime" in general:

> The regime of "capitulation" confirmed by diverse treaties worked out in the nineteenth century, imposed upon the Bey the maintenance of a maximum customs duty of 3 percent ad valorem on imported products. To find new financial resources, the Tunisian government had no alternative but to tax the exports of the country. Thus an absurd system of custom duty was established whereby Tunisian export products were charged between 8 and 25 percent of their value while the national market was left without any protection.[33]

As a result of this, European manufactured goods invaded the country and precipitated the decline of local industries. According to Ganiage:

> In the port of Gouletta, the major Tunisian harbor, in less than fifteen years the total value of imports doubled that of exports, passing from an average of 12 million francs in the three year period, 1846-48, to 24 million francs for the 1860-62 period. This tendency precipitated the decline of the artisanal industries....The industrial corporations were undermined one after another. The English cotton cloth, the woolens and silks of France replaced the indigenous textiles in the interior as well as in the cities. The imports of hardware, weapons, European jewelry, partially ruined the Tunisian metal artisans. The Regency was an easy market for European goods. In 1860 three countries: France, Italy and England monopolized 92% of Tunisian foreign trade.[34]

But when France was freed in 1878 by the Conference of Berlin to have Tunisia for herself, a new era of destruction began. In less than three decades—with the commercial laws of 1890, 1898 and 1905—France was able to eliminate British and Italian competition and to achieve its long-time objective: to reserve Tunisia exclusively for its "capitalists and products," as Jules Ferry himself once put it.[35] The objectives of these three laws were: (1) to free totally, from any tariff barriers the trade between the metropolis and the new colony (although Tunisia was only a protectorate...) by eliminating the taxes imposed on Tunisian exports by the regime of "capitulation" and by the treaties of 1824 and 1830; (2) to eliminate any taxes on Tunisian imports from France; and (3) to suppress the clause of "favored nation" for England and Italy (law of 1905), and therefore to integrate Tunisia totally into what was called "L'Union Douanière Française."[36]

Now what was the impact of all this on the urban economy and especially on the urban social formations and productive forces? According to A. Raymond, the "*chechias*" (woolen caps) industry alone employed 15,000 persons in the late eighteenth century.[37] By 1930 this number was only 5,000, and by 1934 it dropped to less than 1,000.[38] In 1935, in Tunis alone, an estimated 15,000 artisans were unemployed.[39] In the interior, the economies of a large number of cities and small rural towns were undermined one after another by the invasion of French products.[40]

In brief, left without protection, local industries could not compete with French industries. They were literally strangled as Tunisia was, in addition, cut from its traditional markets: the Near-East, Sub-Saharan Africa and even the rest of North Africa.[41] All this resulted in the "pauperization" of urban productive forces and therefore the disintegration of the urban economy. But this was only the beginning. The disintegration of the urban economy was further accelerated when the strategists of the protectorate launched the same barbaric policy of destruction and disintegration on the precolonial rural economy, the traditional market and the supplier of raw materials for the local urban economy.

The Destruction of the Rural Economy. If the destruction of precolonial social formations and productive forces in urban areas was a very important aspect of French economic and political domination in Tunisia, the destruction of social formations and productive forces in rural areas was by far the most important one and did not begin before 1881, date of the official annexation of Tunisia by France. With this annexation crystallized by the Treaty of Le Bardo in 1881 and the Treaty of La Marsa in 1883, the French launched their systematic policy of "pillage" of the resources of the country and of disintegrating its social, political, economic and spatial structures. As Laroui put it, "side by side with a slowly disintegrating society, another society came into being, with its land holdings, its economic system and its administrative organization."[42]

Parallel to the new trade policy mentioned above (laws of 1890, 1898 and 1905), which aimed, as we saw, to transform Tunisia into a supplier of raw materials and an exclusive market (by eliminating British and Italian competition with the law of 1905) for French industries, the administration of the protectorate launched its policy of land colonization.

The Land Colonization Policy. This policy was carried out in two major phases. The first (1885-92) was inaugurated with the law of July 1, 1885. As noted by J. Poncet, this important law set up the whole legislative framework for French colonization in Tunisia:

> The law of 1885 is a fundamental piece not only of the protectorate as it was conceived by Paul Cambon, but of all the colonial enterprise in Tunisia.[43]

Inspired by the Torrens system of land registration, the objective of this law was to secure land for French settlers and to protect them from "Muslim legislation and local customs."[44] Within this new legislative framework, several decrees were devised in order to open to colonization the access to the land. First, there was the decree of May 23, 1886, which was designed to take over the "Habous," the inalienable property of religious institutions. The "Habous" were leased to colonists by the "Habous Association" (El Djemaïa).[45] During this phase the French authorities succeeded in securing, according to Poncet, 402,000 hectares.[46]

But this first phase was very capitalist and speculative. For example, 246,000 hectares were distributed among only 114 properties. The rest, 156,000 hectares, were shared by a few large French companies or banks. In addition, this colonization was "absenteeist." In order to encourage the settlement of small French farmers in order to prevent what was called then, with an obvious racist connotation, the "Italian Peril" (referring here to Italian settlers who outnumbered the French),[47] French authorities launched the second phase of the land colonization policy.

This second phase (1892-1914) was inaugurated with what was called "*La Colonisation Officielle*." Several decrees were devised to this end. The first, issued in 1896, declared all dead lands as being in the public domain. Two years later, the decree of 1898 forced the "Habous Association" to provide the French administration with 2,000 hectares a year. Five years later, the decree of 1903 declared all forest lands as being, too, in the public domain. In 1905, another decree abrogated the decree of 1886 and made the properties leased from the "Habous Association" transferable, an action absolutely against the "Habous" legislation. In addition to this all juridical arsenal, a special fund, the "*Credit Foncier de Tunisie*," was created in 1906 in order to assist the new settlers. As a result of this very elaborated policy, French assets jumped from 402,000 hectares in 1892 to 700,000 hectares in 1914, with a total of 834,000 hectares for all European property.[48]

A decree of fundamental importance in the analysis of the historical roots of the "regional question" has not been discussed yet. This is the decree of 1904, concerning "collective land," belonging to rural communities. As we saw, the objective of the 1885 law was to secure land for French colonists and to protect their "rights"(!!) from "Islamic legislation and local customs" by a new land tenure system. But, as we also saw, the first phase of the land colonization policy was not very successful for the French, especially in terms of "*peuplement*." This first phase was highly capitalist, speculative and absenteeist. Secondly and as of 1892, it concerned mainly the private and the "Habous" lands. But these two types of land represented a limited portion of Tunisian cultivated land. Most of the land was "collective lands" and was located in the richest parts of the country, the interior regions (especially the North-West), a region that has made the reputation of Tunisia as the "granary of Rome." Up to 1892, therefore, these lands were untouched by colonization. But when the French were eager to secure more land for their policy of *colonisation officielle*, they were facing a major obstacle: how to find more land in order to attract more colonists. It is at that time that the *colonisation officielle* began to be concerned by "collective lands." But, here there was another obstacle: the land tenure system of these lands prevented any group or any member of the group to sell any portion of the land. In this system, the land was not in itself a "commodity," with an exchange value. It was valued by its "use value." It was even less valuable than the means of production.[49] This is one of the basic characteristics of the precolonial rural economy in Tunisia and of the tenure system on which it was based. And this is precisely why this tenure system was seen as an obstacle by French legislators and administrators for their land colonization policy. By incorporating the "collective lands" into those of public domain, the decree of 1904 was designed to get rid of a system that had existed in Tunisia for time immemorial and that was the cement, the very foundation of the socioeconomic structures in rural areas. But for the strategists of the protectorate, rural communities, or as they were pejoratively called, "tribes," did not exist! C. Sammut reports that in a trial over a dispute concerning the land of the community of Ouled Slama, the "*Tribunal Mixte*" (a land court dominated, contrary to what its name suggests, by French judges) rendered on February 22, 1904 the following judgment:

> The primary condition to be an owner is to exist; now, in Tunisia the tribes as moral entities, as judicial persons do not exist (!!!).[50]

As we can see, this reflects beyond the land colonization policy itself, the whole philosophy of the "*projet colonial*." We have here the "seeds" of the total destruction of the social formations and productive forces of rural precolonial Tunisia.

After a pause between 1914 and 1939, the *colonisation officielle* continued until 1956, date of independence of the country. At that date, according to Raymond and Poncet, 3,000 Europeans owned 850,000 hectares (the French alone owned 774,000 hectares), about an average of 250 hectares per family, whereas 480,000 Tunisian peasant families owned less than 3,000,000 hectares, an average of less than 6 hectares per family.[51]

Now what were the consequences of the land colonization policy? The direct and first consequence was of course the dislocation of the socioeconomic structures of rural areas. These socioeconomic structures, which were based on a "use value" rather than on an "exchange value" type of relationship, inserted the "Fellahins" (small farmers) in a "mode of production" that prevented them from the need to sell their labor force. This mode of production, as attested to by more and more research now, has nothing to do with the so-called "Asiatic mode of production."[52] Beyond the common property of the land and the kinship lines, at the heart of this mode there was the free union of free human beings. And because of this fundamental difference with the "feudal mode of production" or an imaginary "Asiatic mode of production" (or what has also been called "oriental despotism"), it has been described by many historians and specialists of North Africa as an "agrarian communism" or even "village communism."[53]

The second direct consequence is that by the destruction of this "village communism," the land colonization policy ejected from the best and most fertile land thousands and thousands of peasants. These people, dispossessed from their properties, on which they worked and lived since time immemorial, were forced to relocate on marginal and infertile land, or to become the "labor reservoir" for European agriculture. But this European agriculture, as R. Dumont has shown, was very quickly transformed into "wheat factories" (*usines à blé*), with its excessive mechanization,[54] and needed therefore fewer and fewer workers. This excessive mechanization, which was, according to Dumont, pushed far beyond that of the métropole itself,[55] resulted in the early 1920s in the ejection of about two-thirds of the labor force employed in the agriculture sector. The direct consequence of this, and therefore of the whole colonization land policy, is the appearance of an unknown phenomenon in Tunisia up to that period: a massive rural exodus towards the cities. Thousands and thousands of peasants, who discovered suddenly the unknown notion of "unemployment" ended up in the cities of the coast where slums (*bidonvilles*) began to appear by the late 1920s.[56] This exodus, in turn, has induced the decline of the rural population. According to A. Noushi, from 1931 to 1946, the rural population has declined from 83 percent to 71 percent whereas the total population increased from 2,086,000 to 3,411,000.[57]

In brief, these are some of the consequences of the destruction of precolonial social formations and productive forces in rural areas: the death and pauperization of local communities. The rural economy therefore was disintegrated in parallel with and under the same conditions as the urban economy. But this time, however, the interior, the North-West and the Center-West in particular, because it was there that the "collective lands" were mostly located, suffer more than any other part of the country. But beyond this, it is all of precolonial society that has been destroyed or as Hermassi put it, has ceased to exist:

> Colonialism has unequally but surely transformed the Maghribi societies. Increasing differentiation, tribal erosions, rural exodus, emigration of more than a million people to Europe—such are the incontestable indicators of the "passing of traditional society." If it is true that a tiny minority of Maghribi farmers was converted to modern methods of production and that a small minority of workers was incorporated into industry and modern farming, it also remains true that the majority of the peasant community has been and is being proletarized without being given any possibility of integration into the existing economies and societies. It is important to understand that the colonial impact in the Maghrib introduced not merely a bifurcation between modern and traditional agriculture but also a cultural bifurcation in terms of which traditional society has ceased to exist.[58]

This death of the traditional society, although by far the most important with regard to the historical process of the creation of regional underdevelopment—as well as of course of the underdevelopment of Tunisia as a whole—was not however the only aspect of this process. Another major area of crucial importance was the transformation of the whole space economy of the country through the physical infrastructure policy: ports, railways, roads, etc., the support of the colonial-extractive economy imposed by the protectorate. It is to this important area that the next section is devoted.

## The Destruction of the Precolonial Space Economy and Urban Network

It is true that precolonial Tunisia did not have any railway network, good roads, modern ports, in a word, any "modern" infrastructure. And this has been put forward so many times by colonialists in general and colonial geographers in particular[59] and all those who claim that after all, colonization has had its positive side! My position is clear on this issue. Along with W. Rodney, and many others, "colonialism was a one-armed bandit," as he superbly put it:

> Faced with the evidence of European exploitation of Africa, bourgeois writers would concede at least partially that colonialism was a system which functioned well in the interest of the metropoles. However, they would then urge that another issue to be resolved is how much Europeans did for Africans, and that it is necessary to draw up a balance sheet of colonialism. On that balance sheet, they place both the credits and the debits, and quite often conclude that the good outweighed the bad. That particular conclusion can quite easily be challenged, but attention should also be drawn to the fact that the process of reasoning is itself misleading. The reasoning has some sentimental persuasiveness. It appeals to the common sentiment that "after all there must be two sides to a thing." The argument suggests that, on the one hand, there was exploitation and oppression, but, on the other hand, colonial governments did much for the benefits of Africans and they developed Africa. It is our contention that this is completely false. Colonialism had only one hand—it was a one-armed bandit.[60]

And indeed, as we saw, the colonial project in Tunisia was not to develop the country, but as Jules Ferry himself put it, "to reserve it to its capitalists and products."[61] And this is precisely what J. Marseille has called the "absurd paradox" of the "colonial pact," which imposed on the colonies to buy from, but not to sell to, the métropole.[62] The only thing that the colonies were allowed to do was to provide the métropole with the needed raw materials for its industries.[63] And it is in this colonial economic framework that the "modernization" of the physical infrastructure has to be analyzed, in order, in turn, to understand the roots of the "creation of regional dependency."[64]

The Ports. First and foremost, it must be remembered that only with the discovery of huge mineral resources did the administration of the protectorate launch its program of modernization of existing physical infrastructure (ports and roads) or the creation of new ones (railways). As it was mentioned, in 1881, Tunisia did not have a good road network or any railway at all (except a military line to Algeria and three small local lines around Tunis constructed between 1873 and 1885). But it has, however, and for centuries since Carthage, very dynamic ports. Eighteen major ports existed in 1881.[65] But with the discovery of huge mineral resources in the interior regions: phosphate in 1885 in the South-West; iron, zinc, lead, manganese, lignite, coal as well as phosphate in the Center-West and the North-West, these old ports became inadequate (too small) for a large-scale resource "siphoning" operation such as the one the strategists of the protectorate had in mind. In order to ease the draining of these resources from the interior, the French decided to select a few city-ports well distributed on the littoral. These were: Bizerte and Tunis in the North-East and Sousse and Sfax in the Center-East. The four ports of these cities were modernized and equipped in ten years: 1888-1899, and open to traffic in 1891 for Sfax, 1893 for Tunis, 1898 for Bizerte and 1899 for Sousse.[66] The second phase of this policy was to attribute to each of these ports its zone of "drainage." A law divided the country into four hinterlands and each port was reserved its own economic zone as follows:[67]

| | INTERIOR | LITTORAL |
|---|---|---|
| | North-West | North-East |
| ZONE I: | Minerals of Nebeur and Nefza | Port of Bizerte |
| ZONE II: | Minerals of Kalaat-Senam, Djerissa<br>Cereals of the Tell | Port of Tunis |
| | Center-West and South-West | Center-East |
| ZONE III and IV: | Minerals and Farming Products of Central Tunisia<br>Minerals of the Gafsa Basin | Port of Sousse<br>Port of Sfax |

<u>The Railway Network.</u> In order to link these zones to the ports on the coast, the French launched in parallel a program of railway construction, and financed it, interestingly, with the Tunisian budget.[68] With the exception of a few lines, as mentioned earlier, the development of the railway network falls into two phases (figure 4.3):

Phase I:

—construction of a littoral line connecting 1885-1898 the three ports of Bizerte-Tunis-Sousse (1885-1886);
—then the first portion of a line connecting the port of Tunis to economic Zone II (1897);
—then a line connecting the port of Sfax to economic Zone IV (1896-98);

Phase II:

—the phase of the "mining lines." More than 72 1900-1918 percent of the whole network was constructed during this period.[69] With the exception of the extension of the littoral line from Sousse to Sfax (1908-1911) and from Sfax to Gabes (1916), all the extension of the network was designed to complete the economic penetration of the interior by:
—the extension of the line connecting the port of Tunis with Economic Zone II and to the Algerian border (1906)
—the extension of the line from the port of Bizerte to the mining zones (Economic Zone I) of Nebeur and Nefza (1906-1910)
—the extension of the line of the port of Sousse further west in Central Tunisia to Kasserine and further South-West to the mining zones of Souatir and Moulares (Economic Zone III) (1905-1909).

By the end of the 1914-18 War the network in its main configuration (which remains the same today) was completed. The only extensions added between the two world wars were one line in the north connecting the port of Bizerte to Tabarka near the Algerian border, and another line of military interest connecting Tebessa in Algeria with Kasserine.

Thus, in less than 35 years a typically colonial railway network was constructed. Beyond the classic trilogy of mining zones/railway/port, its colonial character is also reflected by two other main elements: (1) out of a total of 2,065 km constructed, only 500 in the North were of normal gauge; (2) only 18 km (the suburban line of Tunis-Hammam-Iif) were of double track; the rest of the system is composed of single track lines.

<u>The Road Network.</u> Along with the construction of new ports and a railway network, the French launched a program of road construction. Between 1881 and 1914, 4,000 km of paved roads were constructed in the

North of the country.[70] And between 1920 and 1940 another 3,700 km were added.[71] But here again, the configuration (figure 6.4) of the network is similar to that of the railway network. In its design, the objective of the network was to link each of the four ports to its economic zone. Roads, therefore, radiate from the four ports to the interior. The second objective was to link the four ports to each other, as was the case with the railway network. Thus, they were connected by a major coastal road from Bizerte in the North to Gabes and even Ben Gardane close to the Libyan border. So here, the road network, rather than to correct the anomalies of the railway network, reinforced them. There is however a small difference between the two. The road network is fairly dense (secondary roads) throughout the littoral and especially the North of the country. We have to understand here that the objectives were very clear: (1) to irrigate the North with good roads, particularly the North-West, the major zone, because of its good land, of agricultural colonization, and the existence of the "centers of colonization"; and (2) to link the major city-ports, where 80 percent of the French population was found.

Here are, very briefly, the policies of the protectorate in these three areas of infrastructure. Now, what was their impact on the precolonial space economy and the urban network.

The Emergence of a Colonial Space Economy and Urban Network.

Their direct impact, to begin with, was a complete disorganization of the precolonial urban network in its functions as well as in structures. Contrary to the precolonial urban network, which was rooted in the local economy, the main function of the one created by the colonial economy was to serve as a "bridgehead" in the siphoning of the resources of the country by the métropole. In its structure, instead of an integrated and homogeneous urban network, the new one was characterized by, first, the primacy of the capital, also a port, and, second, the emergence of the other three ports of Sousse, Bizerte and Sfax as the largest cities of the country. In a few decades, these cities were literally catapulted at the top of the urban hierarchy. In contrast, the major cities of the interior, which were of no use for the colonial economy, stagnated.

Despite the absence of reliable data on the relative population sizes of Tunisian cities before the French protectorate,[72] I have tried to trace from different sources the changes in the urban network structure, in using available data for major Tunisian cities (table 4.1). The figures from table 4.1 show very clearly, I think, the nature of the structural changes introduced by the colonial economy on the precolonial urban network. While all the cities of the interior grew modestly or stagnated, such as Kairouan, all the cities of the littoral, especially the four city-ports, grew dramatically. Between 1906 and 1956, for example, all four city-ports have more than doubled in size. Between 1880 and 1956, Tunis alone has

Figure 4.3

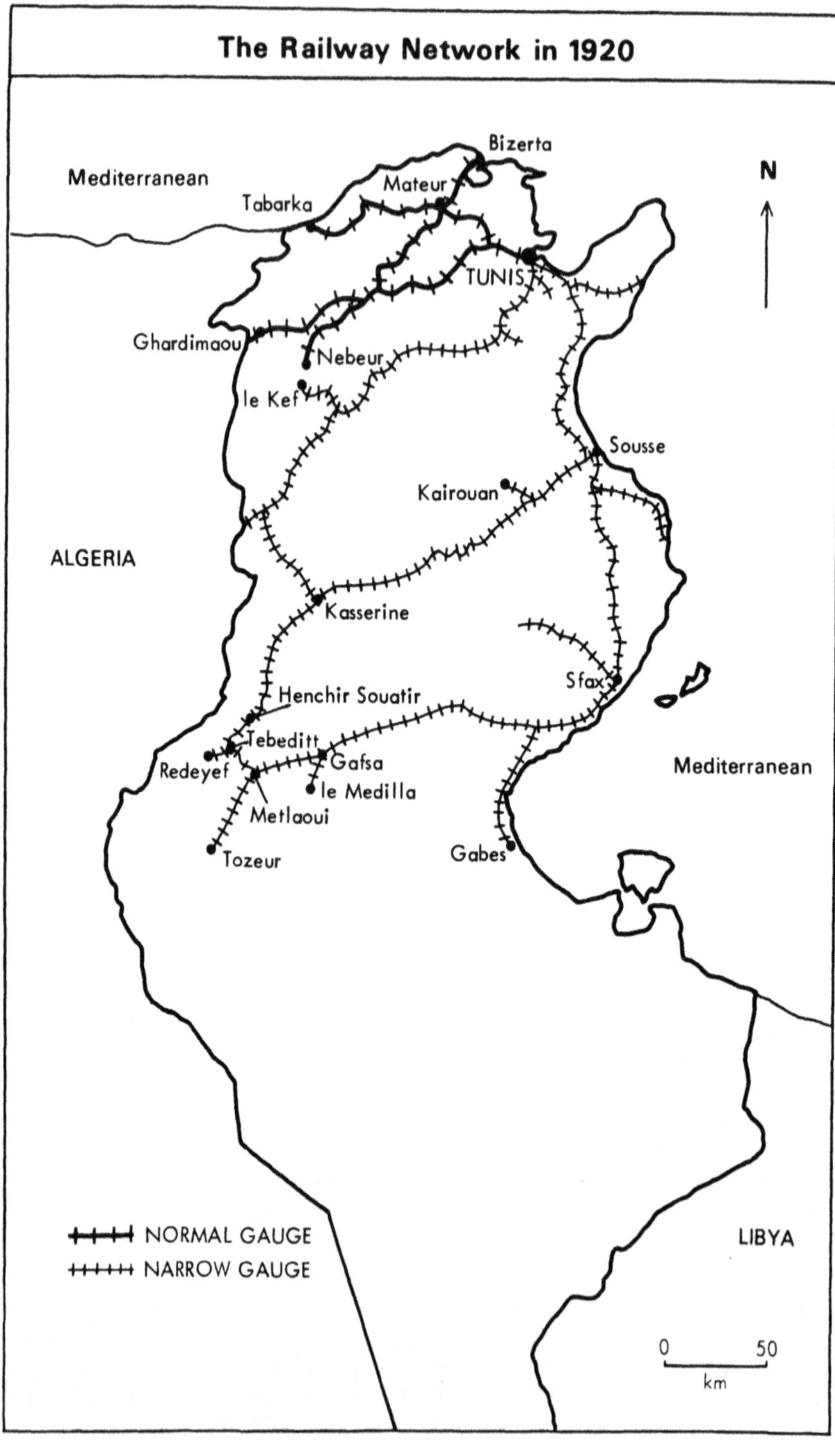


Source: Adapted from: B.G./N.I.D., Tunisia, op. cit., p. 392

Figure 4.4



## The Road Network in 1930

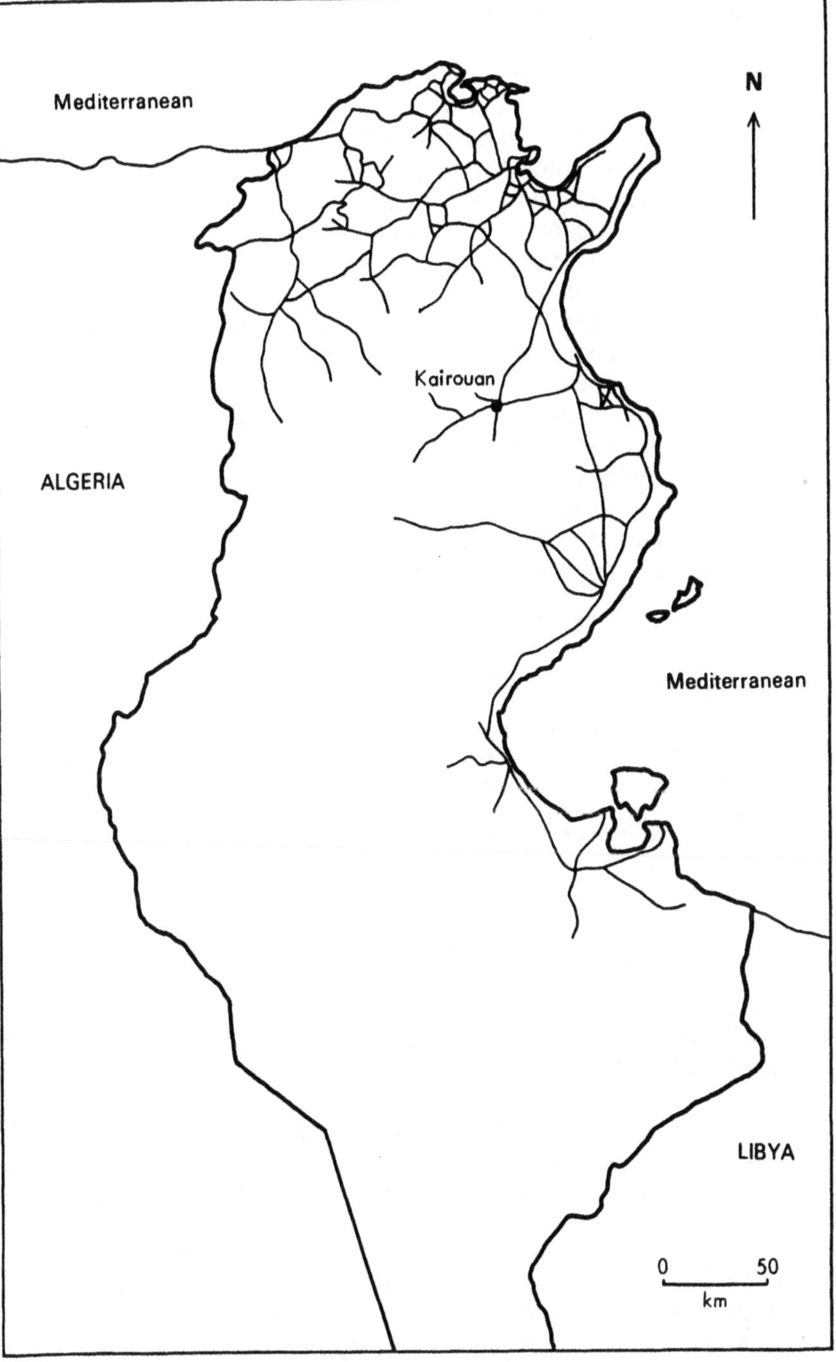


Source: Adapted from: A. Belhadi, Le Chemin de Fer et l'Espace en Tunisie. Publications de l'Universite de Tunis, Tunis, 1980, p.66

multiplied by five its population. And it is interesting to note here that Kairouan, despite the fact that it was supplanted by Tunis as the capital long before the French protectorate, has been able to remain the second city and the métropole of the Center and the South up to 1881. With an estimated population of 20,000 in 1880 it was even larger than the three city-ports of Bizerte, Sousse and Sfax combined! Moreover, and according to Reclus, up to 1880, it was also able to maintain its strategic position in the Tunisian circulation system (figure 4.5).[73] But by 1926 and especially by 1936, when the colonial economy was well in place, Kairouan fell to the fifth place in the urban hierarchy.

The second direct consequence of all this is that in imposing a completely new urban network on top of the previous one, the colonial policies described above have created at the national level, a completely new space economy. The sectoral and regional complementarity that was, as noted by Mahjoub,[74] the base of the coherence of the precolonial economic structures, was destroyed and replaced by the specialization of the extroverted colonial economy. This, in turn, gave birth to a new spatial and economic organization. As a perfect reflection of this extroverted colonial economy, the new space economy was structured upon this classic colonial spatial-economic organization scheme (figure 4.6):

| 1 | | 2 | | 3 | | 4 |
|---|---|---|---|---|---|---|
| Interior Agriculture Mining Zones | → | Links Railway Roads Networks | → | Littoral Major City-Ports | → | France Exports to the Métropole |

## CONCLUSION

In brief, the situation inherited from the French protectorate could be summarized as follows:

1. A few decades after the protectorate was established and the colonial project fully realized, an historical rupture appeared in its most brutal form. And on the eve of independence in 1956, one can even speak of two countries: on the one hand, an urbanized, densely populated and relatively prosperous Tunisia, the littoral, favored by the colonial economy, although it has suffered, but to a lesser degree, the same destruction; on the other hand, an underdeveloped Tunisia, the interior, whose economy and social structures were completely destroyed and whose resources were tapped by the colonial economy. In 1956, for example, five gouvernorats:

Table 4.1

THE TUNISIAN URBAN SYSTEM BEFORE AND AFTER THE FRENCH PROTECTORATE

| Cities | Population | | | | |
|---|---|---|---|---|---|
| | 1860-80[a] | 1906[b] | 1926[c] | 1936[d] | 1956[e] |
| INTERIOR system | | | | | |
| Kairouan | 20,000 | 20,000 | 19,426 | 22,991 | 34,000 |
| Béjà | 3,000 | - | 10,500 | 13,292 | 22,700 |
| Le Kef | 3,000 | - | 7,400 | 8,855 | 14,000 |
| Mateur | 2,000 | - | 7,100 | 7,416 | 14,000 |
| Gafsa | 3,000 | - | 7,800 | 11,266 | 24,000 |
| Tozeur | 8,000 | - | 11,100 | 11,698 | 11,800 |
| Nefta | 8,000 | - | 13,300 | 13,619 | 14,600 |
| LITTORAL system | | | | | |
| Tunis | 80,000 | 204,497 | 185,996 | 219,578 | 410,000 |
| Bizerte | 3,000 | 18,094 | 20,593 | 28,468 | 44,700 |
| Ferry-ville | - | - | 4,500 | 6,300 | 34,700 |
| Nabeul | 4,000 | - | 7,800 | 9,107 | 14,000 |
| Sousse | 8,000 | 20,829 | 21,298 | 28,470 | 48,200 |
| Monastir | 4,000 | - | 8,300 | 10,572 | 12,600 |
| Mahdia | 4,000 | - | - | 8,488 | 10,800 |
| Sfax | 8,000 | 29,069 | 27,723 | 43,333 | 65,600 |
| Gabes | 4,000 | - | 15,100 | 18,611 | 24,400 |

[a] Estimations from: J. Ganiage, *Les Origines du Protectorat Français en Tunisie*, op. cit., pp. 146-48; and L. Valensi, *Fellahs Tunisiens*, op. cit. p. 17.

[b] A. Bernard, "Le Recensement du 1906 en Algérie et en Tunisie," *Annales de Géographie*, no. 91 (1908), pp. 24-33.

[c] J. Clarke, "Tunisia: Population Patterns, Pressures and Policies," in *Populations of the Middle-East and North Africa. A Geographical Approach*, eds. J. Clarke and W. Fisher (London: University of London Press, 1972), p. 366; and A. Bernard, "Le Recensement de 1926 dans l'Afrique du Nord," *Annales de Géographie*, no. 119 (1927), pp. 136-42.

[d] Clarke, op. cit.; and A. Bernard, "Le Recensement de 1936 dans l'Afrique du Nord," *Annales de Géographie*, no. 259 (1937), pp. 84-88.

[e] Clarke, op. cit.; and J. Poncet, "L'Evolution Géographique du Peuplement Tunisien à l'Epoque Récente," *Annales de Géographie*, no. 367 (1959), pp. 247-53.

Figure 4.5

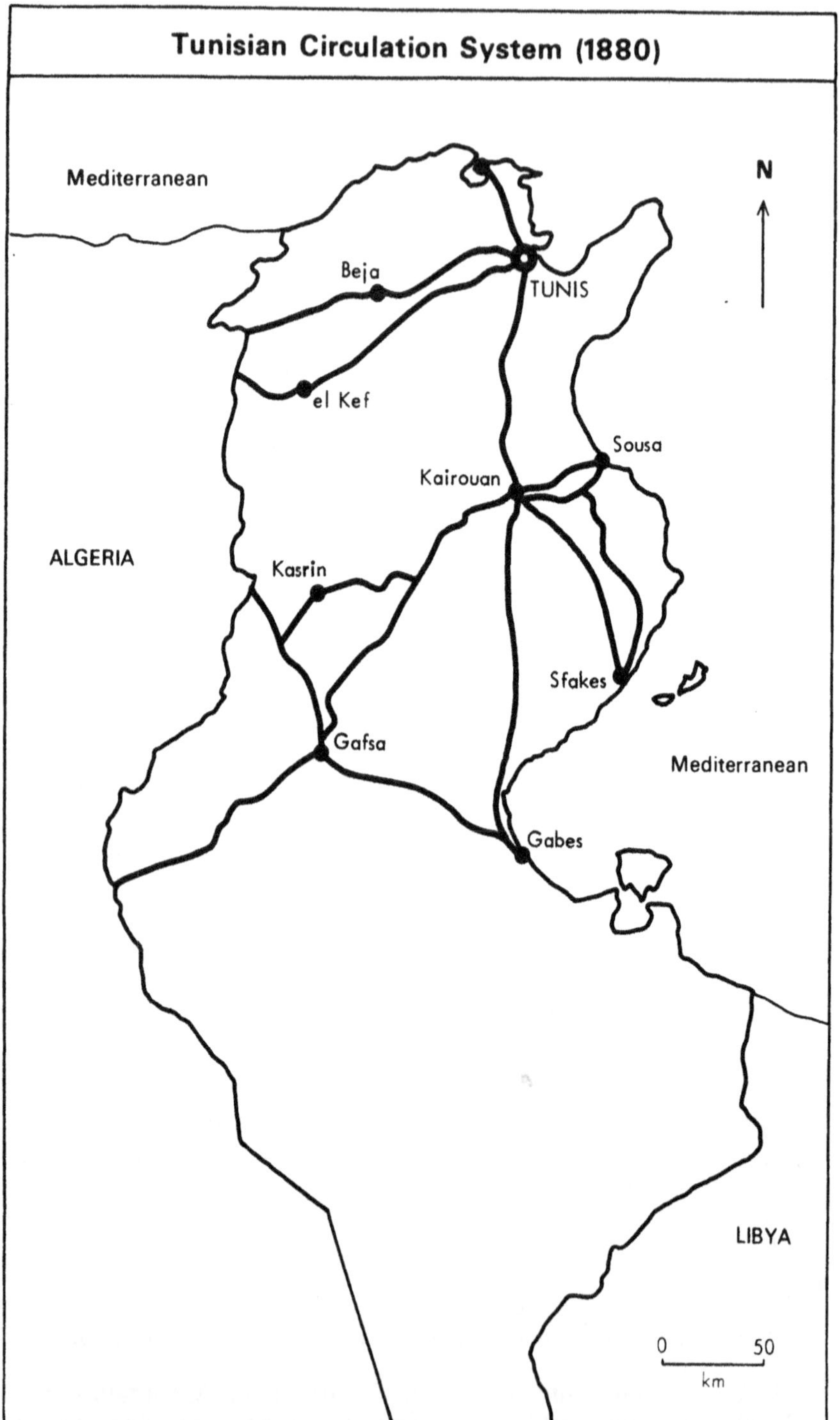


Source: Adapted from: E. Reclus, The Earth and Its Inhabitants. Vol. 2, New York: D. Appleton and Cie, 1887, p. 192

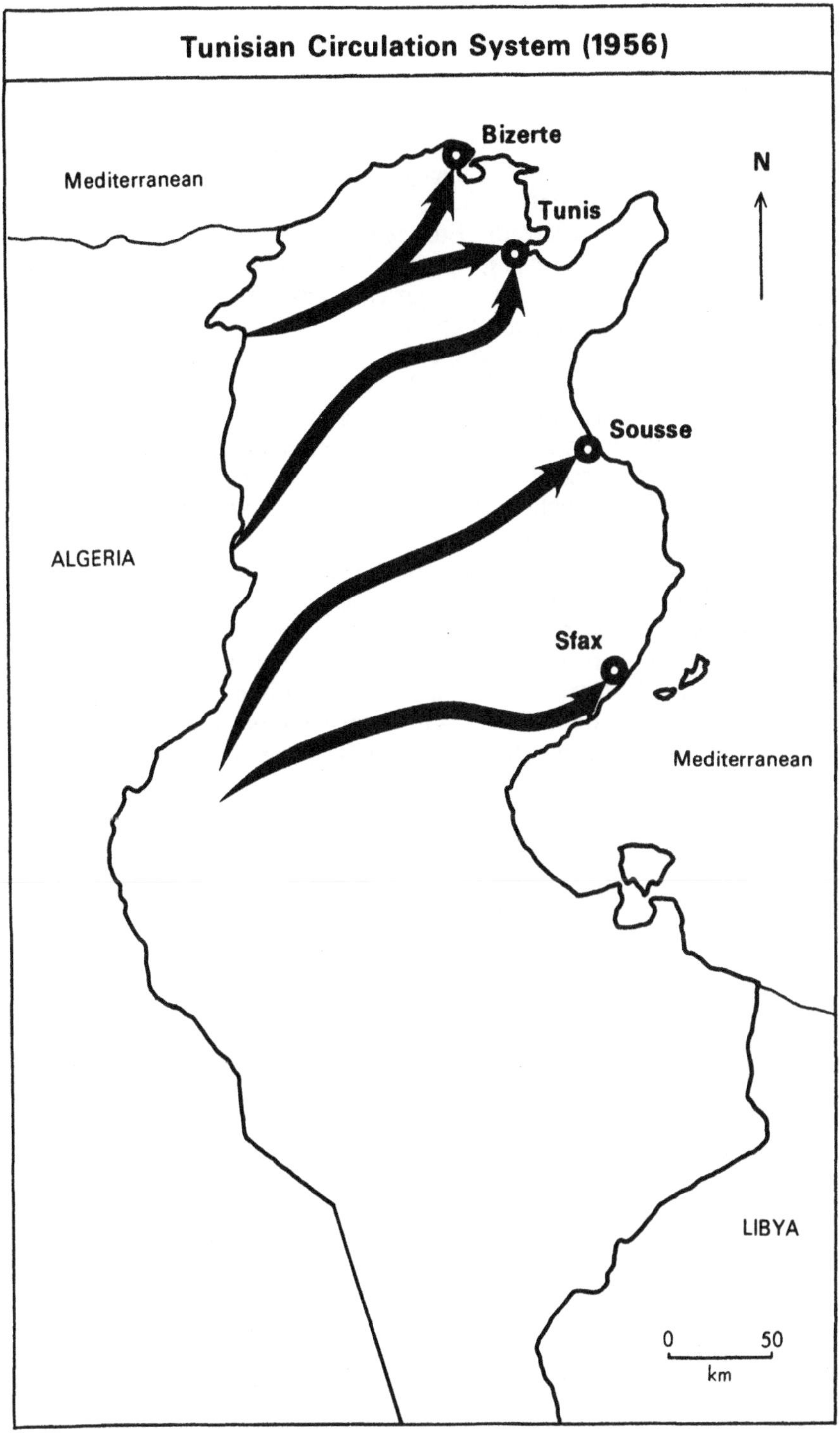
Tunisian Circulation System (1956)
Bizerte
Mediterranean
N
Tunis
Sousse
ALGERIA
Sfax
Mediterranean
LIBYA
0
50
km

Bizerte, Tunis, Nabeul, Sousse and Sfax had 52 percent of the total population. Also, this zone concentrated 90 percent of all industrial activities; Tunis alone had 80 percent of them. Moreover, two-thirds of the national incomes were also concentrated in this zone.[75] This was neither an accident nor the creation of "mother nature!" It is explained rather by the fact that all the investments in the social and economic infrastructure were located in this zone where the European population and economy were heavily concentrated; for example, in 1936, 60 percent of the total European population was to be found in the four city-ports. But Tunis alone had 46 percent of the total European population of 213,000 in the country. In 1956, these percentages were respectively 72 percent and 54 percent of a total of 255,000 Europeans (table 4.2).

2. Finally, and this is the most important element to keep in mind in understanding the historical roots of the "regional question" and regional disparities, in a few decades, French colonialism created new patterns of regional economic and political relationships, based not on complementarity but on *exploitation*. In a few decades, the interior, the core for centuries, became the periphery. And the littoral, the periphery in the precolonial system, became the core in the colonial system.

As we can see from these evidences, regional underdevelopment, as Matthews and others have superbly shown,[76] has nothing to do with "mother nature," or with the, I must say, racist explanation of the Sixth Tunisian Development Plan, which attributes it to "sociological constraints."[77] As this chapter has shown, it can be *historically* explained.

Table 4.2

EVOLUTION OF THE EUROPEAN POPULATION DISTRIBUTION IN MAJOR TUNISIAN CITIES 1936-1956

| Cities | Population | | | |
|---|---|---|---|---|
| | 1936[a] | | 1956[b] | |
| | Tunisian | European | Tunisian | European |
| INTERIOR | | | | |
| Kairouan | 22,128 | 863 | 33,062 | 906 |
| Béjà | 11,360 | 1,932 | 20,425 | 2,243 |
| Le Kef | 7,498 | 1,357 | 12,932 | 1,811 |
| Mateur | 5,792 | 1,624 | 12,552 | 2,089 |
| Gafsa | 10,506 | 760 | 23,028 | 1,317 |
| Tozeul | 11,586 | 112 | - | - |
| Nefta | 13,590 | 29 | 13,423 | 1,161 |
| LITTORAL | | | | |
| Tunis | 120,701 | 98,877 | 272,000 | 138,000 |
| Bizerte | 17,211 | 11,257 | 30,497 | 14,184 |
| Ferry-ville | 446 | 5,864 | 21,358 | 13,374 |
| Nabeul | 8,499 | 618 | 10,000 | 4,000 |
| Sousse | 19,825 | 8,645 | 38,000 | 10,000 |
| Monastir | 10,236 | 336 | 12,000 | - |
| Mahdia | 7,977 | 511 | 10,000 | - |
| Sfax | 34,672 | 8,661 | 55,232 | 10,403 |
| Gabes | 16,854 | 1,757 | 22,663 | 1,757 |

Source:

[a] British Government, p. 193; and A. Bernard, "Le Recensement de 1936."

[b] Poncet, "L'Evolution Géographique," pp. 247-51; and M. Wolkowitsh, "L'Emigration des Français en Tunisie," *Annales de Géographie*, no. 367 (1959), pp. 253-57.

## NOTES

1. For a general discussion on this kind of position, see: R. Matthews, *The Creation of Regional Dependency* (Toronto: University Press of Toronto, 1983). On Tunisia in particular, this kind of perception of regional underdevelopment is illustrated by the *Sixth Five Year Plan (1982-86)* (RT/MPF, 1982) in these terms:

> Most certainly the past twenty years' effort contributed to a noticeable improvement in the standard and conditions of living and to real growth in production and employment in all regions of the country. But comparatively, noticeable disparities still exist. *They could not be totally suppressed for natural, human and sociological constraints* (p. 185, emphasis mine).

2. See J. Poncet, "La Régionalisation en Tunisie," *Tiers-Monde*, no. 55 (1972), pp. 597-614; H. Attia, "L'Urbanisation de la Tunisie," *Revue Tunisienne des Sciences Sociales*, nos. 28-29 (1972), pp. 9-32; J. Abu-Lughod, *Rabat: Urban Apartheid in Morocco* (Princeton, NJ: Princeton University Press, 1980) (see especially Chapter 2, pp. 30-51).

3. See M. Lombard, "L'Evolution Urbaine pendant le Haut Moyen Age," *Annales: Economies, Sociétés, Civilisations*, no. 1 (1957), pp. 7-28.

4. Poncet, op. cit.; see also P. Bonnefant, "Béjà, de la Conquête Musulmane à 1881," *Revue de l'Institut des Belles Lettres Arabes*, no. 127 (1971), pp. 3-33.

5. Eric Wolf, *Europe and the People Without History* (Berkeley: University of California Press, 1982) (see especially pp. 37-41).

6. F. Braudel, *The Mediterranean and the Mediterranean World in the Age of Philip II*, vol. 1 (London: Collins, 1972), p. 467.

7. Abu-Lughod, op. cit., p. 31.

8. On this very important issue, see: A. Laroui, *The History of the Maghrib: An Interpretative Essay* (Princeton, NJ: Princeton University Press, 1977); E. Hermassi, *Leadership and National Development in North Africa* (Berkeley: University of California Press, 1972); and Wolf, op. cit.

9. L. Valensi, *On the Eve of Colonialism: North Africa before the French Conquest* (New York: Africana Publishing, 1972), p. 80.

10. Ibid; see especially Appendix 2 (pp. 111-20), in which Valensi provides a summary of these racist and colonial interpretations.

11. Among the many contributors to this effort, see for example: M. Sahli, *Décoloniser L'Histoire* (Paris: Maspero, 1965); Y. Lacoste, *Ibn Khaldoun: Naissance de l'Histoire Passé du Tiers-Monde* (Paris: Maspero, 1969); idem, "General Characteristics and Fundamental Structures of Mediaeval North African Society," *Economy and Society*, no. 1 (1974), pp.

1-17; J. Poncet, "Le Mythe de la Catastrophe Hilalienne," *Annales, Economies, Sociétés, Civilisations*, no. 5 (1967), pp. 1099-1120; A. Mahjoub, "Analyse Historique du Sous-Développement en Tunisie," *Annuaire de l'Afrique du Nord (AAN) 1979*, vol. 18 (Paris: CNRS, 1980), pp. 443-56; and idem, "Analyse Historique du Sous-Développement en Tunisie," *Annuaire de l'Afrique du Nord 1981*, vol. 20 (Paris: CNRS, 1982), pp. 509-22; M. Bdira, *Relations Internationales et Sous-Développement: La Tunisie 1857-1864* (Uppsala: Almquist and Wiksell International, 1978); Laroui, op. cit.; and Hermassi, op. cit.

12. Abu-Lughod, op. cit., p. 43.

13. Poncet, "Le Mythe."

14. V. Berdoulay, *La Formation de l'Ecole Française de Géographie (1870-1914)* (Paris: Bibliothèque Nationale, 1981) (see especially Chapter 2, pp. 45-76). Among those French geographers who have popularized the "Hilali myth" the most are: E.F. Gauthier, *L'Islamisation de l'Afrique du Nord: Les Siè*cles Obscurs du Maghreb (Paris: Payot, 1927) (see the critique of this work by Laroui, op. cit.); A. Bernard, "Afrique du Nord," in *Géographie Universelle*, eds. P. Vidal de la Blache and L. Gallois (Paris: Armand Colin, 1937); and J. Despois, *L'Afrique du Nord* (Paris: Payot, 1949).

15. Poncet, "Le Mythe"; idem, *La Tunisie à la Recherche de Son Avenir: Independance ou Néocolonialisme* (Paris: Les Editions Sociales, 1974) (see especially the historical chapter, "La Tunisie dans l'Histoire," pp. 21-56, where Poncet delivers the most devastating critiques of the work of Gauthier and his followers).

16. Abu-Lughod, op. cit., pp. 43-44.

17. Braudel, op. cit., p. 468.

18. Abu-Lughod, op. cit., p. 44.

19. See, for example: I.D. Latham, "Towns and Cities in Barbary: The Andalusian Influence," *The Islamic Quarterly*, nos. 3-4 (1972), pp. 189-204; and M. De Epalza and R. Petit, *Etudes sur les Moriscos Andalous en Tunisie* (Tunis: Société Tunisienne de Diffusion, 1973).

20. Latham, op. cit.

21. Braudel, op. cit., pp. 462-69.

22. Ibid.; see also Wolf, op. cit.

23. Abu-Lughod, op. cit., p. 31.

24. Ibid., p. 32.

25. E. Reclus, *The Earth and Its Inhabitants*, vol. 2 (New York: D. Appleton and Cie, 1887), p. 159.

26. This historical process is not unique of course to Tunisia. It has to be re-placed in the whole historical context of the colonization of Africa and the Third World in general. But for Africa and for further discussion,

see for example: R.A. Obudho and S. El-Shakhs, eds., *Development of Urban Systems in Africa* (New York: Praeger, 1979); M.C. McNulty, "West African Urbanization," in *Urbanization and Counter-Urbanization*, ed. B.J.L. Berry (Beverly Hills: Sage, 1976), pp. 213-32; and in the same book, E. Soja and C. Weaver, "Urbanization and Underdevelopment in East Africa," pp. 233-66; D. Slater, "Colonialism and the Spatial Structure of Underdevelopment: Outlines of an Alternative Approach, with Special Reference to Tanzania." Progress in Planning, 2 (1975) pp. 137-167.

27. See for example: A. Findlay et al., *Tunisia*, World Bibliographical Series, vol. 33 (Oxford: Clio Press, 1982).

28. See on this particular issue, F. Stambouli and A. Zghal, "Urban Life in Precolonial North Africa," *British Journal of Sociology*, no. 1 (1976), pp. 1-20.

29. See, A. Raymond, "North Africa in the Precolonial Period," in *The Cambridge History of Islam*, eds. P.M. Holt et al., vol. 2 (London: Cambridge University Press, 1970), pp. 266-98; see also Bdira, op. cit., and Mahjoub, *AAN 1979* and *AAN 1981*.

30. Mahjoub, *AAN 1979*, p. 448.

31. Ibid.

32. Valensi, op. cit., p. 69.

33. J. Ganiage, *Les Origines du Protectorat Français en Tunisie* (Paris: Presses Universitaires de France, 1959), pp. 44-55 (the English translation is from: N. Bennouna "Primary Capital Accumulation in Colonial Tunisia," *Dialectical Anthropology*, no. 2 [1979], pp. 87-88).

34. Ibid.

35. Jules Ferry in a speech on July 28, 1885, declared that the objective of France in Tunisia was not "to create jobs and shelters" for an "exuberant population" of a "poor country"(!!!), but "to reserve to its capitalists and its products this technologically and economically backward country" (quoted in J. Poncet, *La Colonisation et l'Agriculture Europeennes en Tunise deput 1881* (Paris/La Haye: Mouton, 1961), p. 141 (translation mine); for further discussion on the colonial policy of Jules Ferry and the Third Republic in Tunisia and Africa in general, see among others: D. Thomson, *France: Empire and Republic, 1850-1940* (New York: Walker and Cie, 1968).

36. See. C. Sammut, *L'Impérialisme Capitaliste Français et le Nationalisme Tunisien* (Paris: Publisud, 1983) (see especially Chapter 8, "La Réforme de la Législation Commercial Tunisienne," pp. 101-109); see also Mahjoub, *AAN, 1980*, p. 513.

37. Raymond, op. cit., p. 290.

38. See C. Coquery-Vidrovitch, "L'Afrique Coloniale Française et la Crise de 1930: Crise Structurelle et Génèse du Sous-Développement," *Revue Française d'Histoire d'Outre-Mer*, nos. 232-233 (1976), p. 395.

39. See, C. Liauzu, "Un Aspect de la Crise en Tunisie: La Naissance des Bidonvilles," *Revue Française d'Histoire d'Outre-Mer*, nos. 232-233 (1976), p. 610.

40. See, J. Poncet, *Paysages et Problèmes Ruraux en Tunisie* (Paris: Presses Universitaires de France, 1962); and idem, "La Régionalisation en Tunisie."

41. See Raymond, op. cit., pp. 290-91.

42. Laroui, op. cit., p. 327.

43. Poncet, *La Colonisation*, p. 147.

44. Statement by Paul Cambon, first "Résident Général" of the protectorate in Tunisia (quoted from Poncet, *La Colonisation*, p. 147).

45. For the clarity of the discussion, a few words about the land tenure system of precolonial Tunisia must be said. Apart from a very small portion of "private" land called *Melk* (see Poncet, *La Colonisation*, p. 133), there were three major types of land tenure systems in 1881 in Tunisia: (1) the property of the sovereign, called the *Domaines*; (2) the *Habous*, property of religious institutions. There are two types of Habous: (a) "public Habous," land effectively owned and managed by religious institutions, and (b) "private Habous," land "donated" to religious institutions but still owned by private persons until their death and the death of their descendants. (3) The most important type of land tenure system, in any aspect, is that of "collective lands" (*terres collectives*). These are the lands of an indeterminate, juridically speaking, status. And here too we have two subcategories: (a) "dead lands"; these produced nothing and are the property of no one; (b) "rejuvenated" lands; which were developed, worked and appropriated by a given community and transmitted through generations. They are as such recognized as the property of that community and have even its name. For example, in this particular area, even today, you hear that these lands, thousands and thousands of hectares, are the property of the *Fraichich* or of the *Ayar*, or *Cherif*, etc. Of course, and juridically speaking, according to the "Roman Civil Code," from which derives the "Napoleonic Code," this land belongs to the State, to the sovereign. But the sovereign's power on this type of land was severely limited by what Hermassi called, the "sanctity of tradition" (op. cit., p. 77). In other words, the collective property of the group was recognized and unchallenged by the rulers and by the society as a whole, precisely because this society itself was structured along communal and kinship lines. Therefore, *group rights* were predominant over *individual* rights. It is crucial to understand the "rationality" of this land tenure system in order to

be able to understand the precolonial productive system; the whole spatial organization that supported it; the whole and devastating impact of the introduction by force (violence) through colonialism of the capitalist mode of production on precolonial social formations and productive forces; and the complexity of the "question of transition" as discussed in Chapter 2.

46. Poncet, *La Colonisation*, p. 164.

47. On this issue, see Poncet, *La Colonisation*; and Sammut, op. cit., pp. 87-99, 149-62.

48. A. Raymond and J. Poncet, *La Tunisie* (Paris: Presses Universitaires de France, Collection Que-Sais-Je?, 1971), p. 32.

49. A. Zghal, "L'Economie Paysanne de la Tunisie Pré-Coloniale," *Revue Tunisienne des Sciences Sociales*, no. 61 (1980), pp. 11-30.

50. Sammut, op. cit., p. 157 (translation mine).

51. Raymond and Poncet, op. cit., pp. 33-34.

52. On this fundamental issue, see the monumental work of Poncet, to whom I owe so much on this particular subject, *La Colonisation*, pp. 64-83; see also S. Amin, *Unequal Development: An Essay on the Social Formations of Peripheral Capitalism* (New York and London: Monthly Review Press, 1976) (see especially Chapter 1, "The Precapitalist Formations," pp. 13-58; R. Luxembourg, *The Accumulation of Capital* (New York: Monthly Review Press, 1968); J. Ziegler, *Le Pouvoir Africain* (Paris, Le Seuil, 1979); see also my discussion in Chapter 2.

53. See Poncet, *La Colonisation*; Lacoste, "General Characteristics," Sammut, op. cit., especially pp. 149-62.

54. D. Dumont, *Paysanneries aux Abois* (Paris: Le Seuil, 1972), p. 126; see also Poncet, *La Colonisation*, pp. 404-14.

55. Dumont, op. cit.

56. See F. Stambouli, "Sous-Emploi et Espace Urbain: Les Bidonvilles au Maghreb," *Espaces et Sociétés*, nos. 6-7 (1972), pp. 165-80; see also, Lianzu, op. cit. By 1936, the population of the bidonvilles in Tunis was estimated at 10,000; in 1946 at 50,000 and in 1956 at 150,000, one-fourth of the population of the capital in 1956.

57. A. Noushi, "North Africa in the Period of Colonization," in Holt et al. (eds.), op. cit., p. 317.

58. Hermassi, op. cit., p. 88.

59. See in particular, Bernard, op. cit., Despois, op. cit.; and Basset, A., et al., *Initiation à la Tunisie* (Paris: Adrien-Maisonneuve, 1950).

60. W. Rodney, *How Europe Underdeveloped Africa* (Washington, DC: Howard University Press, 1982), p. 205.

61. See n. 35.

62. J. Marseille, "L'Industrialisation des Colonies: Affaiblissement ou Renforcement de la Puissance Française," *Revue Française d'Histoire d'Outre-Mer*, no. 252 (1982), pp. 23-34.

63. See, Sammut, op. cit., Chapter 8, "La Réforme de la Législation Commercial Tunisienne," pp. 101-109.

64. See Matthews, op. cit.

65. See Basset et al., op. cit., p. 362; A. Belhadi, *Le Chemin de Fer et l'Espace Tunisien* (Tunis: Publications de l'Université de Tunis, 1980), p. 48; for an historical review of the development of Tunisian ports, see the British Government, Naval Intelligence Division, *Tunisia*, Geographical Handbook Series (Oxford: Oxford and Cambridge University Presses, 1945).

66. Basset et al., op. cit., pp. 362-71.

67. For further details, see: Belhadi, op. cit., pp. 47-56; and British Government, op. cit.

68. See Sammut, op. cit.

69. See Belhadi, op. cit.; and E.D. Brant, *Railways of North Africa* (Newton Abbot: David and Charles Publishers, 1971).

70. See Basset et al., op. cit., p. 378.

71. Ibid.

72. The lack of reliable data on this particular period shows very clearly, I think, how much the study of precolonial urban networks in North Africa and in Africa in general has been neglected in the past. The need for some systematic studies on this particular issue will help us in Africa to learn more, empirically, about the processes of the destruction by colonization. I am not (thank goodness!) an empiricist! But this would help to support further what we already know about the processes, and most important would help us to study further African precolonial urban systems on their own.

73. Reclus, op. cit., p. 192.

74. Mahjoub, *AAN 1979*.

75. P. Aydalot, "La Restructuration de l'Espace Economique Tunisien," *Revue Tunisiennes des Sciences Sociales*, no. 5 (1966), pp. 65, 67.

76. Matthews, op. cit.; Obudho and El-Shakhs (eds.), op. cit.; Abu-Lughod, op. cit.; Soja and Weaver, op. cit.; Slater, op. cit.;

77. See n. 1.

# 5
# REGIONAL DISPARITY AND REGIONAL DEVELOPMENT POLICIES IN THE POSTCOLONIAL PERIOD: 1960-1980

## INTRODUCTION

Chapter 4 dealt with the historical roots of the "regional question" in Tunisia. In focusing on the policies that transformed the whole economic and spatial structures of precolonial Tunisia—and have, therefore, through this process "created" regional disparity—during the French protectorate it has been shown that regional underdevelopment is not, contrary to dominant thinking, a "natural" phenomenon.

The objective of this chapter now is to test the validity of the second premise of the study: that all societies have their own productive systems and related spatial organizations that have to be analyzed, understood and planned for in terms of their proper structural logic and rationality. It is hoped that the following documentation and analysis of the policies that have tried to eliminate the disparities inherited from the colonial period will provide a thorough understanding of the roots of the "regional question" in Tunisia today.

But before doing that, a few words will be said about the periodization adopted in this chapter. Between 1960-69, or what is also called the "Ben Salah" period,[1] regional development policy corresponded to the nature of the national development strategy itself: a very centralized strategy, based on direct State control and intervention in the economy and society. But after nearly ten years of "structural reforms" of the Tunisian economy and the whole society, this strategy was suddenly stopped in 1969 (see below and Chapter 3). From this date Tunisian development strategy shifted to economic laisser-faire and even, less than 15 years after independence, in favor of direct foreign investments in the Tunisian economy. This period (1970-80) was also called the "Nouira" period.[2]

As a direct consequence of this shift, regional development policy itself shifted in 1970 from a centralized policy in which the State played an important role, to a policy in which the State intervened indirectly, if at all. This whole reorientation in ideological and economic terms of the role of the State has had a tremendous impact, as we will see, on the evolution of regional disparities during the last 25 years. In order to fully understand all the ramifications of the "regional question" today, it is important to distinguish between these two periods. And it is for this reason that I will document and analyze postcolonial regional development policies on the basis of this periodization and from the perspective of each of the two development strategies and ideologies.

Because they have constituted the major components of the two regional policies and have, therefore, a direct and important impact on the evolution of regional disparities, special attention is given to the following areas: (1) the growth pole policy in the industrial and urban sectors and the cooperative program in the agricultural and rural sectors (the two major components of the regional policy until 1969); and (2) the industrial decentralization policy and the rural development program (the two major components of the regional policy between 1970-80). In addition to these, some other areas, because their importance, will be examined, although briefly.

## THE REGIONAL POLICY DURING THE "BEN SALAH" PERIOD: 1960-1969

### The Growth Pole Policy

The political commitment of Tunisian leaders during the "Ben Salah" period to the elimination of regional disparities inherited from the French protectorate was very clearly stated in the first and most important Tunisian planning document, the *Perspectives Décennales 1962-1971*, published in 1962. In this document, it was stated that the development of the industrial sector should also contribute to regional development and the restructuration of the spatial system inherited from the protectorate:

> The industrial development should correct the current disparities between the regions, and thus should eliminate one of the most important obstacles to economic development.[3]

And it was during the period of the first two Tunisian plans, the Three Year Plan (1962-64) and the Four Year Plan (1965-68) that Tunisian leaders launched the projects that were supposed to achieve this objective. Between 1961 and 1969, investments in the industrial sector had absorbed 265.7 MTD (million Tunisian dinars), nearly 30 percent of all public investments (not including tourism, construction and public works) of that period. The efforts to eliminate regional disparities in the industrial sector were translated into the localization of three projects (among the four most important industrial projects of the period) in the interior and the South-East. These four projects absorbed alone nearly 50 percent of all industrial investments of that period. Two of them were located in the interior: the sugar-refinery of Béjà in the North-West and the paper-mill industry of

Kasserine in the Center-West; and two were located in the littoral: the chemical industry of Gabes (a port) in the South-East and the steel industry of Menzel-Bourguiba (ex-Ferryville and also a port) in the North-East (figure 5.1). Based on François Perroux's theory it was believed that the creation of these *pôles de croissance*, especially those of the interior, would generate the development of their respective regions in a few years. As the authors of the *Sixth Development Plan (1982-1986)* recently said, these industrial units

> were meant to constitute real growth poles capable of radiating over the whole region where they are located and to induce the development of several related activities.[4]

But according to all the information available now, none of this has been achieved.[5] In what follows, I will try to explain, one by one, all the reasons that have been considered the main factors of the failure of these projects in respect to interregional disparities.

To begin with, the projects were criticized for their highly capital-intensive character.[6] For example,for 132 MTD of that time (the total cost of the four projects), only 3,000 permanent jobs were created: the growth pole of Gabes cost 100 MTD and created 2,000 jobs; in the steel industry of Menzel-Bourguiba 23 MTD were invested for only 200 jobs; and in the two growth poles of the interior 9 MTD were invested for only 800 jobs.[7]

The second major criticism addressed to this growth pole policy was that it was not conceived in function of the real needs of the regions where they were located, but in function of the national and international markets. Within the national industrial development strategy of that period it was merely a "localization" of some projects. In other words, it was a "*parachutage*" of certain industries in certain cities. This was particularly true for the two projects of the interior in Béjà and Kasserine, as well as that of Gabes in the South-East. All three of these industrial units depend heavily on foreign technology, know-how, equipment and personnel for their inputs and production, and not on the existing resources of their respective regions. This explains why, for example, that in the paper-mill of Kasserine among the 570 workers in 1966, only 150 unskilled workers (*manoeuvres*) were from the region.[8] Also, and when the headquarters (*siège social*) of the companies are outside the pole itself, as with the case of the chemical industry in Gabes, all the "cadres" were located in Tunis.[9] This means that a substantial part of the salaries that these jobs would have brought to the regions benefit, in fact, another region. That is why, therefore, these poles have been called "*enclaves economiques*": they were not integrated into the economies of their regions. Their location was commanded simply by the existence or the proximity of the raw materials needed by the industries: the phosphate of the South-West for the pole of Gabes, the "alfa" (esperato grass) of Central Tunisia for the industries of

Figure 5.1

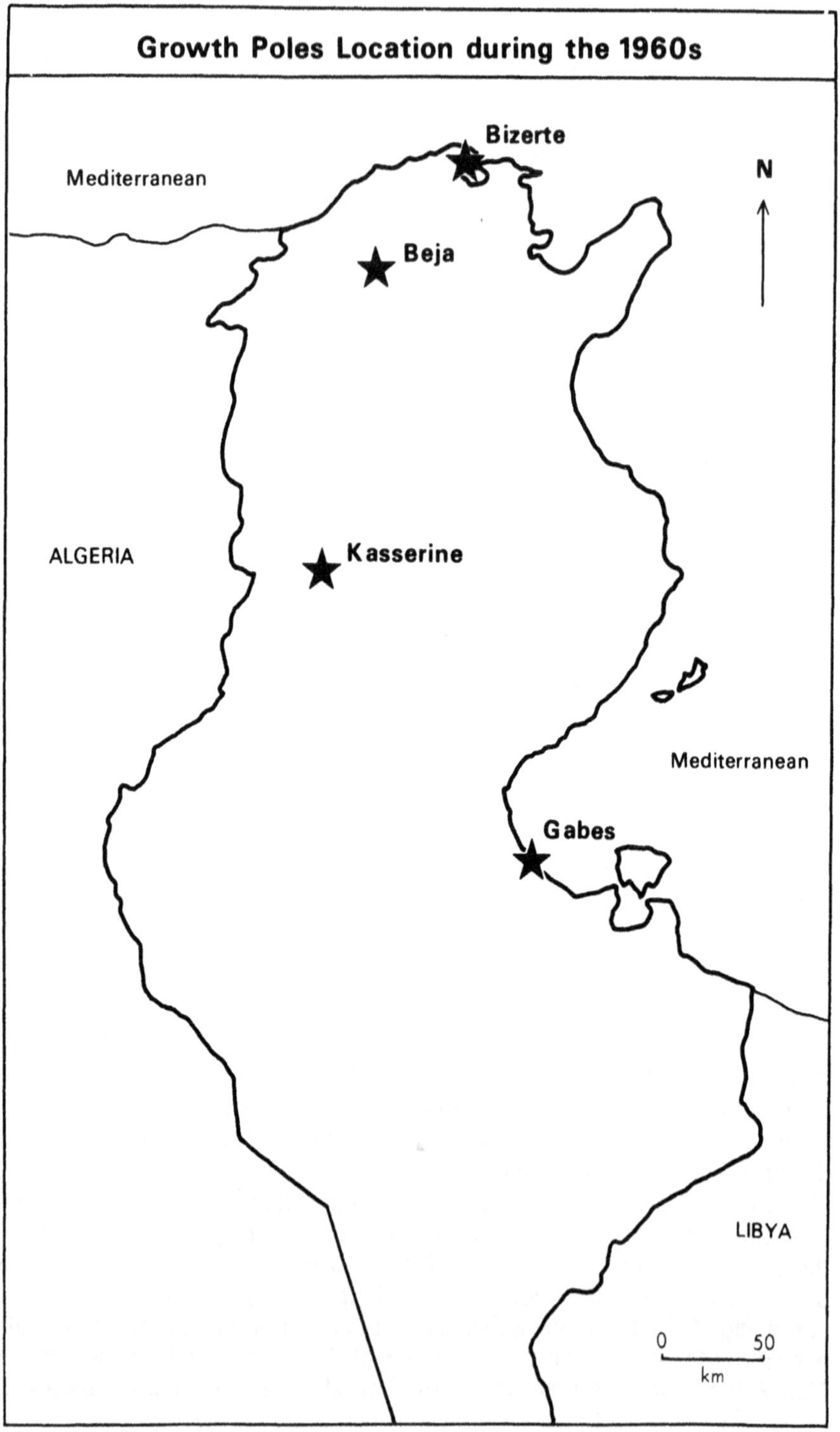
Growth Poles Location during the 1960s
Bizerte
Mediterranean
N
Beja
ALGERIA
Kasserine
Mediterranean
Gabes
LIBYA
0
50
km

Kasserine or the iron of the North-West for the steel industry of Menzel-Bourguiba in the North-East.

These criticisms led some observers and advisers of Tunisian planners at that time to publicly question the validity of the growth pole approach in a country that was so poorly industrialized in the early 1960s.[10]

The final critique was that not only was the policy based on a dubious theory (see Chapter 2), but all the efforts to diffuse the "industrial phenomenon" in the interior regions and to use it as a catalyst for the "take off" of their economy, were simply a "joke."[11] As we saw, among the four major projects of the decade only two were located in the interior. These cost 9 MTD for only 800 jobs; whereas the two located in the littoral cost 123 MTD and created 2,300 permanent jobs. Based on this evidence, it was argued that this policy has reinforced the gap between the littoral and the interior. This argument is further illustrated when we look at the localization of total investments in the industrial sector for the whole "Ben Salah" period. During the 1962-71 decade, the littoral regions received 77 percent of all industrial investments. Tunis alone received 20.4 percent. Whereas the interior regions received only 23 percent (table 5.1). This investment distribution resulted in a heavy concentration of industrial employment by 1972 in the littoral regions (table 5.2), where 76 percent of all employment was concentrated, with Tunis having 45 percent.

So here we can see the gap between the objectives of the *Perspectives Décennales* and their realization. And this is despite the fact that four-fifths of the investments in the industrial sector were public. In brief, not only was the approach inadequate but the efforts to reduce regional disparities in the industrial sector have strengthened the dominance of the littoral.

Now, one may ask: but did these growth poles have had any positive effects at all? The answer, of course, is yes! Of course they generated some positive effects: jobs, to begin with, salaries, taxes, infrastructure, housing, etc., especially in the cities where they located. No one can deny that. And without them the situation in the cities where they were located would be worse today. But this is not the point here. We are not talking about "city development." We are talking about *regional development*. And the point therefore is: was the growth pole policy an appropriate approach for a country that has been kept so poorly industrialized by the "colonial pact?" Is it adequate for a country that was having a huge unemployment problem to create in rural areas highly capital-intensive industries where the cost of only one job would have created hundreds more? Strongly related to this: is it adequate for a country, despite the high unemployment at home, to subsidize employment abroad by buying equipment and licenses, and to find itself in a few years, consequently overwhelmed by the burden of the debt and a dangerous dependence on foreign technology and experts? Let me give an example to illustrate this. With the paper-mill of Kasserine, this dependence was from

Table 5.1

DISTRIBUTION OF INDUSTRIAL INVESTMENTS
BY REGION BETWEEN 1962 AND 1971

| Regions | Investments in MTD | Percentage |
|---|---|---|
| North-East | 97.3 | 36.2 |
| Center-East | 33.8 | 12.9 |
| South-East | 74.8 | 27.9 |
| LITTORAL | 205.9 | 77.0 |
| North-West | 12.5 | 4.8 |
| Center-West | 27.7 | 10.7 |
| South-West | 19.6 | 7.5 |
| INTERIOR | 59.8 | 23.0 |
| TOTAL TUNISIA | 265.7 | 100 |

Source: Adapted from: H. Dlala, *L'Economie Industrielle dans les Villes-Ports du Nord-Est Tunisien* (Tunis: Publications de l'Université de Tunis, 1981), p. 279.

Table 5.2

EMPLOYMENT DISTRIBUTION IN THE INDUSTRIAL SECTOR BY REGION IN 1972

| Regions | Employment | Percentage |
|---|---|---|
| North-East | 50,000 | 56 |
| Center-East | 16,000 | 18 |
| South-East | 2,600 | 2 |
| LITTORAL | 68,600 | 76 |
| North-West | 9,000 | 10 |
| Center-West | 2,000 | 2 |
| South-West | 10,400 | 12 |
| INTERIOR | 21,400 | 24 |
| TOTAL TUNISIA | 90,000 | 100 |

Source: Adapted from République de Tunisie, Ministère de l'Equipement, Direction de l'Aménagement du Territoire (DAT), *Schéma National et Schémas Régionaux d'Aménagement du Territoire*, vol. 1 (Tunis, 1983), p. 80; and vol. 12 (1984), p. 202.

the beginning, in 1963, the major problem for the project. The project was designed by an American group called "Parsons Whittemore Industries." Due to errors in the design and to some defects in equipment, production was stopped for several months.[12] The losses due to these problems were estimated in 1965 by a mission of USAID at 4 MTD (1965 value). But this is the past. New problems are facing the plant today and threatening its very existence. In 1978, for example, the possibility of shutting down the plant was even publicly mentioned by the Prime Minister.[13] This extreme solution was mentioned because of the increasing technical, financial and socioeconomic problems that the company was facing for the last 15 years. But one of these problems is by far the most important for the existence of the enterprise and the city of Kasserine itself, and this is the slow but irreversible reduction of the areas covered by "alfa," the raw material needed for the production of paper. This reduction of alfa is due to two other related problems: one is ecological and the other is socioeconomic. The ecological problem is explained by the intensive use of alfa during the last two decades, which caused a grave problem of erosion, which, in turn, resulted in a serious reduction of the areas where alfa used to grow. As the journal of the company has put it, this "desertification" caused the disappearance of 175,000 hectares of alfa between 1961 and 1976.[14] During this period, from a total of 625,000 hectares, the area covered by alfa was reduced to 450,000 hectares. The socioeconomic part of the problem is the difficulty the company has had finding workers to collect the product during harvest periods. Due to rural exodus, certain *régions alfatières* of Central Tunisia have been literally depopulated.[15] Searching better salaries and better life, people emigrated to the cities in the littoral or even abroad. The combination of these two problems has forced the company to close the plant that produces the *pâte à papier* several months a year. During a second visit to Kasserine in October 1984, the "cellulose" plant was closed for four months, and it was expected to be closed for six months in 1985.[16] Here are, then, to mention just a few, some of the problems, the neglect of the milieu, a critique that was often addressed to the growth pole approach as a major instrument of a regional development policy.

Here are, then, the problems and shortcomings of the regional policy in the industrial sector during the "Ben Salah" period. And they illustrate very well, I think, the problem of the transfer of traditional spatial models to Third World countries as discussed in Chapter 2.

## The "Modernization" and "Destruction" of the Rural Economy: the Cooperative Program

The second major sector that Tunisian leaders, during the "Ben Salah" period, used in their attempt to eliminate the regional disparities inherited from the French protectorate was the agricultural sector.[17] Within the whole framework of the structural reforms of the economy, the "modernization" of the "traditional" sector was seen as the sina qua non condition for the increase of productivity and therefore of incomes and living conditions in the former French-dominated agricultural regions of the interior. And as "Tunisian Socialism" was "authentic" and anti-Marxist,[18] the cooperative system was seen as the most adapted form to achieve these objectives, and which, at the same time, it was believed, would reconcile Tunisia with its very old communal traditions. In a speech in 1962, at a seminar on the philosophy and political objectives of the cooperative system, Mr. Ben Salah, in a very "Proudhonien" accent, said:

> The cooperative movement responds better to the objectives of our economy and social beliefs. It is perfectly adapted to our circumstances and means. In our national plan, *it is explicitly stated that Socialism in Tunisia must have a*

*national vocation: the revival of the communal tradition of our people.*[19]

The following analysis will focus on only three aspects of the program: (1) the establishment of the cooperatives and the adherence of the *cooperateurs* to the program; (2) the organization and management of the cooperatives; and (3) the impact of the experience and its failure to improve incomes and living standards (in order to reduce rural exodus from the interior to the littoral—another important objective of the program).

## The Establishment of the Cooperatives and the Adherence of the Cooperateurs

**The Establishment of the Cooperatives.** It was with the first Tunisian plan, the Three Year Plan (1962-64), that the cooperative program was initiated. A Direction of Cooperation office was created in the "Secretariat d'Etat au Plan" in July 1962 for this purpose. Under the supervision of its director, a "Union Régionale des Cooperatives" (U.R.C.) was established in each gouvernorat (13 in 1963) and placed under the authority of the Governors. Each U.R.C. was responsible for the supervision and coordination of the establishment of all cooperatives in its gouvernorat. Its main role was to provide instructions and managerial advice—to channel central government directives to all cooperatives under its control.

By the end of 1966, aided by government technicians and local political leaders of the P.S.D., the U.R.C. were able to establish 779 cooperatives with a total membership of 206,633, about 12 percent of the total active labor force of the country at that time.[20] By August 1968, 38 percent of the nation's cultivated land was in the cooperative system, which had more than 900,000 people and represented 30 percent of the rural population.[21] In the discussion that follows, the focus will be placed on one type of cooperative: the "*cooperatives de production.*" But first, a few words will be said about the different types of cooperatives.

There were two major types of cooperatives: (1) the *cooperatives de production*, which are the most important and have been established mainly in former French-dominated and rich agricultural regions of the interior in the North-West and the Center-West. That is why, therefore, they are the main focus of this section; and (2) the *pré-cooperatives* and the *cooperatives de service*. These were specialized in marketing, storage, construction, credit facilities, etc. Because of this difference in the nature and objectives of each group of cooperatives, their internal organizations and structures did not follow the same sequences in all gouvernorats. Suffice to say here, as E. Hermassi has put it: "there were two types of cooperatives: those who are integrated within a State-supervised unit and who are supposed to exercise direct management of the land, and those who work on their own land and who are encouraged indirectly to improve their management or to market their production through State offices."[22]

Now, concerning more specifically the cooperatives of production, 682 cooperatives were established by 1966-67 with a total of 614,000 hectares of the best land of the country (table 5.3).

**The Adherence of the Cooperateurs.** As we saw, the first objectives of the program were, within the framework of the development of Tunisian agriculture, the "modernization" of the traditional sector in order to improve productivity, to increase incomes in order to improve the living standards of the peasantry and thus to reduce regional disparities and to stop rural exodus from the interior to the littoral. Secondly, and this is very important to keep in mind, the objective, on the political and ideological level as stated by the father of the whole strategy of development during the 1960s, was "the revival of the communal traditions of our people."[23] Now, and in respect to the principles of adherence of the cooperateurs, the idea of farms regrouping that was advanced by the Three Year Plan (1962-64) was fairly simple. Prior to the creation of the cooperatives, between 1958 and 1963, 570,000 hectares of land occupied by the colonists and French companies were bought by the Tunisian government. In 1964, with the "Crisis of Bizerte" (the recuperation of the military base of Bizerte in a bloody confrontation with France), President Bourguiba decided to nationalize the remaining 400-500,000 hectares of French-held land. All these lands were composed of very large estates and highly mechanized large farms on the best land of the country in the North-West and some in the Center-West. Both their division among the thousands of small farmers (whose fathers and grandfathers, it is important to stress and remember, were the owners before their expulsion by French colonization land policy [Chapter 4]) and their rent or sale to private Tunisian large farmers were ruled out. The first alternative was rejected on the grounds that this would have an adverse effect on productivity because, it was believed, the small "Fellahins" would not be able to use "modern," "rational," "efficient" methods of production! The second solution was also rejected on the basis that this would be contrary to the objectives and philosophy of "Tunisian Socialism" because it would inevitably accentuate the concentration of wealth and would aggravate, therefore, the disparities in the countryside. In a speech in October 1962 before the National Assembly, President Bourguiba himself expressed these views in the following terms:

> The objective of the reform of the agricultural structures is the modernization of agriculture. It is not an agrarian reform in the classical meaning of the term. It is not concerned with private properties managed with modern techniques and norms. It is introduced essentially in order to increase the productivity of the farms that do not have the possibilities of acquiring the technical skills of modern agriculture. As traditional agriculture is mainly concentrated in very small farms, the reform of the agricultural structures is therefore in

the beginning a regrouping of traditional farms to help them to adopt modern techniques.[24]

Table 5.3

GROWTH OF THE "COOPERATIVES DE PRODUCTION"

| Year | Number of Co-ops | Membership | Area per 1,000 hectares |
|---|---|---|---|
| 1963-64 | 128 | 12,852 | 148 |
| 1964-65 | 177 | 14,348 | 205 |
| 1965-66 | 246 | 17,745 | 279 |
| 1966-67 | 682 | 37,496 | 614 |

Source: Hermassi, *Leadership and National Development in North Africa*, p. 188.

So, here, importantly, it is only the "traditional" sector that is concerned by the reform. And large Tunisian farmers, who are considered, by definition, "modern," are not concerned by the "revival of the communal traditions of our people" as Mr. Ben Salah has put it! As noted by J. Simmons, this reflects very well the obsession with modernization of Tunisian leaders of that time, for whom "agricultural modernization means big farmers and machines."[25] It also portrayed, I think, their view of the peasant and peasant society, a view based on the stereotype of the "ignorant peasant" and one that refuses to acknowledge that "the peasant may be ignorant about the agricultural plans, but not about farming."[26] This is what E. Wolf has called the "disease of modernization."[27] And beyond the Tunisian case itself, this reflects the "fetishism" of many African "modernizers," or what A. Schawrz calls "les dupes de la modernisation" in Africa,[28] about technology and its role in the process of development as well as about the whole issue of "transition" (Chapter 2). It is important to understand this whole problem in order to comprehend not only the way the program was imposed on the peasant, but also, more important, the roots of its failure.[29]

On the basis of this modernist perception of the problems inherited from the French protectorate in the rural economy, Tunisian planners decided to opt for an intermediate solution of farm grouping. They decided to use former colonist farms as models and bases for the grouping of the surrounding small farms. On the criteria of efficient mechanization and a minimum number of work days per year per cooperateur (in order to guarantee a minimum income per cooperateur), Tunisian planners, along with the engineers of the Secretariat d'Etat à l'Agriculture decided on the optimum size of the cooperatives of production and the optimum number of cooperateurs per cooperative.

A cooperative of production was to be composed of a small portion (200 hectares) from ex-colonists' farms that were managed by the "Office des Terres Domaniales," and of 300 hectares of small private parcels. Thirty families were to farm this optimum unit. Priority, however, was given to ex-colonist workers. This was explained by the need to make full use of the equipment and machinery. And it is from here that the major problems of the cooperatives began. Tunisian "planistrators," as R. Apthorpe called them,[30] never thought to ask, at least, the cooperateurs their opinion on all or some of these decisions. And in May 1962 a cooperative legislation (completed in December 1964) was introduced that enabled the government to purchase or to rent (from very small farmers, who had less than five hectares, who were too small to be allowed to join the cooperatives and who were therefore called, elegantly, "*membres indirect*") lands falling within the area of a cooperative. This legislation was designed to establish the legal base for the cooperative system. As D. Ashford observed, its main objective was to make certain that no cooperative would be initiated without close control by the central Ministry of Planning, in other words, by the peasants themselves:

> Contrary to the prevailing philosophy in Co-ops..., the Tunisian cooperative structure was organized from the top-down. Moreover, the cooperatives were not viewed as products of voluntary, cumulative efforts at the local level, but were to be the products of carefully coordinated and planned action by the political and administrative hierarchy. No argument is made more forcefully by Tunisian officials than the absolute necessity for an "Etude Technique" prior to the consideration of any new coop.[31]

In brief, not a single peasant or group of peasants, because they were assumed to be ignorant, were allowed to initiate a cooperative on their own. Contrary to any principle of cooperation as Proudhon and others have taught us, the cooperatives were imposed from ABOVE; and all this for the good of the peasant and in the name of the "revival of communal traditions" of Tunisia!!

## The Organization and Management of the Cooperatives

The nature of the legislation mentioned above, and the ways the cooperatives were initiated bring us now to another related issue: the organization and management of the cooperatives.

Officially each cooperative has a "*Conseil d'Administration*" elected by the cooperateurs. This board of directors elect, in turn, a president. But in reality, three officials have the real power in the cooperatives. And these people are not elected! First, there is the "*Directeur Technique*," appointed by the Ministry of Planning; second, the "*Ingenieur Agronome*," appointed by the Ministry of Agriculture; and finally, the most important personage is the "Sécretaire Général du Comité de Coordination Régional du Parti" who is not a member of any cooperative but is present in all cooperatives in the gouvernorat.

So, although the cooperateurs elected the board of directors, in reality the cooperatives were managed through a State hierarchy of technicians and politicians.[32] For example, the program of production of the cooperatives was not designed by the *Conseil d'Administration*, but by the *Directeur Technique* and the engineer, who receive their orders from Tunis. As noted by many observers, even "the cultivation plan, the system of crop rotation, the number of cows per farm," were decided by the technicians of the ministries in Tunis.[33] And this sometimes reached a surrealistic dimension: "even the hours at which the cattle had to be milked (...) were planned and imposed by the technicians of the Ministry of Agriculture"(!!)[34] Indeed, we are in the surrealistic world of Franz Kafka.[35]

That is why, therefore, for the "Fellahins," the State has simply took their land, as the French did before to their fathers. And for those who were lucky enough to become "*cooperateurs directs*," their status was that of employees reduced to selling their labor on their own land for a miserable salary. And it is with this "Stalinist" system that Mr. Ben Salah wanted the "revival of the communal traditions" of Tunisia. Here is what Hermassi wrote about this totalitarian system:

> In all this reorientation of the rural economy, there was one fundamental drawback that arose from the nature of its inception: the reform had been handed down from above by the power elite and was never the object of a power struggle in which those who would be the beneficiaries could later appreciate its value and its cost. Also, at no time were the organizers able to arouse the enthusiasm of the rural masses, which was indispensable to the formula's success. Although the *cooperateurs* were represented on the administrative records, in reality the units were managed through the state hierarchy of organizations and technicians.[36]

This central conflict between true self-management and a Stalinist-Jacobin system imposed on the "Fellahins," on a peasantry that has already been "mutilated" by colonization, has to be understood within the frame of first, the power structure of the single-party system and the ideology of development (Chapter 3) of the leaders of that time. As C. Micaud has noted:

> In the Tunisian approach to modernization, a choice place has been given to the "psychological revolution," in the belief that it is necessary first to "transform attitudes," establish a "new scale of values," create a "revolutionary spirit." The frequent use of the words "mobilization," "attack," "campaign," and "war" in connection with routing prejudice, inertia, ignorance, and fatalism implies a concerted and all-out effort. This effort itself is based on the conviction that it is possible to transform attitudes, tear down the mental obstacles to progress, broaden horizons, and commit men to the fight for a better society.[37]

And this approach to modernization of Tunisian leaders has its roots in:

> The values held by Bourguiba and his followers have made them, in fact, true interpreters of the French revolutionary tradition—including the convenient Jacobin mystique of the general will.[38]

All this brings us to the discussion of the impact of the program on: (1) the improvement of the living conditions of the rural masses of the interior and therefore (2) the reduction of rural exodus from the interior to the littoral and the reduction of the disparities in general between the two areas.

## The Impact of the Experience and its Failure

According to a study of several cooperatives of production in the North-West, undertaken by a Tunisian social scientist in 1969, the real incomes of the peasantry during the cooperative program declined.[39] K. Zamiti, the author of the study, found that in 1969, the highest income per capita in the cooperatives he surveyed was 57 millimes (about 10-20 cents at that time) and the lowest was about 10 millimes. Moreover, Zamiti found that among the cooperateurs interviewed, the average number of days worked per month was 13. And as paid work outside the cooperative was very rare, mainly because of the general unemployment in the region and because of the cooperatives occupying most of the land, these incomes were the only source of revenues for the cooperateurs. This low number of average days of work, and therefore of incomes, is explained by the excessive mechanization of the cooperatives and the financial problems it has created for them. For example, in one cooperative, Zamiti found that the total annual debt represented exactly the cost of renting a tractor for the cooperative.[40] This mechanization, which another Tunisian researcher has called "*une mecanisation outrancière*,"[41] is therefore responsible for the reduction of work and incomes.

Another more important reason for the decline of real incomes of the peasantry is that two of the three major sources of incomes were no longer available with the cooperatives. Before the cooperatives, small farmers had three major sources of revenue: land, labor and equipment (allowing them to work outside their own farms), and animals. In the early months of the initiation of the program, they began to fear the confiscation of their assets. Many began to sell their animals and their equipment. As usual in these cases, large farmers were the buyers. But the results of this insidious phenomenon was that they lost an important source of revenue and food.[42] The imposition of the cooperatives and consequently, the small farmers' "proleteriazation" left them worse off in real terms than they were before under the former household economy. Zamiti's conclusion is that this transformation of the rural economy overall resulted in a substantial decline in the living conditions of the peasantry. In brief, this is some of the evidence about the impact of the program in terms of the improvement of the living standards of the rural masses of the interior.

Related to this, the impact of the experience in general, but of its failure in particular, in terms of reducing the rural exodus from the interior to the littoral, was very negative. When in 1969 the Ben Salah team in a kind of "*fuite en avant*," wanted to extend the program beyond the former French-dominated regions into the Sahel and Sfax, where "5000 families" (3 percent of all farmers) possessed one-half of all arable land (and for many of them close ties in Tunis and the government), the experience was suddenly stopped in September 1969.[43] The same month (9 September) Mr. Ben Salah was arrested and accused, with his team, for "crimes against the State and high treason." The direct consequence of these "*règlements de compte*" between the leadership and the sudden end of the program was that thousands and thousands of small farmers found themselves with nothing. Even those who took back their small parcels from the cooperatives were facing the following cruel dilemma. In order to survive on their own land, they were forced to accept the "*métayage*" system, the only condition for them to obtain the "help" (advance in cash on the harvest) of large farmers. In this system, however, and in exchange of this "help," the small farmers kept one-third of the harvest and gave two-thirds to the large farmers. The second alternative was even more cruel: sell the land to the large farmer (who was waiting since 1962 for this) and migrate to the cities. This drama of the destruction of the rural economy by the "*dupes de la modernisation*," was summarized by a small farmer: "We have only one dream left: to work our land ourselves, and only one means to survive: to yield it under *métayage* to our rich neighbours."[44] Another farmer put it more bluntly: "The generosity of the large farmer is both the solution of our problems and a knife held to our throats."[45] These statements and many others,[46] show very clearly I think, the devastating impact of the program on the rural milieu as a whole. What was achieved therefore, was simply the "extinction" of the traditional sector. And how was this extinction manifested? By a massive rural exodus from the interior regions to the littoral, especially to Tunis, where the population of the *bidonvilles* grew from 160,000 in 1966, to 225,000 in 1970 and to 275,000 in 1975.[47] According to the report of the "Comité de Reflexion sur l'Aménagement du Territoire et la Décentralisation Industrielle," published in April 1979, between 1970 and 1975, the gouvernorat of Béjà alone (the gouvernorat where Zamiti undertook his research) lost 10,660 persons, whereas Tunis gained 40,100 people.[48] Out of 37,790 people that the interior lost to the littoral, the North-West alone lost 31,790! (table 5.4). And this does not include the estimated 80,000 people that simply left the country between 1970 and 1975. The report does not give any indication on the geographical origins of these immigrants. We can only guess!

In brief, the overall results of this disastrous experience were not only that small farmers of the interior regions were "as poor in 1970 as they had been 15 years earlier, but their real income level had declined and the gap with the urban populations had widened even more rapidly since 1956."[49] Conceived of and imposed from ABOVE, it was shown to these "wretched of the earth," that the "freedom that came with independence meant the freedom of the new urban elite to restrict the freedom of the rural peasantry."[50]

Here are, then, the two major components of regional policy and the results up to 1969. Before moving on to two other areas of lesser importance, but which have had better results, I would like to stress that beyond the Tunisian case, the failure of this experience of modernization illustrates very well I think, the problems that these types of socioeconomic reforms create in the process of development.[51] It also illustrates the "inadequacy" of past development strategies and the theories upon which they were based (Chapter 2), as well as the alienation of Third World leaders and planners from their own national societies and the impossibility of them understanding that each society has its own productive system and its related spatial organization that have to be analyzed, understood and planned for in terms of their proper structural logic and "rationality." The growth pole policy was simply a *parachutage* of some industrial units into a milieu that did not need this kind of industry. The "rationality" of the cooperative program was not that of the household economy. The problem of the peasantry was not the lack of tractors and fertilizers, but the lack of land, land from which they have been ejected by French capitalists. But Tunisian technocrats, obsessed by their own rationality and blinded by the "disease of modernization," could see nothing positive in rural society. The real objective of the Third Year plan (1962-64) was not as Ben Salah said, "the revival of communal traditions of our people," but, and according to the Director of the Plan and Cabinet of Mr. Ben Salah until 1969:

Table 5.4

NET MIGRATION BY REGION
BETWEEN 1970-1975

| Regions | Net Migration (in thousands) |
|---|---|
| North-East | + 29,850 |
| Center-East | + 6,110 |
| South-East | + 1,830 |
| LITTORAL | + 37,790 |
| North-West | - 31,790 |
| Center-West | - 3,470 |
| South-West | - 2,530 |
| INTERIOR | - 37,790 |

Source: Adapted from République de Tunisie, Premier Ministère, *Rapport du Comité de Reflexion sur l'Aménagement du Territoire et la Décentralisation Industrielle* (Tunis, April 1979), p. 17.

> The major objective of the Plan was to reform the archaic and obsolete structures of the country in order to adapt them to an accelerated rhythm of development. The modernization of the country would not be achieved, without introducing the radical change into traditional ways of life (...); the Government was aware that in order to succeed to get the country out from the state of lethargy within which it was *its actions must touch the heart of this fatalist and resigned society*.[52]

We can't be more clear. And indeed as we saw this objective was fully achieved.

## The Policy in the Tourist Sector

The third economic sector that Tunisian planners have used in their attempt to eliminate the disparities between the interior and the littoral is the tourist sector. In 1960, the development of this sector was seen as a way to diversify the Tunisian economy. And as with the industrial sector, the State played an important role in its development. For example, in the early years of its development, 90 percent of all investments in tourism were public.[53]

In 1959, a public enterprise called the "Société Hotelière et Touristique de Tunisie" (SHTT) was created and 92 percent of its capital was public.

The beginning of the activities of the SHTT coincide with the adoption of the Perspectives Décennales 1962-71. And as this document, as we saw, stated very clearly the intention of the government to reduce regional disparities, three hotels were built by the SHTT in the interior: the "Cillium" in Kasserine, the "Aghlabites" in Kairouan and the "Jurgurtha" in Gafsa. These were the only investments in the tourist sector in favor of the interior during the decade 1962-71.

From 1965, because of increasing difficulties in finding sources of capital, the State encouraged, through fiscal and loan facilities, the private sector to invest in tourism. Since the private sector was not at all interested in the industrial sector or the agricultural sector because of government controls, investors found in these government encouragements a safe and very profitable way to invest. Therefore private investments rose from 10 percent in 1962-64 to 50.8 percent in 1965 and 74.6 percent in 1968.[54] This shift in the government policy in this sector ended the efforts in favor of the interior. Seeking the most attractive regions, the private sector invested exclusively in the littoral. This evolution in tourist investments policy since 1965 had resulted, by 1970, in the concentration of all new equipment, created during that period, in the littoral. In 1970, for example, more than 90 percent of all the tourist installations were found in the littoral.[55]

In conclusion, as with the industrial sector, tourist sector policy did not contribute to the reduction of regional disparities. On the contrary, its development resulted in their intensification. The two sectors were developed, but did not benefit all regions.

## The Policy in the Social Sectors

Two other sectors in which the State played a very important role are those that have contributed much in the reduction of regional disparities during the 1956-70 period. The different reforms in the administration and the whole public sector, and the massive investments in the social sectors: education, health, housing, sociocultural equipment, the physical infrastructure, have had, in spatial terms, a tremendous effect on the reduction of the disparities. The reform of the colonial administration, through the creation of new administrative structures, or the extension of others, created new jobs in the administration and the public sector, almost exclusively in the interior. These new jobs were fundamental to the survival of some urban centers and to the tremendous growth of a number of small cities in the interior (table 5.5). This relation between the urban growth and the public investments for some cities of the interior, especially the gouvernorats' capitals, is shown by the very high percentage of public employment in the employment distribution by sector (table 5.6).

Investments in social services, schools, roads and hospitals have been another factor in the growth of these small centers and cities. For example, between 1957 and 1967, 159 primary schools were built in the gouvernorat of Le Kef, 135 in the gouvernorat of Gafsa, 123 in the gouvernorat of Kairouan, 94 in the gouvernorat of Kasserine and 107 in the gouvernorat of Béjà.[56] A more important change was made at the secondary education level. In 1957, three gouvernorats of the interior: Béjà, Kasserine and Gafsa did not have any secondary schools. By 1967 they had four, one and six secondary schools respectively.[57] In terms of percentage, the increase in education at the secondary level reached 400 percent between 1962 and 1970 for five of the interior gouvernorats: Jendouba, Kairouan, Béjà, Gafsa and Kasserine.[58]

Table 5.5

POPULATION CHANGE OF SOME CITIES AND TOWNS IN THE INTERIOR BETWEEN 1956-1975

| | 1956 | 1966 | 1975 | % Change |
|---|---|---|---|---|
| Kairouan | 33,968 | 46,199 | 54,546 | 60.6 |
| Le Kef | 14,743 | 23,244 | 27,939 | 89.5 |
| Gafsa | 24,345 | 32,408 | 42,225 | 73.4 |
| Kasserine | 2,705 | 9,852 | 22,594 | 735.3 |
| Sidi Bou Zid | 1,855 | 3,257 | 8,843 | 376.7 |
| Siliana | 3,431 | 5,322 | 6,982 | 103.5 |
| Maktar | 4,021 | 5,393 | 6,068 | 50.9 |
| Thala | 4,301 | 6,412 | 8,908 | 107.0 |
| Sbeitla | 3,409 | 5,846 | 8,039 | 135.8 |
| Sbiba | - | 1,096 | 4,891 | 346.2 |
| Rouhia | - | 807 | 9,592 | 1,088.6 |
| Jelma | - | - | 4,449 | - |
| Foussana | - | - | 3,912 | - |
| Kesra | - | - | 3,891 | - |
| Jedliane | - | - | 3,441 | - |

Source: Frank W. Young, Fernando Bertoli and Sandra Bertoli, *A Baseline for Rural Development in Central Tunisia*, Macrosocial Accounting Project (Ithaca, NY: Cornell University, 1981), p. 19.

Table 5.6

IMPORTANCE OF THE EMPLOYMENT IN THE TERTIARY SECTOR IN FIVE CITIES IN THE INTERIOR IN 1966 (in percentage)

| | Kairouan[a] | Kasserine[b] | Le Kef[b] | Béjà[b] |
|---|---|---|---|---|
| Tertiary | 40 | 58 | 56 | 53 |
| Secondary | 50 | 30 | 11 | 19 |
| Marginal & Underemployment | - | 10 | 25 | 13.5 |

Source:

[a] H. Sethom and A. Kassab, *Les Régions Géographique de la Tunisie* (Tunis: Publications de l'Université de Tunis, 1981), p. 31.

[b] H. Attia, "L'Urbanisation de la Tunisie," *Revue Tunisienne des Sciences Sociales*, nos. 28-29 (1972), p. 30.

All these efforts in the social sector, combined with those in the administrative sector have been much more important than those in the industrial and the tourist sector, in the reduction of regional disparities and the diffusion of urbanization towards the interior. The city of Kasserine is the most typical case of this change. From a small village of 2,700 persons in 1956, it was transformed into a city of 22,000 persons by 1975: an increase of 735 percent in 20 years. But, as table 5.5 shows, most small towns and cities of the interior have benefited from these investments.

It is therefore in the social sector that the regional policy during the Ben Salah period had the most positive impact on the evolution of regional disparities. This suggests very clearly that public investments can affect the patterns of inequalities in general and the evolution of the formation of urban systems in particular.[59] This also shows, and I would like to stress this again and again, that rural-urban inequalities, urban primacy, pathological urban processes, and regional underdevelopment in general are not "natural"; rather they are the by-product of given policies. Here are therefore, the failures and successes of the regional development policy during the Ben Salah period.

# REGIONAL POLICY DURING THE "NOUIRA" PERIOD: 1970-80

With the shift in 1969 in the Tunisian development strategy and the abandonment therefore of the socialist options of the Ben Salah period, Tunisian regional development itself shifted radically. As M. Chaker put it, it will change in its "foundations and methods.[60]" To be fully understood, this change has to be placed within the frame of the new development strategy and the ideology behind it. For example, during the Ben Salah period the State was perceived as the main actor, the promoter and the "engine" of development. In the "Nouira" strategy, the role of the State was seen mainly as a "palliative" to the private sector. This perception of the new leadership was very clearly expressed through many public speeches and statements during the 1970s. For example, in the first economic plan, the Fourth Plan 1973-76, of the "Nouira" period, it is stated that the role of the State must be reduced to that of a simple "regulator of the economic system," of which the main task is simply "to incite, to orient and to motivate the economic actors."[61] This new perception of the role of the State is expressed more bluntly in a public declaration by the first "Président Directeur Général" of the "Agence de Promotion des Investissements" (API) (a public agency created in 1972 in order to "promote" Tunisia abroad—see below): "The role of the State is to fill emptiness: to build roads, to bring water; in a word to allow the private sector to function."[62] This radical shift in the perception of the role of the State in the economy was not, as we will see, without consequence on the perception of the "regional question" itself and of the solutions to it. Based on a very restrictive, I would even say, a blind and dogmatic, notion of *profitability*, the new economic strategy saw any localization constraints as unacceptable strain to a true and pure policy of *laisser-faire*! For example, in an important speech delivered in 1972, Mr. Hédi Nouira, the Prime Minister, declared: "We must consider the choice of the localization of a project only from the angle of its profitability and not from a sentimental one..."[63] And that is why he made the decision (announced in his first and most important speech as Prime Minister—"Discours Programme" of November 17, 1970 at the National Assembly) "to put an end to the so-called growth pole investments."[64] Several years later, coming back to this notion of profitability, Mr. Nouira declared: "In order to make more profitable our limited resources, the accent has been on the development of the coastal zones at the risk of provoking the aggravation of regional unbalance..."[65] I think this statement, more than any other, reflects very clearly the philosophy behind the new economic strategy during the Nouira period and the nature of the radical rupture with the Ben Salah period.

Here are then some of the statements of the new leadership that show very clearly this shift in the perception of the role of the State in the economy and the consequences of this shift on the perception of the "regional question." In what follows, I will document and analyze, as I did for the Ben Salah period, the major components of the regional policy after 1969 and try to assess their impact on the evolution of regional disparities during the Nouira period.

The Industrial Decentralization Policy

Within the new ideological framework, the major objective of the new leadership was to promote an economic policy that—in order, it was argued, to promote exports and create the maximum of jobs—create a "positive climate" for local and foreign investors. To achieve this, incentives were offered and protection and control were eliminated (see below). In the industrial sector this was concretely translated into the two public laws mentioned in Chapter 3. First, the law 72-38 of April 27, 1972, was designed exclusively for export industries and offered very generous incentives to foreign investors that even during French colonization they could never dream of. Some of these are: total profits repatriation; exemption from customs duties for all imports; and tax exemptions of all kinds for the first ten years and at a very reduced rate for the second ten years. The list continues. Suffice to say that in order to attract foreign investors, the Nouira government, as Entelis put it, "virtually abdicated a portion of Tunisian sovereignty."[66] Second, the law 74-74 of 3 August 1974 was designed for all manufacture industries and, with the law of 1972, completed the legislative framework of the industrial strategy of the Nouira period. It offered fiscal, financial and commercial incentives: tax exemptions on profits, on customs duties, on imported equipment, on turn-over, and on all kinds of registration fees. In addition to these two laws, a public agency "L'Agence de Promotion des Investissements" (API) was set up by the law of 1972 as the intermediary between the administration and the investors. Within this new legislative framework and in respect to regional development, the law of 1974 provided, in Article 15, some incentives, such as the payment of the cost of infrastructure work, pending on location. The law of finance of 1973, however, in Article 45, mentioned the creation in 1974 of the "Fonds de Promotion et de Décentralisation Industrielle" (FOPRODI).[67] The objectives of the fund were to take charge of all the expenditures resulting from the incentives provided for in Article 15 of the law of 1974.[68] In reality, and contrary to what its name suggests, the FOPRODI was set up mainly to encourage the creation of small industries. As noted by the "Direction de l'Aménagement du Territoire," among the 15 articles of the decree creating the fund, only one (Article 14) is concerned with decentralization.[69] Moreover, and this illustrates further the real concern of the new leadership about regional disparities, the fund was not operational until 1977! It is only then that a new decree (Decree 77-578 of July 6, 1977) fixed the regional zoning according to locational advantages. It is only then, therefore, after seven years Mr. Nouira was Prime Minister, that the whole legislative base of the industrial decentralization policy was in place.[70] Let us now look at the results of the new regional policy in the industrial sector.

As was expected by many economists and geographers,[71] this shift in the industrial strategy had, as early as 1976, a disastrous impact on regional disparities. For example, during the Fourth Plan (1973-76) and within the frame of the two public laws mentioned earlier, 91.5 percent of the investments and 96.3 percent of the jobs created under the law of 1972 were located in the littoral regions. 88.6 percent of the investments and 91.3 percent of the jobs created under the law of 1974 (and this in spite of Article 45) were located in the littoral regions (tables 5.7 and 5.8).

If we look now to overall industrial investments (all the data in tables 5.7 and 5.8 are about the private sector only) in the public and private sectors combined, we find that out of a total of 284 MTD invested during the Fourth Plan period (1973-76) in the industrial sector, 94 percent were invested in the littoral regions.[72] This constitutes, as shown in table 7.9, a dramatic shift from the 1962-71 period.

Table 5.7
REGIONAL DISTRIBUTION OF INVESTMENTS, PROJECTS AND JOBS CREATED UNDER THE LAW 72-38 OF 1972 BETWEEN 1973-76 (in percentage)

| Regions | Projects | Investments | Jobs |
|---|---|---|---|
| Tunis (gouvernorat) | 40.6 | 17.7 | 28.3 |
| Other Littoral Gouvernorats | 50.9 | 78.6 | 61.8 |
| TOTAL LITTORAL | 91.5 | 96.3 | 90.1 |
| TOTAL INTERIOR | 9.5 | 3.7 | 9.9 |

Source: H. Dlala, "Développement Economique et Action Régionale en Tunisie." *Revue Tunisienne de Géographie*, no. 6 (1980), p. 77.

Thus, we see that the total industrial investments during the Ben Salah period in the interior regions fell from 23 percent to 6 percent during the first half of the Nouira period. This dramatic decrease is a clear consequence of the drastic reduction of the role of the State in the industrial sector and in the economy in general. For example, during 1962-71, 80 percent of the industrial investments were made by the State. During the Fourth Plan, the State invested only 23 percent.[73] Moreover, when we look at the geographical distribution of these investments, we find that 83 percent of them were invested in the littoral regions.[74] So here, not only has the State reduced its role, but—and this is the most striking aspect of the economic philosophy during the Nouira period in respect to the regional problem—has, in the name as we saw of a very narrow perception of "profitability," favored the littoral regions at the expense of those of the interior, which were not attractive at all to the private sector.

This tendency during the Fourth Plan has been further accentuated during that of the Fifth Plan (1977-81) as the available data on the localization of investments and jobs created in the industrial sector during that period can show. Out of 900 MTD invested and an estimated 100,000 jobs created in the industrial sector between 1977 and 1981, 80 percent of the investments and 85 percent of the jobs created were located in the littoral regions.[75] Three littoral gouvernorats alone (Tunis, Sousse and Sfax) share 40 percent of the investments and 56 percent of the jobs created.

Here is then one of the consequences of the shift in the economic policy since 1970: the concentration in the littoral of the industrial development during the Nouira period. This explains, therefore, why the total share of development jobs created in the littoral was 93 percent whereas the interior regions had a symbolic 7 percent (table 5.10).

Table 5.8

REGIONAL DISTRIBUTION OF INVESTMENTS, PROJECTS AND JOBS CREATED UNDER THE LAW 74-74 OF 1974 BETWEEN 1973-76 (in percentage)

| Regions | Projects | Investments | Jobs |
|---|---|---|---|
| Tunis (gouvernorat) | 43.7 | 36.1 | 44.7 |
| Other Littoral Gouvernorats | 46.5 | 52.5 | 46.6 |
| TOTAL LITTORAL | 90.2 | 88.6 | 91.3 |
| TOTAL INTERIOR | 9.8 | 11.4 | 9.7 |

Source: Dlala, op. cit., p. 78.

In brief, the clear results of the industrial decentralization policy during the Nouira period was a widening of the gap between the littoral and the interior. Let us now look at the second major component of regional policy during the Nouira period.

The "Programme de Dévelopment Rural" (PDR)

Initiated also with the Fourth Plan (Decree 73-310 of June 20, 1973) the main objectives of this program were: (1) to create new employment opportunities and to develop vocational training in rural areas; and (2) to improve living conditions in the interior regions in order to achieve the final objective of the program: (3) to stop rural exodus from the interior regions.[76] One hundred sixty-three MTD were allocated to the PDR during the period of two plans: 63 MTD during the Fourth Plan and 100 MTD during the Fifth Plan.[77] In terms of the sectoral distribution of funds, two-fifths of the 63 MTD for the Fourth Plan were allocated to the improvement of living conditions: construction of rural housing, rural electrification, rural health centers, rural roads, adduction of water, etc. One-fifth was allocated to vocational training and the other two-fifths were allocated to the creation of jobs for unemployed young rural people.[78]

With 100 MTD, the Fifth Plan changed this sectoral distribution. The emphasis was put on vocational training and job creation. These two sectors alone received two-thirds of the funds during 1977-81.[79] This shift was due to the seriousness of unemployment in most poor interior regions by the end of the Fourth Plan.

In terms of the geographical distribution of the funds, the gouvernorats were divided into categories: the littoral gouvernorats and the interior ones. During the Fourth Plan period, each gouvernorat received a fixed sum of 700,000 TD (about US$1,750,000). But those of the interior received an extra 1 MTD each (a total therefore of about US$3.5 million). During the Fifth Plan, the government decided to increase the sums for the poorest gouvernorats of the interior. In addition to the normal funds, a special fund of 25 MTD (about US$70 million) were allocated to four border gouvernorats in the interior (Le Kef and Jendouba in the North-West; Kasserine in the Center-West; and Gafsa in the South-West) and one border gouvernorat in the South-East, Mednine, on the Libyan border.[80]

The Implementation and Institutional Framework of the Program. Before discussing the results of the program a few words about the organization and implementation of the program are necessary.

In comparison with the cooperative program of the Ben Salah period, the PDR could be seen as a relatively "decentralized" program. As we will see, this is, unfortunately, not true. I have tried to trace the processes of the implementation of the PDR in order to see how it really works. Despite the difficulties of doing such a thing in the chaotic Tunisian administrative system (not to mention the quasi-obsession with secrecy!) I have been able, through different interviews, to gather some information. The organization and implementation of the program, according to the information I have, fall in four major phases (figure 5.2):

Table 5.9

REGIONAL DISTRIBUTION OF INDUSTRIAL INVESTMENTS BETWEEN 1962-71 AND 1973-76
(in percentage)

| Regions | Investments | |
|---|---|---|
| | 1962-71[a] | 1973-76[b] |
| North-East | 36.2 | 43.6 |
| Center-East | 12.9 | 20.4 |
| South-East | 27.9 | 30.1 |
| LITTORAL | 77.0 | 94.1 |
| North-West | 4.8 | 2.7 |
| Center-West | 10.7 | 0.8 |
| South-West | 7.5 | 2.4 |
| INTERIOR | 23.0 | 5.9 |

Source:

[a] See table 5.1;

[b] M. Toumi, *Tunisie: Pouvoirs et Luttes* (Paris: Le Sycomore, 1978), p. 442.

Table 5.10

GROWTH OF INDUSTRIAL EMPLOYMENT BY REGION BETWEEN 1972 AND 1980

| Regions | 1972 Employment | % | 1980 Employment | % | % of Total Increase | Variation in % |
|---|---|---|---|---|---|---|
| North-East | 50,000 | 56 | 89,000 | 57 | 58 | + 78 |
| Center-East | 16,000 | 18 | 35,000 | 22 | 28 | +120 |
| South-East | 2,600 | 2 | 7,000 | 5 | 7 | +170 |
| LITTORAL | 68,600 | 76 | 131,000 | 84 | 93 | + 91 |
| North-West | 9,000 | 10 | 10,000 | 6 | 1.5 | + 11 |
| Center-West | 2,000 | 2 | 3,000 | 2 | - | + 50 |
| South-West | 10,400 | 12 | 13,000 | 8 | 4.0 | + 25 |
| INTERIOR | 21,400 | 24 | 26,000 | 16 | 7 | + 21 |
| TOTAL TUNISIA | 90,000 | 100 | 157,000 | 100 | 100 | + 75 |

Source: Adapted from DAT, *Schéma National*, vol. 1 (1983), p. 80; vol 2 (1983), p. 224; and vol. 12 (1984), p. 202.

Phase I: Definition of the overall objectives and orientation of the program by the National Committee of the PDR. Headed by the Prime Minister, it includes the ministries most concerned by the activities of the PDR.

Phase II: Sectoral and technical coordination of the program by the National Technical Committee of the PDR. This committee is headed by the Minister of Plan and Finance and includes technical ministries.

Phases I and II are at the national level and include very few people and no popular participation at all.

Phase III: This phase involves the preparation of project proposals and includes different participants. It is located at the gouvernorat level as well as at the délégations level (subdivisions of the gouvernorats). During this phase, representatives of different national organizations, the local party officials, members of the National Assembly representing the area, and different local representatives of various ministries participate in the preparation and discussion of the project proposals. This process starts at the delegation level, and then moves on to the gouvernorat level. Project proposals therefore go through two major selection processes. All project proposals selected by each delegation are examined at the gouvernorat level.

Only those that pass the selection process at the gouvernorat level are sent to Tunis for approval and financing. Each at their own level, the délégué and the gouverneur have the final word on the selection of the projects.

Phase IV: Each gouvernorat has a PDR official who has the rank of a delegué. After selection of the projects, this delegate is in charge of all the negotiations with Tunis; the gouverneurs intervene only when it is really necessary. For example, when a phone call to the Prime Minister may become inevitable and the only alternative to make the powerful Minister of Plan more reasonable, because no project can be launched without the green light of the "Budget Direction" of the Ministry of Plan. Each PDR délegué must consult with the PDR office of that direction where the project proposals are carefully scrutinized and controlled. Project costs are checked several times and, if necessary, are reduced. In October 1984, I attended one meeting at which several PDR delegates from various gouvernorats were forced "to defend" all the items in the proposals "millimes" by "millimes" (equivalents of cents). And I must confess here, that whatever "finesse" and diplomacy (and I really mean it) the Budget Direction's officials have, the kind of "rapport de force" in favor of these officials was quite disturbing and somehow "humiliating" for the PDR's délegués. While I was listening to the discussion, I couldn't avoid thinking about Third World countries when they negotiate with organizations such as the IMF!! After the PDR delegates left, one official of the Budget Direction, obviously embarrassed by his own power, confesses,

> Si [Mr.] Ezzeddine, believe me, I wish we haven't to do this at all. I wish that the funds were annually allocated to the gouvernorats and managed by them under the direct control of the gouverneur and the gouvernorat council. This would reduce the tensions and would simplify the procedures by avoiding to the delegates to come to Tunis every time there is a problem with a project. And what we can do here is to control afterwards.[81]

In brief, when the project proposals were finally accepted by the Ministry of Plan, the realization process began. This is the task of the local level, with the technical assistance of the local technicians of the different ministries at the gouvernorat level.

Here is then, very schematically, the structural organization of the PDR. In spite of the differences with the very centralized cooperative program, the structural organization of the PDR is still a very "Jacobin" structure based on a classic top-down organization type, in which the center holds the keys (especially the money) of the game and the beneficiaries (the rural population) are excluded from any form of participation. And this will be one of the reasons (see below) why the program was severely criticized.

Figure 5.2
THE STRUCTURAL ORGANIZATION OF THE PDR

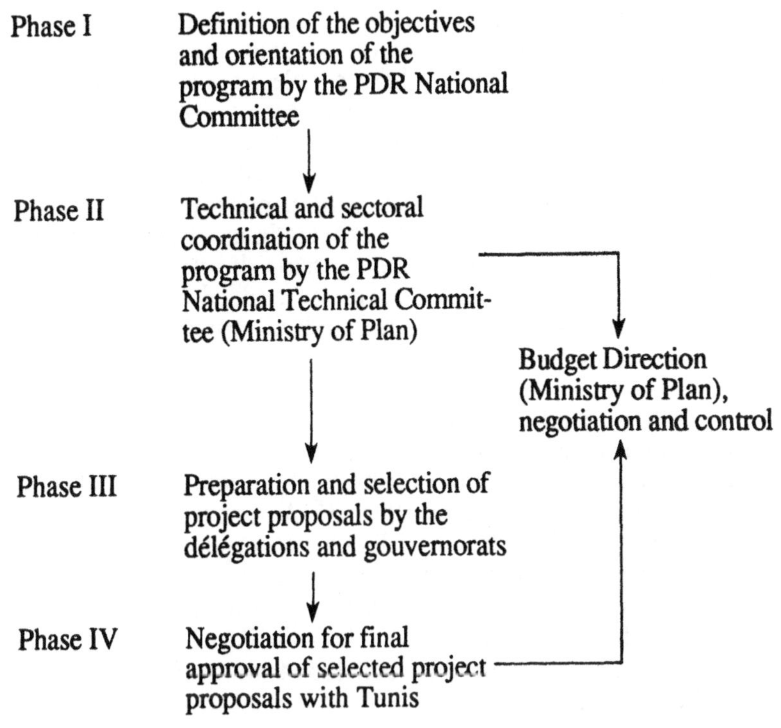


Source: Author's fieldwork.

## The Results of the Program

Between 1973 and 1981, according to the Sixth Plan (1982-86), 136,000 jobs were created; 133,000 young rural people were enrolled in vocational training programs; 5,500 km of rural roads were built or improved; water was adducted to 525 villages; 1,075 villages received electricity; 1,479 wells were drilled; and 386 basic health centers and 264 cultural facilities were established.[82] All this, transpired for a total cost of 163 MTD. These are, indeed, non-negligible results. But the question to be asked here is: was the PDR, as an instrument of a regional policy (in the rural sector), a success? Among the several critiques of the program, one was a direct answer to this question. In the only available and most comprehensive evaluation of the program, a Tunisian geographer, A.

Belhadi, dismissed the PDR as being too small relative to the huge and real needs of the rural population of the interior regions. He even called it a political operation of "sprinkling" (*saupoudrage*).[83] Belhadi's criticism was repeated almost word for word in the Sixth Plan:

> Disintegration and "sprinkling" were probably inevitable at first. The rural population's needs were so great, the rightful aspirations of these people were so compelling in most districts and rural places that it was very hard to classify needs, to satisfy the most urgent ones, since all were necessary and urgent. The limited supplies available constrain us to this almost egalitarian distribution to satisfy, even in part, everyone's expectations. Furthermore the studies needed for a general vision did not exist or were insufficient and the political pressure added to our difficulties so that we had to "act rapidly," sometimes even to "squander" slightly.[84]

The second major criticism addressed by Belhadi was the total absence of a spatial vision in the program—a spatial vision, he argued, that would have had an integrated dimension of the action undertaken in order to generate a minimum of spread effects.[85] A third critique, and this is a very serious charge, Belhadi had regarding the conception of the program, is that it was conceived as "aid" to the interior regions, and, as such, favored the insidious phenomenon of "clientelism" and "favoritism."[86] He even found that in certain areas, the local officials of the P.S.D. illegally used the PDR to become richer![87] He then concluded his evaluation with this very negative statement:

> In conclusion, it appears very clearly that the objectives of the PDR were far below that which the rural world expects in order to get out from its paralysis...The problem is crucial, the stake is big and rural development is more than some limited sprinkling operations of a centralizing and sectoral vision.[88]

Belhadi's conclusion was repeated to me, although in other terms, by an official of the Ministry of Plan.

> "You see, Si Ezzeddine, what can you expect from a drop in the sea? Is it going to change the sea? The 163 MTD spent on the program from 1973 to 1981 do not represent even one-tenth of the cost of one of the several dams built in the interior regions in order to transfer water from these regions to the littoral ones for the needs of industries and tourism!

Yes, of course, the PDR is necessary, but don't expect a drop to change the sea!"

When I asked why, therefore, the PDR was not changed or even replaced by something else, he said: "Si Ezzeddine, you want a revolution? We can't abolish the PDR, simply because it became so popular among the rural masses. Let me tell you something else: without the PDR, the Gouverneurs will simply cease to exist!"[89] For these reasons in spite of its shortcomings, the PDR was not abolished. The government, however, introduced with the assistance of the World Bank, a new program announced in the Sixth Plan (1982-86) called the "Programme de Développement Rural Integré (PDRI). The novelty of the PDRI is that it is supposed to insure a better "coordination and integration" of the actions undertaken. One hundred MTD were made available in 1983 by the Sixth Plan for integrated rural development projects in "poverty pockets," as the poorest areas of the interior regions are called.[90] Whereas the PDR continued to be supervised by the Budget Direction, the new program was placed under the control of a new public agency: the "Commissariat Général au Développement Régional" (CGDR). Also under the tutelage of the powerful Ministry of Plan, the CGDR was created in 1981 (see Chapter 6). Here are then the results of the PDR, the second major component of the regional policy during the Nouira period.

Policy in the Tourist Sector

The evolution of this sector is very similar to that of the industrial sector. All the efforts in favor of the interior regions during the Ben Salah period were abandoned. During the Nouira period, all the investments were concentrated in the littoral regions. In 1972, for example, four littoral zones were declared "priority zones." These zones were: Tunis and Nabeul-Hammamet in the North-East; Sousse-Monastir in the Center-East; and the Jerba-Zarzis in the South-East. Between 1972 and 1981, 215 MTD were invested and 103,000 jobs were created in the tourist sector. They were concentrated in these four "priority zones." This explains why the share of the total tourist capacity of the country in these regions jumped from 80 percent in 1972 to 93 percent in 1980 (table 3.9). Thus, in 1980, only 7 percent of the tourist capacity of the country was found in the interior regions. And this represented the realizations of the Ben Salah period. This evolution in the tourist sector is a perfect reflection of the new economic philosophy during the Nouira period and its consequences: the dramatic reduction of the role of the State in this sector.[91] Here too then, the development of the tourist capacity of the country did not benefit all regions and has, therefore, contributed to further widening the gap between the littoral and the interior.

Policy in the Social Sectors

In addition to the PDR and in spite of the reduction of its role in the social sectors (for example, between the Fourth Plan and the Fifth Plan in the administration alone, jobs creation has dropped by 5,000 jobs[92]), the State has been forced to maintain its presence at a minimum level. And the major action in this area during the Nouira period was the creation in 1974 of five new gouvernorats: Zaghouan in the North-East; Siliana in the North-West; Monastir and Mahdia in the Center-East; and Sidi Bouzid in the Center-West. The fact that these five small cities were designated as gouvernorat capitals stimulated certain public investments in the social and tertiary sectors: administration, housing, public services, infrastructure, etc. For example, in 1980, employment in the administration and services sectors represented in their total employment: Mahdia, 81.2 percent; Monastir, 70.1 percent; Zaghouan, 82.9 percent; Sidi Bouzid, 87.1 percent; and Siliana, 77.8 percent. This is a clear indication of how important public investments, generated by their designation as capitals, have been in terms of job creation (table 3.17).

This is therefore the only action in these sectors during the Nouira period. But as we can see here too the littoral was favored. For example, three of the five gouvernorats created were in the littoral: Zaghouan, near Tunis, in the North-East; Monastir and Mahdia, near Sousse, in the Center-East. So here not only has the State reduced its role, but even in those sectors where it has decision-making power, it did not play a corrective role by focussing on those regions that were not attractive to the private sector. And that is why, by the end of the decade, just one year before Mr. Nouira was replaced in 1980 by Mr. M. Mzali, a blunt warning came from an official report published in 1979 by the "Direction de l'Aménagement du Territoire":

> The industrialization of the country has first of all benefitted the region of Tunis, second, the other coastal regions; and the development and modernization of agriculture have only slowed the rhythm of the widening of the gap between the interior regions and the coastal regions, but did not, however, succeed in reversing the tendency towards the aggravation of the disequilibrium...In other words, if the jobs creation continues to be regionally localized as in the past, we will reach very rapidly a situation that could be characterized as *explosive*.[93]

And indeed the authors of the report had good reasons to worry (and the political events mentioned in the introduction and that have seriously shaken Tunisia, have shown that they were right) because the gap in living standards, for example, has not ceased to widen between the littoral and the interior regions. For example, the gap between the most privileged region (the North-East) and the poorest one (the Center-West, or Central Tunisia) will be between 270 and 300 percent in the year 2000 if the tendency observed by the authors of the report continues. Whereas it was 113 percent in 1966 and 167 percent in 1975! And if the same tendency continues, say the authors of the report, all littoral regions will see their living standards exceed those of the interior regions by more than 100 percent.[94]

The direct consequence of the aggravation of regional disparities during the Nouira period was the continuing flow of the population from the interior to the littoral and even directly abroad. For example, between 1975 and 1980 the interior regions lost 30,400 people to the littoral (the North-West alone lost 23,000) and another 31,926 who immigrated abroad.[95] This makes, if we include the loss between 1970 and 1975 (table 5.11), a total net loss for the interior regions of 100,116 people between 1970 and 1980, without taking into account, because of the lack of reliable data, those who have immigrated from the interior between 1966 and 1975 to Europe and Libya. The second consequence, strongly related to the first, is that the population of the *bidonvilles* (slums) of Tunis alone grew from 275,000 to 300,000 between 1975 and 1980, representing in 1980 more than one-fourth of the total population of the capital.[96]

Table 5.11

NET MIGRATION BY REGION
BETWEEN 1970 AND 1980

| Regions | Migration 1970-75 | Migration 1975-80 |
|---|---|---|
| North-East | +29,850 | +10,700 |
| Center-East | + 6,110 | +10,400 |
| South-East | + 1,830 | +10,000 |
| LITTORAL | +37,790 | +30,400 |
| North-West | -31,790 | -23,000 |
| Center-West | - 3,470 | - 6,200 |
| South-West | - 2,530 | - 1,200 |
| INTERIOR | -37,790 | -30,400 |

Source: Adapted from: DAT, *Schéma National*, vol. 2 (1983), pp. 43, 45.

# CONCLUSION

Now, what one may conclude from all this? The first thing to emphasize is that during the Nouira period, with the exception of the PDR (in spite of all the criticisms of the program), there was no regional policy at all! In the name of, and it is important to stress this again and again, a blind, and I would say a pseudo notion of "profitability," the Nouira government deliberately aggravated regional disparities. Based on a dogmatic philosophy of laisser-faire (that is why it is hard for me to call it a policy, because the expression "laisser-faire" means precisely to laisser-faire!) this has deliberately undermined the efforts of the Ben Salah period. What a contrast between the two periods! Having said that, it is, however, important to remember that the regional policy of the Ben Salah period too was, inadequate, despite the colossal efforts of that time. Because it was based on dubious theories of development and social change and of regional development and planning (Chapter 2) it failed to grasp the rationality and complexity of the productive system of the regions of the interior and the spatial organization of this system.

The third observation I would like to make is that this documentation and analysis of the regional policies in Tunisia reinforce further the conclusion of Chapter 4: that regional underdevelopment is not a natural phenomenon, but rather is fundamentally a by-product of policies, which create it, reduce it or aggravate it. This brings me to my final observation: this review of the Tunisian case illustrates remarkably, I think, the dilemmas of centralized, jacobin development strategies, regardless if they were inspired by "socialist" or "capitalist" economic policies. The next chapter will illustrate this further.

# NOTES

1. Ahmed Ben Salah was the father of the socialist experiment of the 1960s. And it is in the usage in Tunisia as elsewhere to associate the sixties with his name. Ben Salah is one of the great, and most controversial figures, of the Tunisian left. When the socialist strategy was suddenly stopped in 1969, Ben Salah was arrested and accused of "crimes against the State and high treason." He was condemned to ten years of forced labor. He escaped from jail in February 1973 and has since lived in exile in Europe, where he has many friends in the "*Internationale Socialiste*" (Willy Brandt, Bruno Kriesky and of course the late Olaf Palme). In 1974 Ben Salah created the "Mouvement de l'Unité Populaire" in Paris. For further information on this great *patriote*, see: P. Judet, "Ben Salah et le Développement Tunisien," *Esprit*, no. 397 (1970), pp. 805-16; M. Nerfin, *Entretiens avec Ahmed Ben Salah sur la Dynamique Socialiste dans la Tunisie des Années 1960*. (Paris: Maspero, 1974); see also the excellent analysis of J.P. Entelis, *Comparative Politics of North Africa* (Syracuse, NY: Syracuse University Press, 1980).

2. This period is also associated with the name of Hédi Nouria, Prime Minister from 1970 to 1980. An old militant of the P.S.D. Governor of the Central Bank during the 1960s, he was known as the most virulent opponent of the policies of Ben Salah. He is also considered as the father of the "open door" policies of the 1970s.

3. République Tunisienne, Sécrétariat au Plan et aux Finances, *Perspectives Décennales 1962-1971* (Tunis: Imprimerie Officielle, 1962), p. 87; see also the declaration of Ben Salah in, Nerfin, op. cit., pp. 96-111.

4. République Tunisienne, Ministère du Plan et des Finances, *Sixth Five Year Plan 1982-1986* (Tunis, 1982), p. 183.

5. See among others: P. Aydalot, "La Structuration de l'Espace Economique Tunisien," *Revue Tunisienne des Sciences Sociales*, no. 5 (1966), pp. 65-93; H. Attia, "L'Evolution des Structures Sociales et Economiques dans les Hautes Steppes," *Revue Tunisienne des Sciences Sociales*, no. 6 (1966), pp. 5-41; J. Poncet, "La Régionalisation en Tunisie," *Tiers Monde*, no. 55 (1972), pp. 597-614; M. Seklani, *Economie et Population du Sud* (Paris: CNRS, 1976); K. El Manoubi, "Le Pôle Industriel de Gabes et son Impact sur le Développement du Sud Tunisien," *Revue Tunisienne des Sciences Sociales*, nos. 48-49 (1977), pp. 115-36; M. Sethom, "Les Tentatives de Remodelage de L'Espace Tunisien depuis l'Indépendance," *Méditeranée*, nos. 1-2 (1979), pp. 119-25; H. Dlala, "Développement Economique et Action Régionale en Tunisie," *Revue*

*Tunisienne de Géographie*, no. 6 (1980), pp. 67-85; H. Sethom and A. Kassab, *Les Régions Géographiques de Tunisie* (Tunis: Publications de l'Université de Tunis, 1981).

6. Sethom, op. cit., p. 120; Sethom and Kassab, op. cit., pp. 188-89; and El Manoubi, op. cit., p. 120.

7. Sethom, op. cit., p. 120.

8. Attia, op. cit., p. 28.

9. El Manoubi, op. cit., p. 121.

10. This was the case of P. Aydalot for example (op. cit, pp. 87-93).

11. Sethom, op. cit.; and Sethom and Kassab, op. cit.

12. All the information in this section has been provided from several interviews with officials of the "Société Nationale de Cellulose et de Papier Alfa" (SNCPA): in Tunis, with Ms. M. Ridane, Director of the "Département Etudes et Controle de Gestion"; Mr. M. Besbes, Directeur Technique of the plant at Kasserine and Mr. N. Mraid, Director of "Relations Publique et Presses." Outside of the SNCPA, a son of the region, Mr. A. Mansouri, President Directeur Géneral of the "Société Régionale de Transport de Kasserine," provided me with valuable information for which I would like to extend all my thanks.

13. See Dlala, op. cit., p. 74.

14. Société Nationale de Cellulose et de Papier Alfa (SNCPA), "Le Complexe Industriel de Pâte et de Papier Eteint sa 20ième Bougie." *Journal du Papier*, no. 11 (1983), pp. 28-29.

15. Ibid., p. 29.

16. From my interview with Mr. Besbes, Directeur Technique of the SNCPA at Kasserine.

17. Sethom, op. cit., p. 120; and Dlala, op. cit., pp. 72-73.

18. On this particular issue, see Judet, op. cit., pp. 809-10.

19. Quoted from M. Toumi, *Tunisie: Pouvoirs et Luttes* (Paris: Le Sycomore, 1978), pp. 236-37 (translation and emphasis mine). On this particular aspect of the experience, see also Ben Salah's preface to M. Guen, *La Cooperation et l'Etat en Tunisie* (Tunis UGTT, 1964).

20. E. Hermassi, *Leadership and National Development in North Africa* (Berkeley: California University Press, 1972), p. 187.

21. J.L. Simmons, "Agricultural Cooperatives and Tunisian Development," *The Middle East Journal*, no. 4 (1970), pp. 455-65; and no. 1 (1971), pp. 45-57.

22. Hermassi, op. cit., p. 187.

23. See note 19.

24. Quoted from A. Zghal, "Changements de Systèmes Politiques et Réformes des Structures Agraires en Tunisie," *Revue Tunisienne des Sciences Sociales*, no. 12 (1968), pp. 9-32 (see p. 27; translation mine).

25. Simmons, op. cit., 1971, pp. 53, 57.

26. Ibid., p. 53.

27. E. Wolf, *Europe and the People without History* (Berkeley: University of California Press, 1982), p. 5.

28. A. Schawrz, *Les Dupes de la Modernisation* (Montreal: Nouvelle Optique, 1983).

29. I will not discuss here all the factors that have contributed to the failure of the cooperative system. For further discussion of these, see E. Moudoud, *Modernisation, Centralisation et Destruction de l'Economie Rurale: L'Experience des Cooperatives Agricoles en Tunisie 1962-1969*, U.B.C. Planning Papers, no. 7, School of Community and Regional Planning, University of British Columbia, Vancouver, 1983.

30. R. Apthorpe, "Peasants and Planistrators: Rural Cooperatives in Tunisia," *The Maghreb Review*, no. 1 (1977), pp. 1-18.

31. D. Ashford, "Organization of Cooperatives and the Structures of Power in Tunisia," *The Journal of Developing Areas*, no. 1 (1967), pp. 317-32.

32. See. L. Ben Salem, "L'Encadrement des Unités de Production Agricole," *Revue Tunisienne des Sciences Sociales*, no. 26 (1971), p. 143.

33. Apthorpe, op. cit., p. 8.

34. Ibid., p. 8.

35. F. Kafka, *The Trial* (New York: Knoff, 1960).

36. Hermassi, op. cit., p. 187.

37. C. Micaud et al., *Tunisia: The Politics of Modernization* (New York: Praeger, 1964), p. 140.

38. Ibid., p. 137.

39. K. Zamiti, "Les Obstacles Matériels et Ideologiques à l'Evolution Sociale des Campagnes Tunisiennes," *Revue Tunisienne des Sciences Sociales*, no. 21 (1970), pp. 9-50.

40. Ibid., p. 50 (it is important to note here that the tractor is not produced in Tunisia but imported!).

41. E. Makhlouf, "Les Cooperatives en Tunisie: Structures et Difficultés," *Revue Tunisienne des Sciences Sociales*, no. 26 (1971), pp. 79-114. In this excellent article, Mahlouf noted that even the ex-colonist workers never saw so many machines (imported of course) in their life!

42. Zamiti, op. cit., p. 50.

43. For further details, see Entelis, op. cit., pp. 136, 159.

44. Zamiti, op. cit., p. 50 (translation mine).

45. Ibid., p. 53 (translation from Simmons, op. cit., (1971), p. 46).

46. See Moudoud, op. cit.

47. See E. Moudoud, "L'Urbanisation et la Politique du Logement Social en Tunisie," (MA Thesis, Institut d'Urbanisme de l'Académie de Paris, Université de Paris VIII, Paris 1980), p. 56.

48. *Rapport du Comité de Reflexion sur l'Aménagement du Territoire et la Décentralisation Industrielle* (Tunis: DAT, April 1979), p. 17.

49. Simmons, op. cit., (1971), p. 45.

50. Ibid., p. 50.

51. For other case studies, the literature is vast. However, one of the best books I ever read in the last few years on this issue is: G. Hyden, *Beyond Ujamaa. Underdevelopment and Uncaptured Peasantry* (Berkeley: University of California Press, 1980.

52. S. Bahroun, "La Plannification: Outils et Techniques," in *La Politique Economique de la Tunisie*, ed. Ecole Nationale d'Administration (Tunis and Paris: Centre de Recherche et d'Etude Administratives, 1974) (translation and emphasis mine).

53. See Sethom, op. cit., p. 124; and P. Rouillé, *Le Tourisme en Tunisie* (Tunis: Ecole Nationale d'Administra-tion, 1970).

54. Sethom, op. cit., p. 124.

55. Ibid., p. 124.

56. N. Sraïeb, "Mutations et Réformes des Structures de l'Enseignement en Tunisie," *Annuaire de l'Afrique du Nord 1968*, vol. 8 (Paris: CNRS, 1968), p. 93.

57. Ibid., p. 124.

58. P. Signoles, "L'Armature Urbaine Tunisienne: Forces et Faiblesses, et son Rôle dans le Développement National," *Revue Tunisienne de Géographie*, no. 1 (1978), p. 86.

59. For further discussion, see, for example: D. Rondinelli, *Secondary Cities in Developing Countries* (Beverly Hills: Sage, 1983).

60. M. Chaker, "La Problématique de la Régionalisation en Tunisie," *Servir*, nos. 25-26 (1980), pp. 7-26.

61. RT/MPF, *Fourth Plan 1973-1976* (Tunis, 1973), p. xxxvii (translation mine).

62. Declaration of Mr. Tijani Chelli, first PDG of the API, quoted from : M.T. Maschino and F. Mrabet "La Tunisie Vingt Ans Après," *Le Monde Diplomatique*, December 1975. The French version is: "Le rôle de l'Etat c'est de combler les vides: construire des routes, amener l'eau; en un mot, permettre au privé de fonctionner."

63. Speech reported by the PSD daily newspaper *L'Action* of June 25-26, 1972 (translation mine).

64. Discours Programme of the Prime Minister of November 17, 1970, published in *La Presse*, November 18, 1970.

65. Speech published in *La Presse*, July 7, 1977.

66. Entelis, op. cit., p. 177.

67. For further information on all this legislation see: Agence de Promotion des Investissements, *1973-1983: Une Décennie au Service du Développement Industriel de la Tunisie* (Tunis: API, 1984), pp. 6-13.

68. RT, Ministère de l'Equipement, Direction de l'Aménagement du Territoire, "Organisation de l'Espace Tunisien" mimeographed (Tunis: DAT, 1979), p. 6.

69. Ibid., p. 6.

70. The decree of 1977, divided the country in three zones called A, B and C. This zoning is based on the principles of digressive advantages from A to C. In other words, all the gouvernorats (except some delegations within them) of the littoral are classified as zone A. They benefit only of the advantages of this zone (exemption from several taxes, registration fees, and taxes on profits for one year, etc.), but do not benefit from any of the advantages offered in the other two zones. On the contrary, in zones B and C, all the gouvernorats of the interior benefit from the incentives provided in zone A in addition to their own. For example, if investors would like to take advantage of all the incentives offered by the decree they will have to locate in zone C, where the poorest gouvernorats are grouped. If they want only to take advantage of the incentives offered in zone B (taking charge of interest rate on loans up to 5 percent and payment of infrastructure work) and A (see above), they can locate their projects in zone B. But if they do not want to locate in neither C nor B (in other words in the interior) they can only have that which is offered in A (the littoral).

71. See for example: J. Poncet, *La Tunisie à la Recherche de Son Avenir: Indépendance ou Neo-Colonialisme* (Paris: Editions Sociales, 1974).

72. See special dossier of the RT/Ministry of National Economy, "Industrial Decentralization Policy," *Conjoncture*, no. 59 (1981), p. 4.

73. P. Signoles, "Les Déséquilibres Urbains en Tunisie," *Aujourd'hui l'Afrique*, no. 20 (1980), pp. 21-30.

74. Ibid., p. 26.

75. RT/Ministry of National Economy, op. cit., p. 5.

76. *Fourth Plan 1973-1976*, pp. 145-68.

77. Ibid., p. 167; and RT/MPF, *Fifth Year Plan 1977-1981*, (Tunis, 1977), pp. 43-44.

78. *Fourth Plan*, p. 167.

79. *Fifth Plan*, pp. 43-44.

80. For further discussion see: A. Belhadi, "Le Programme de Développement Rural: Les Illusions et la Réalité," *Revue Tunisienne de Géographie*, no. 7 (1981), pp. 9-45; J. Nellis, *Decentralization, Regional Development and Local Public Finance in Tunisia*, Occasional Paper, no. 79, Metropolitan Studies Program, Maxwell School, Syracuse University, 1984.

81. Interview with a PDR official in the Budget Direction, Ministry of Plan and Finance, Tunis, October 1984.

82. RT/MPF, *Sixth Plan 1982-1986* (Tunis, 1982), p. 184.

83. Belhadi, op. cit., p. 21.

84. *Sixth Plan*, p. 200.

85. Belhadi, op. cit., p. 21.

86. Ibid., pp. 21-22.

87. Ibid.

88. Ibid (translation mine).
89. See note 81.
90. *Sixth Plan*, p. 201; RT/MPF, *Note sur le Nouveau Programme de Développement Rural Integré* (Tunis, 1983).
91. See A. Kassab and H. Sethom, *Géographie de la Tunisie: Le Pays et les Hommes* (Tunis: Publications de l'Université de Tunis, 1980), p. 221.
92. Signoles, "Les Déséquilibres Urbains," p. 28.
93. Report published by the Direction de l'Aménagement du Territoire, Comité de Réflexion sur l'Aménagement du Territoire et de la Décentralisation Industrielle (Tunis, 1979), pp. 17-19 (translation mine).
94. Ibid., pp. 16-19.
95. DAT, *Schéma National*, vol. 2 (1983), pp. 34, 45.
96. Moudoud, *L'Urbanisation*, p. 56.

# PART THREE
# TOWARDS RETHINKING THE REGIONAL QUESTION

> Il faut bien que certains se disent ceci: jamais cette société ne trouvera d'issue s'il n'existe pas de gens prêts à renoncer à une part au moins de leurs pouvoirs et de leurs privilèges. Sinon, ils perdront tout et nous perdions avec eux. Je redoute sincèrement pour ce pays un destin comme celui du Tchad ou du Liban, ou même de l'Iran. Cela arrive toujours par défaillance de l'intelligence et du caractère. Que ceux qui se sentent une responsabilité la prennent. L'intellectuel a la sienne, qui est de réflechir et de faire don de la substance de sa pensée à son pays.
>
> Hichem Djait,
> "Tunisie: Dérive ou Renouveau?,"
> *Jeune Afrique*, nos. 1207-1208 (1984), p. 33.

Part Two examined the validity of the two first premises as well as answered the two questions of this study. We therefore can see now: (1) why the overall "good" economic performance of Tunisia during the last three decades did not benefit all regions of the country; and (2) why past regional development policies, whether they were based on centralized economic policies or on economic laisser-faire, failed.

The objective of this third part is first to discuss the validity of the third premise of the research: that the major causes of regional underdevelopment are not the lack of human and natural resources, or the lack of the "attributes of development," but rather the continued polarization of political power through the control of state apparatus by hegemonic political elites and bureaucracies organized on a regional basis.

In doing this, it is hoped that this final part of the study which covers the period 1980-1982 will (1) illustrate further the arguments developed in Chapters 4 and 5, and (2) provide a new framework for rethinking the "regional question" in Tunisia, and hopefully through the Tunisian case itself, in other developing countries in general, the second objective of this study.

# 6
# THE IMPOSSIBLE "JACOBIN" REGIONALIZATION

As a continuation of Chapter 5, this chapter has two objectives: (1) through the analysis of the failure of a recent development project in Central Tunisia, to restate the "regional question" in Tunisia in order to contribute to the progress of the debate on this very sensitive question; (2) to show, through the Tunisian case itself, the limits and the impasses towards which centralized and technocratic approaches—conceived and imposed from "above" in the best "Jacobin" traditions—in regional development always lead; (3) to stress the urgent need in Tunisia for a truly radical regional reform that would seriously deal with the issue of the redistribution of *power* between the *State* and the *region*.

## THE CENTRAL TUNISIA DEVELOPMENT PROJECT

As we saw in Chapter 5, the impact of the past two regional policies on reducing the regional disparities created during the French protectorate has not been impressive at all. And it is in this context that in April 1979, the blunt warning of the "Rapport du Comité de Réflexion sur l'Aménagement du Territoire et de la Décentralisation Industrielle," brought to the attention of the Nouira government the danger of its policy in respect to regional disparities.

It is also in this context that a few months later an important regional development project, the "Central Tunisia Development Project," was launched by the Nouira government with the assistance of the United States Agency for International Development (USAID).[1] Before continuing with the analysis of this experience and the political significance of its failure with regard to the "regional question," I would like to raise a few questions:

One. Considering the failure of past regional development policies and the fact that the gap between the littoral and the interior has widened especially during the Nouira period, is it true, as suggested in the *Sixth Plan (1982-1986)*, that regional disparities "cannot be totally suppressed for natural, human and sociological constraints?"[2] In other words, is it true that the main *causes* of regional underdevelopment in Tunisia lie within the underdeveloped regions themselves?

Two. My second question is strongly related to the previous one. Given the centralized power structures in Tunisia today, is it reasonable to assume that the real *causes* of regional underdevelopment in Tunisia *are not* the lack of whatever kind of resources nor, to paraphrase Ralph Matthews, whatever "attributes of development"[3] (as the authors of the Sixth Plan have suggested)? On the contrary then, is the cause the continuing domination and exploitation of the interior regions through the monopolization of political power by the regions of the littoral?

Three. My third and final question is: is it reasonable to assume that without this domination and exploitation, and given the considerable resources (agricultural, mineral, human, financial etc.) (for example: the interior regions have the monopoly on all the mineral resources of the country) the interior has, would the interior regions be able to sustain a reasonably high standard of living and rapid development *if left alone*?

These are the fundamental questions to be asked if we want to understand first of all the political significance of the failure of Central Tunisia Project and second and beyond, all the ramifications of the "regional question" in Tunisia today.

## Brief Description of Central Tunisia.

In order to understand fully the importance of the project and the hopes that it has generated in the region,[4] a brief presentation of Central Tunisia is necessary.

The area covered by the project is composed of the poorest region of the country (figure 6.1). Contributing to this are many factors. The most often mentioned in the various studies of the region are:

— the physiographic factors: poor soils, low and irregular rainfall, topographic and other climatic factors;

— sociohistorical factors, such as the recent transition from pastoralism to sedentary settlement. This is still manifested in the dispersed settlement pattern and the lower level of urbanization, the lowest in the country (21 percent in 1980; see table 5.11);

— the very unequal land tenure system and as a corollary of this, the very unequal income distribution within the region. In 1979, according to an unpublished study for USAID-Tunis by Nicholas Hopkins,[5] 80 percent of the region's farmers were mainly subsistence producers having average cash incomes of less than 100 TD a year and unable, therefore, according to Hopkins, to purchase any agricultural inputs. In contrast, 12 percent of the farmers had incomes of between 100 and 360 TD a year, and 6 percent with average incomes between 360 and 1,000 TD a year. The unequal income distribution is closely associated with the highly concentrated land tenure system. For example, Hopkins estimated that given the climatic conditions in the region, 40 hectares per family was a minimum for family survival. But very few farmers possess anywhere near this amount of land. In 1962, 38 percent of the farms had less than 10 hectares.[6] In 1976 this percentage jumped to 64 percent, and another 20 percent of the farms were in the 10-20 hectares range[7];

— the very poor level of social and physical infrastructure in the region. For example, despite all the efforts of the Ben Salah period, in 1980 the region had the least water adduction, electrification, and telephone density; the lowest percentage of beds and doctors per inhabitant; and the lowest level of household incomes as measured by household cash consumption. On the other hand, it has the highest rates of illiteracy in the country and the highest percentage of population living in "absolute poverty" (see the second part of Chapter 3 for further comparison with other regions).

— the low level of industrialization, despite the resources of the region. Industrialization is almost nonexistent and the region's share of total industrial employment in the country is the lowest in 1980: 1.8 percent (see table 3.8). Only 55 establishments were counted in the industrial activities census of 1979. Were it not for the paper industry in Kasserine created during the Ben Salah period, one could hardly speak about any industrial activities in the region. This is illustrated by the fact that out of the 55 establishments, 29 were in the food processing industry, including 24 bakeries!![8]

— the "dependent" position of the region from a national perspective, which is seldom mentioned, as noted by L. Jakobson, but which has contributed the most to the underdevelopment of the region. This is explained by historical and political factors. First, the French colonization, which, by destroying the precolonial socioeconomic structures and by siphoning the region's natural resources, transformed it into an "export" region (see Chapter 4). Second, since independence, the postcolonial policies (see Chapter 5) which perceived the problem of the region mainly to be one of "*rattrapage*" (adopting therefore the "gap approach" of modernization theories), have maintained it in its subordinate position. L. Jakobson, an American regional planner, wrote of this particular issue in 1981:

> Looking at Central Tunisia from a national perspective, we see an "export" region with a skewed output-input balance. The region exports oil and minerals and also a considerable amount of water to the coastal cities of Sfax and Sousse. There is no tangible return from these export commodities to the region.[9]

In addition, the region exports its labor force, because of unemployment and underemployment. This has not only created an undesirable dependency on external income but has deprived the region of its youth and therefore compromised its future. Twenty years ago, H. Attia, a Tunisian geographer and specialist on the region, put his finger on this insidious phenomenon of the dependence of this region, which he called "parasitisme régional," when he wrote:

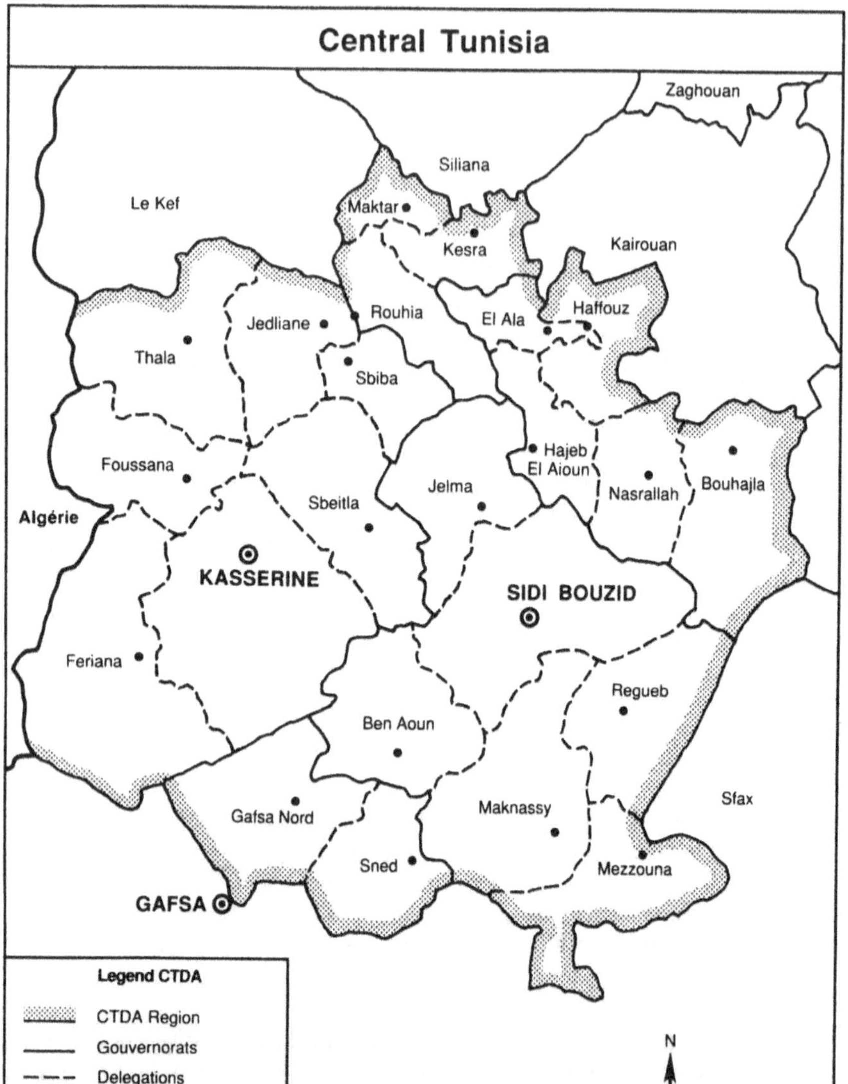
Central Tunisia
Zaghouan
Siliana
Le Kef
Maktar
Kesra
Kairouan
Rouhia
El Ala
Haffouz
Jedliane
Thala
Sbiba
Hajeb El Aioun
Foussana
Jelma
Nasrallah
Bouhajla
Sbeitla
Algérie
KASSERINE
SIDI BOUZID
Feriana
Regueb
Ben Aoun
Sfax
Gafsa Nord
Maknassy
Sned
Mezzouna
GAFSA
Legend CTDA
CTDA Region
Gouvernorats
Delegations
Gouvernorats Capitals
Delegations Seats
N
0 10 30 40
kms

> The non-agricultural activities totally escape the people of the region and are monopolized by Sfax and secondly by the Saheliens who fight over the region of Kasserine with Sfax.

> The Sfaxiens buy the olives and almond-tree before the harvests, and share with the jobbers of Sousse and Tunis the sheep market. In addition, they supply the High Steppes where the Sfaxien commercial network is present everywhere and dominates by far the few Sahelien or Djerbien merchants established in Sbeitla and Kasserine. Even the utilitarian handicraft and service sectors are set up by the Sfaxiens and they are: hairdresser, carpenter, coppersmith, *gargotiers*....

> Among the 570 workers employed by the paper mill, only 150 manual workers are from the region. There is here a phenomenon of *interregional parsitism*, aggravated by the fact that the people of the Steppes sell everything unmanufactured and by all what they need, even the plow from Sfax. The wealth is not only rare but it is in great part levied by foreign merchants in the region, and thus there is *no accumulation* of wealth in the region.[10]

This phenomenon of "interregional parsitism" has also been observed in another gouvernorat of the region—Sidi-Bouzid. The Sfaxiens monopolize all nonagricultural activities, especially commerce and small industries.[11] So, here, 20 years after Attia wrote his penetrating statement, the situation has not changed. For example, and in addition to the exports mentioned by Jakobson earlier, the "surplus" produced in the region is not reinvested in the region. H. Attia, in a recent study on the region published in 1982, found that in the gouvernorat of Sidi-Bouzid, the smallest one in the region, the funds entering in the gouvernorat in 1979 through the postal and banking network totalled the sum of 241,670 TD (about US$360,000). But the funds that went out of the gouvernorat totalled 5,538,540 TD (about US$8,300,000)!! Most of this important amount, interestingly, went to Sfax and Tunis.[12] I think it is important to stress that these figures are for only one year and one gouvernorat!

In brief, here is, in addition to all the factors mentioned earlier, the most important factor in the underdevelopment and constant "impoverishment" of the region, which once had, due to its agricultural and artisan resources as well as to its strategic position, a key role in the development first of Carthage and then for centuries, of Kairouan and all of North Africa (see Chapter 4).

<u>Presentation of the Project</u>

Now, after this brief socioeconomic profile of the region, let us go back to the project itself and the analysis of its failure. One may ask at this stage why this interest in the project in the first place and what its failure has to do with the "regional question?" My objective in analyzing this project is to look at the lessons that one may draw from its failure. I believe that beyond the Tunisian case itself there are some very useful lessons for other Third World countries, especially in Africa.

What was very interesting in the whole experience is the fact that it was a very innovative project, in the sense that it introduced in Tunisia a completely new approach to regional development and planning when it was launched in 1979. Given the objectives that were set for the project and the new and unusual type of institution specially created, the "Central Tunisia Development Authority" (CTDA), the new approach has marked a significant rupture with the past regional policies.

It is true that in 1978, when the CTDA was legally created in August, there were other "authorities" (*offices* in French) in existence in Tunisia. But these were primarily technical units with limited responsibilities. The CTDA was different;it was a quasi-autonomous authority with a civil personality and financial autonomy, the mission of which was to promote the "integrated development" in *its region*, says the law establishing it, . And this is the second aspect of the rupture with previous policies I mentioned earlier. Contrary to these policies, it is not the gouvernorat, a strictly administrative unit with no historical, geographical or economic base, which is the focus of intervention, but a whole region. For several political reasons (some of them were briefly explored in Chapter 3, such as the ideology of development and the conception of "national unity" of the Tunisian elites) a whole region was never before taken as the focus of a regional development policy. I would even say that because of this obsession with "national unity" and what was called pejoratively "tribalism," the word "region" itself was almost taboo!

The third aspect of the rupture was the mission of the CTDA itself as defined by the law. With previous policies, each ministry was in charge of "portion" of the policy that corresponded to its sectoral activities, through its local departments at the gouvernorat level. Because of this technocratic and centralized approach, regional policies were a superimposition of programs and projects, sometimes if not always duplicating projects without an overall vision and in which the spatial dimensions were very often neglected as we saw for the PDR, for example. With the Central Tunisia Project, one authority, and only one, was in charge of the whole development (multisectoral development) of a whole region. For example, the project's area included five gouvernorats: two totally—Kasserine and Sidi-Bouzid and 3 partially—Siliana, Kairouan and Gafsa. With a total of 22 délégations, the project's area corresponded thus to the historical and geographical limits of Central Tunisia. Also, the CTDA's mission was to act in both rural and urban sectors as well as in both agricultural and nonagricultural sectors. In brief, all this makes the new approach unusual in the chaotic and centralized Tunisian planning system. Both the nature and the scale of the intervention were thus the most important aspects of this rupture with past policies. And that is why I said that the project generated much hope when it was launched in 1979.

The Activities of the CTDA. In the fall of 1978, the Chef de Cabinet of the powerful Ministry of Plan was appointed as Président Directeur Général (PDG) of the CTDA. In January 1979, the CTDA was officially established in its offices in the city of Kasserine; this also was unusual in Tunisia, where everything is Tunis. As J. Nellis noted: "that an official of Chef de Cabinet rank was appointed to the post of PDG was itself significant; that this official agreed to reside permanently in Kasserine even more so."[13] During the summer of the same year and after the signing in May 1979 of a US$25 million project agreement with USAID,[14] a team of consultants from the "Regional Planning and Area Development Project" of the University of Wisconsin-Madison, was hired to assist the CTDA. While this assistance was contracted to provide technical assistance and training in general, it was specifically concerned with assistance to the Planning Unit of the CTDA in the preparation of a development plan for the region by the end of 1981, which would feed into the Sixth Plan then in preparation.[15]

A few months later, the CTDA produced its first "Program for the Integrated Development for Central Tunisia—Budget for the Year 1980," which spelled out in detail its operating objectives and actions. These were:

— to create conditions that would expand the regional economy;

— to mobilize local resources, especially in the agricultural sector in order to increase production;

— to survey and give titles to land holdings in the area;

— to improve rural living conditions and prevent migration of the region's population to the coastal cities and abroad;

— to create new employment opportunities as a remedy against unemployment as well as a means of increasing family incomes;

— to undertake community development activities in adult literacy, family planning and cooperative formation projects;

— to improve credit facilities for small farmers; and finally

— to promote nonagricultural industries and enterprises.

Some 27 specific projects were proposed and each of the areas listed above was scheduled to receive at least one project in 1980. In addition to this ambitious program, in October 1980, after several months of preparation, the CTDA with the assistance of the Wisconsin team, presented to the government a development plan for the region.

Here is, briefly, an overview of the project, the context within which it was launched, the nature of the new approach it introduced into

Tunisia in the field of regional development and finally, a summary of its first two years of activities.

The Impossible "Jacobin" Regionalization.

As we have just seen, in addition to its "Budget Program," and after several months of hard work, the CTDA proposed a plan for the region in October 1980. And it is from here that all the problems originated. This plan was categorically rejected by the powerful Ministry of Plan and Finance. The reasons of this rejection are clearly given to us by the Project Evaluation Report (evaluation prepared in June 1981 by a team composed by two Americans and three Tunisian experts hired by the Tunisian government and USAID–Tunis):

> Without entering into a debate on the abstract intellectual merits of the sketch plan approach it must be said that its emphasis on socio-spatial, as opposed to micro-economic issues, and its key assumptions regarding regional level decision-making powers do not fit into the present Tunisian system. Thus, respondents said of the approach:
>
> — It is too early to undertake this kind of planning in Tunisia.
>
> — It is a noble idea but premature.
>
> — We must await a truly decentralized policy.
>
> — It is something for the future.
>
> — These are fascinating ideas, but it must be said that ideas like these require radical changes.[16]

This pertinent analysis of the evaluation report was confirmed to me in an interview with the new PDG of the CTDA in Kasserine in September 1984, in these terms: "The Wisconsin team wanted Tunisia to make a jump of 20 years ahead in the field of planning! They did not take into account the current political-administrative structures in Tunisia..." But, as correctly noted by Nellis, the American consultants were doing exactly what they had been expressly charged with:

> American technical assistance to the CTDA's Planning Unit ran into great difficulty by proposing a regional plan (they had been expressly charged with the task by the project agreement) that assumed the CTDA was precisely what the

> law said it was: an independent planning and implementation body able to act without close central supervision and committed to the notion of a regional locus of planning and power.

Nellis then adds this very pertinent and significant observation:

> But when the *rhetorical bluff* was called and a preliminary strategy produced expressing these assumptions concretely, the central-level Tunisian officials withdrew with alarm. They claimed the CTDA and its advisers were exceeding their authority, and they characterized the draft strategy as "premature" and as not based on existing political realities. Eventually the Tunisian central officials sent a second team into the area to produce *an acceptable plan*, that is, *one that discussed the mobilization of local resources to fit the Tunis-set objectives* of the national plan.[17]

As we can see, Nellis has put his finger not only on the real reasons for the rejection of the strategy proposed by the CTDA, but also on the real causes of regional disparities in Tunisia. For me, this proves in the clearest manner that the real problem of the interior regions is not the "lack of human or natural resources" or whatever imaginary "sociological constraints," but rather the lack of *political power*. It is very important to stress this: the strategy proposed by the CTDA was not refused for any reason other than it did not fit the current political-administrative structures!

Here are, then, the reasons of the failure of this promising and very innovative experiment. Now, to go further in the analysis of the political significance of the project, one may ask: but why did the Tunisian government launch the project in the first place? It is difficult to answer this question with certainty. Some suggestions, however, are possible. First and foremost, as we saw, the impact of past regional policies has not been impressive at all, and regional disparities were even aggravated during the Nouira period. This aggravation was, as many official documents can show (see Chapter 1), at the base of the political events that shook the country between 1978-84 and threatened its unity and stability. At the same time, the Tunisian government became aware of the dangers of its economic policy and of the rising political unrest, especially in the regions of the interior. I believe that all these were very sufficient reasons to do something, or at least to give the impression of doing something. Others observers have suggested other reasons. For example, according to the Project Evaluation Report, several respondents most critical of the project, have argued that the CTDA and its regional planning focus were American ideas imposed on the Tunisian government by USAID.[18] Frankly, this is nonsense, of course! It is not the way Tunisian officials do business with USAID or with any foreign agency. Others have argued that "the Tunisian government accepted the project mainly to obtain American money, and that there was no strong commitment among central-level Tunisian decision-makers to the supposedly key operating principles or innovative aspects of the venture."[19] Perhaps, but I still believe that the very reason that forced the Nouira government to do something to be highly political. This belief is supported by someone who was closely associated, on the USAID–Tunis side, with the project from the beginning, P. Demongeot, who, in an unpublished report on the project, wrote:

> The GOT [government of Tunisia] became aware of serious dissatisfaction and incipient political unrest in some of the interior regions, including Central Tunisia. It became conscious of the fact that the local populations were fed up with studies and promises and were becoming increasingly vocal in their demands for action. The GOT, therefore, perceived US support and advocacy of a "basic human needs" approach focused on the "rural poor" as an opportunity to make good its past promises and to improve its standing with the Central Tunisia citizenry.[20]

I think that anyone who has visited the region during the last five or six years would understand the pertinence of this statement. It is reasonable to assume, therefore, that the real intentions of central planners were to calm down the "political unrest" of the "increasingly vocal" local populations. This assumption is further sustained by the fact that while the CTDA and the American team were working hard on the preparation of a regional plan, Tunis central planners were working on another project: the creation of a "Commissariat Général au Développement Régional" (CGDR), the creation of which was announced by the *Note d'Orientation pour la III eme Décennie de Développement et le VIème Plan*, an important document published by the Ministry of Plan in November 1980[21] (in other words, just a month after the CTDA proposed its plan of development for Central Tunisia!).

Under the tutelage of the Ministry of Plan, the principal functions of the newly created CGDR are: (1) to conceptualize regional development strategies; (2) to insure coherence of planning within and among gouvernorats; (3) to monitor the implementation of integrated rural development projects, etc. In addition, says the *Note d'Orientation*, the CGDR's mission is:

> to help the gouvernorats to prepare for the Sixth Plan at least some embryo of regional plans and for the Seventh Plan (1987-1991) of truly regional plans.[22]

This return to the scale of the gouvernorat is a dramatic and clear setback for decentralization in Tunisia. It is true that some six regional units of the CGDR were planned. But when I asked the "Commissaire Général" of the CGDR in October 1984 to explain to me the exact role and functions of these regional units, the response was very frank but astonishing: "data gathering" (!!), and that the conception and formulation of the strategies will be done at Tunis.[23]

And it is here that the promising experience of the Central Tunisia Development Project ends. Almost two years after the creation of the CGDR by the law of August 9, 1981, two new "development authorities" (*offices*) were created in the gouvernorats of Sidi-Bouzid (formerly included entirely in the CTDA's area) and Kairouan (formerly included partially). And when I visited Kasserine in September-October 1984, I discovered that from "Office de Développement de la Tunisie Centrale" the CTDA became the "Office de Développement de Kasserine."

Here are then, what I believe to be the real intentions of Tunisian central officials in launching the project in 1979: to buy time and to counterattack with the creation of the CGDR—despite the fact that the strategy proposed by the CTDA and the American team was simply assigning the use of local resources for the benefit of the region they were working for. Concluding his remarks on the lessons that one may draw from this experience in respect to decentralization and regional development, Nellis wrote:

> Strengthening regional and local responses to centrally set goals—that is as far as "decentralization" goes in Tunisia today.[24]

In the same vein, a Tunisian social scientist, H. Charrad-Rouissi, writing about the political significance of the creation of the CGDR, noted:

> in spite of the political discourse, it is always the central power who detains the keys to regional development in Tunisia. This situation has been consolidated by the creation of the "Commissariat Général au Développement Régional."[25]

## CONCLUSION

In conclusion, what may all the evidence from the previous section suggest? What lessons can be drawn from the failure of the Central Tunisia Development Project?

To begin with, and I would like to stress this, it is no longer possible to assume that the major causes of regional underdevelopment lie in the underdeveloped regions themselves. It is no longer possible to assume that regional disparities cannot be eliminated due to the lack of resources or to whatever imaginary "sociological constraints." But on the contrary, and based on all the evidence, it is more than reasonable to assume that the only cause of regional underdevelopment is the continuing domination and exploitation of the interior regions by the littoral ones through the continuing monopolization of economic and political power. And it is, therefore, more than reasonable to assume that what the interior regions are really lacking is political power, what I call "regional power." This is the only resource they don't have—a resource that would allow them, at the national level, to have their word in the allocation of the national pie to which, due to their huge resources, they contribute more than the littoral regions. Let me illustrate this further. Seventy-one percent of all investments in the Sixth Plan (1982-86) are located in the littoral regions. And this, as noted by Nellis: "is a plan supposedly devoted to regional equilibrium!"[26] This regional investment distribution is justified by the Sixth Plan on the grounds that 58.3 percent of the total population is to be found in the littoral![27] What, however, the authors of the Sixth Plan don't say is that, as we saw in Chapter 5, because of past regional policies, the interior regions have not ceased through the years to lose their population to the littoral regions and abroad. So paradoxically, the depopulation of the interior becomes a self-justification for fewer investments, which itself will lead to further depopulation (because of fewer jobs and opportunities) and again to fewer investments ...etc! But beyond this, my position is that there is another explanation. The littoral regions have been always favored due to political factors. For example, despite all the official rhetoric of the last 30 years against "regionalism" and "tribal reflexes,"[28] a study published in 1972 by the Centre de Recherches et d'Etudes sur les Sociétés Méditerranéenes, on the theme of the "Formation des Elites Maghrébines," found that 73 percent of Tunisian elites were originally from four littoral gouvernorats: Tunis, Sousse, Sfax and Mednine-Jerba.[29] Other studies have since stressed this curious aspect of Tunisian politics in respect to the analysis of the "regional question." For example, W. Zartman, focusing on the core elite in Tunisia, found that among government and Party Political Bureau members in 1956, 65 percent of them were from two regions: Tunis and the Sahel (the region of Sousse-Sfax). In 1980, this percentage was slightly increased to 69 percent.[30] A more recent study, published by the magazine *Jeune Afrique* in 1985, found that 83 percent of all political and administrative elite were originally from the littoral regions—from Bizerte in the North-East to Zarzis in the South-East.[31] But what is more interesting is that the authors of the study found that in contrast, the interior regions were overrepresented in labor unions, the opposition parties and student unions.[32] In brief, as noted by an American specialist on Tunisia, R. Stone, "regionalism is an integral part of Tunisian political life," and that "there exists some corresponding regional favoritism in economic investments and development programs" and regional disparities in the geographical distribution of Tunisian elites in the State apparatus.[33] What is more striking is that even in those institutions that are supposedly dealing with regional disparities, the same insidious phenomenon is occurring. For example, one of my respondents in the Ministry of Plan and Finance mentioned that 80 percent of the personnel of the newly formed Commissairat Général au Développement Régional were from the city of Sfax (a fact that I have observed, but couldn't of course check statistically, through several visits to the CGDR). The only explanation of this is that the Commissioner himself was from...Sfax! As we can see, this has nothing to do with what is called in French the *ragots* (gossips) of the "Café du Commerce!" Unfortunately it is a very dangerous sociopolitical phenomenon, which Michel Camau, writing about the Tunisian State, called the "privatization of the State,"[34] by a few interest groups organized on regional and "tribal" bases. It is this insidious phenomenon that explains, therefore, the continuing polarization of economic and political power in favor of the littoral regions. We have here, a typical "hegemonic" elite, to use Gramsci's terminology, which in the name of an hegemonic conception of "national unity" uses the State apparatus for its own "self-interest," to paraphrase J. Nellis.[35]

My conclusion, therefore, based on this evidence, is that regional underdevelopment in Tunisia is due to the continuing monopolization of economic and political power by some regions at the expense of others. Secondly, my belief is that without a radical regional reform, the main objective of which must be to recognize the region's right to existence and to consider seriously, therefore, the issue of the distribution of *power* between the *State* and the *region*, there is no way to avoid further violence and destabilization and to resolve today's regional disparities "dilemma."

It is the objective of the final and concluding chapter to outline some of the elements with which this urgent reform should be concerned.

## NOTES

1. In what follows, I will limit my discussion to the major factors in the project's failure. But for a detailed discussion of the whole experience, see my "Le Développement Régional en Tunisie: Le Cas du Gouvernorat de Kasserine" (unpublished Memoire de "Diplome d'Etude Approfondie" (DEA), Institut de Géographie, Université de Paris IV-Sorbonne, Paris, 1981; idem, *Le Développement Régional en Tunisie: Le Projet de Développement de la Tunisie Centrale*, UBC Planning Papers, no. 2, School of Community and Regional Planning, University of British Columbia, Vancouver, May 1982; idem "L'Impossible Régionalisation 'Jacobine' et le Dilemme des Disparités Régionales en Tunisie," *Canadian Journal of Regional Science*, no. 3 (Autumn 1985), pp. 413-58.

2. RT/MPF, *Sixth Plan 1982-1986* (Tunis, 1982), p. 185.

3. R. Matthews, *The Creation of Regional Dependency* (Toronto: University of Toronto Press, 1983).

4. I have been working on the project for six years now. In an interview with the first Président Directeur Général of the Office de Développement de la Tunisie Centrale (authority created specially for the implementation of the project) in July 1980, he called the project a "pioneer project" for the region and for the country as a whole in terms of regional development and planning.

5. N. Hopkins, *Social Soundness Analysis: A Report on Central Tunisia Rural Development Project* (Tunis: USAID, 1978) (quoted from J. Nellis, "Rural Development Technical Assistance and Migration. A Tunisian Case Study" [Paper presented at the Conference on Rural Development and the Retention of the Rural Population in the Countryside of Developing Countries, Institute for International Development and Cooperation, University of Ottawa, Ottawa, Canada, October 1981], pp. 10-11).

6. H. Sethom and A. Kassab, *Les Régions Géographiques de la Tunisie* (Tunis: Publications de l'Université de Tunis, 1981), p. 114.

7. L. Jakobson, *An Illustrative Strategic Plan for Central Tunisia*, Regional Planning and Area Development Project, Country Report no. 6 (Madison: University of Wisconsin, 1981), p. 18.

8. Ibid., p. 16.

9. Ibid., p. 14.

10. H. Attia, "L'Evolution des Structures Sociales et Economiques dans les Hautes Steppes Tunisiennes," *Revue Tunisienne des Sciences Sociales*, no. 6 (1966), p. 28. (translation mine).

11. P. Bonnefant and R. Laudy, "Gammouda: Essor d'un Centre Urbain dans la Steppe Tunisienne," *Revue de l'Institut des Belles Lettres Arabes*, no. 130 (1972), pp. 332-34.

12. H. Attia, *Propositions pour l'Elaboration d'un Plan de Développement Régional pour la Région du Nord Ouest de la Tunisie Centrale* (Tunis: Commissariat Général au Développement Régional, 1982), pp. 12-13.

13. Nellis, "Rural Development, Technical Assistance," p. 16.

14. Ibid.

15. RT/Ministère de l'Agriculture/USAID-Tunis, *An Evaluation of the Area Development Sub-Project: Central Tunisia Development Project* (Tunis, 1981), p. 13.

16. Ibid (end statements in French; translation mine).

17. J. Nellis, "Decentralization in North Africa: Problems of Policy Implementation," in *Decentralization and Development: Policy Implementation in Developing Countries*, eds. G.S. Cheema and D.A. Rondinelli, pp. 127-82 (Beverly Hills: Sage, 1983), p. 165 (emphasis mine).

18. RT/ Ministère de l'Agriculture/USAID, op. cit., p. 4.

19. Nellis, "Rural Development, Technical Assistance," p. 23.

20. P.D. Demongeot, "*The Central Tunisia Rural Development Project: Lessons of Experience*," (Tunis: USAID-Tunis, October 1982), p. 8.

21. RT/MPF, *Note d'Orientation pour le IIIème Décennie de Développment et le VIème Plan* (Tunis, 1980), p. 114.

22. Ibid.

23. Interview with the Commissioner of the CGDR, Tunis, October 5, 1984.

24. Nellis, "Decentralization," p. 165.

25. H. Charrad-Rouissi, "Le Commissariat Général au Développement Régional," *Servir*, nos. 31-32 (1983), pp. 55-81 (see p. 75).

26. J. Nellis, *Decentralization, Regional Development, and Local Public Finance in Tunisia*, Occasional Paper, no. 79, Metropolitan Studies Program, Maxwell School, Syracuse University, March 1984, p. 7.

27. RT/MPF, *Sixth Plan 1982-1986*, p. 191.

28. Ibid., p. 193.

29. Quoted from K.Chamari, "L'Alerte Tunisienne," *Le Monde Diplomatique*, March 1980, p. 19.

30. I.W. Zartman, "Political Elites in Arab North Africa: Origin, Behavior and Prospects," in *Political Elites in Arab North Africa*, eds. I.W. Zartman et al, pp. 1-34 (New York and London: Longman, 1982), p. 27.

31. S. Bessis and S. Belhassen, "Les Elites Tunisiennes," *Jeune Afrique*, nos. 1284-85 (1985), p. 56.

32. Ibid.

33. R. Stone, "Tunisia: A Single Party System Holds Change in Abeyance," in Zartman et al., eds., op cit., pp. 144-76 (see p. 148).

34. M. Camau, "L'Etat Tunisien de la Tutelle au Désengagement," *Maghreb-Machrek*, no. 103 (1984), pp. 8-38.

35. Nellis, "Decentralization," pp. 138-39.

# 7
# CONCLUSIONS: RETHINKING THE REGIONAL QUESTION

Une Région ne doit pas être définie mais reconnue
—Vidal de la Blache

As stated in Chapter 1, the objectives of this study were twofold: (1) to answer the following related questions: why didn't the overall good economic performance of Tunisia during the last three decades benefit all regions of the country, and why have past regional development policies in Tunisia failed? (2) Based on the answers to these two questions, the second objective was to draw some conclusions from the Tunisian case and to provide a new framework for rethinking the "regional question" in Tunisia, and hopefully elsewhere in Africa.

To this end the study was organized in three parts. Part One provided a theoretical discussion of the issues underlying the whole problematic of the study. Adopting an epistemological approach and focusing on Africa, its objective was to look at the evolution of ideas and theories about development in general, and about the question of "transition" in particular at the national and the subnational levels. This allowed us to see why, when and how, "theories" of development were discredited and how, therefore, the question of transition was reopened in the late 1970s. This then led us, to use a Kuhnian terminology, to see very briefly in Chapter 2 some of the major paradigm shifts that occurred in the late 1970s. As this study is concerned mainly with regional disparity and therefore with the issue of the transition at the subnational level, the focus in this brief survey was on those new theories that emerged in response to the failure of modernization theories in general, and to that of traditional spatial top-down strategies in particular. With this discussion, therefore, Part One thus framed the theoretical issues underlying the discussion of Part Two and allowed us to avoid analyzing our "case study" in a vacuum.

Within this theoretical framework, Part Two engaged in discussion of the historical and contemporary roots of the regional question in Tunisia. My effort in this discussion was, by showing the real *causes* of regional underdevelopment in Tunisia today, to maintain a dialectical analytical perspective with the discussion of Part One. In other words, I have tried to avoid a classic and simplistic "policy analysis." The discussion focused on all factors—historical, ideological, political, etc.—that have a fundamental role in the creation and perpetuation of "regional dependency." And that is why, for example, I devoted a whole chapter to the analysis of the historical roots of the "regional question." As we saw in Chapter 2, some of the most important and devastating critiques of the "bourgeois" model of development, as well as of that of the classic Marxist model, is that they are ahistorical. For these two models, non-European societies, as Eric Wolf put it, are "without History." As we also saw, the same criticism has been addressed to orthodox regional science for which a *region* is a pure "economic" space. Beyond, then, the idea, and this is a "vérité de Mr. de La Palice," that we cannot understand the present if we don't understand the past, Chapter 4 is meant to be a direct response to these fallacies. In testing the validity of my first premise, it was clearly shown that regional underdevelopment has nothing to do with "mother nature" but can be *historically* and *politically* explained. It is important to stress this again and again; because not only can our perceptions of the problem change, but, and more important, our answers to the "regional question" depend on this simple truth.

In the same vein, focusing on postcolonial policies, Chapter 5 showed that "Jacobin," top-down strategies, which adopt uncritically the basic—ideological, political, economical, and spatial—tenets of modernization theories, perpetuate the same exploitative structural relationship between social and territorial entities. Beyond the fact that they differ radically in their ideological discourse and economic policies, both regional policies examined in Chapter 5, because they saw in the regional "dependence" created by French colonization as a mere "economic" problem, have avoided any serious historical-political analysis of the regional problem. Adopting, therefore, the "gap approach," they were clearly based on the following stereotypes: Interior = poor, rural; and the people of the interior = peasants, bedouins, nonreceptive to "modern" life, to a "modern" society and economy (i.e., opposed to their exploitation by an urban elite and its State apparatus). This perception of the underdeveloped regions of the interior and their populations, because of its repetition over and over for 30 years, became, as noted by H. Attia, "an apparently objective truth."[1] One of the major contributions of this study is that it has clearly shown how that this is not the case. Rather, regional underdevelopment is fundamentally a political phenomenon, a by-product of given policies, which create it, reduce it or aggravate it. Rather than understanding rural societies and their productive systems, with their rationality and their related spatial organization, "Stalinist-Jacobin" regional policies (whether they adopt capitalist or socialist rhetoric), "help" them by imposing on them policies that in fact, as Chapter 6 showed, perpetuate their domination and exploitation. By demonstrating this, Chapter 6 has very clearly shown, I hope, the true nature of the "regional question" today in Tunisia. And this is the other major contribution, I believe, of this study: to shed new light on this so vital question, in order to end, among other things, "*le temps du mépris*" (the era of despite and contempt), as Attia superbly put it.[2] It is in order to contribute to this that I stressed the need for a radical regional reform. The following section will briefly outline some of its most important elements.

## Rethinking the Regional Question

To begin with, I want to stress in the strongest possible terms that I have no magic recipe or blueprint answer to the "regional question." What this study is all about is precisely that there is no "universal" solution to the problems discussed here. In addition, it would be foolish, and I would say, "arrogant" and "contradictory," for an anti-Stalinist, anti-Jacobin to claim to have *the* answer. If this study succeeds in providing a new perception of the "question," then and only then I would consider that all my efforts were not in vain.

But does this mean that I have nothing to say? Not at all! For example, few years ago, while working on the urbanization of Tunisia and its consequences,[3] I proposed that:

—In order to stop the human "hemorrhaging" that the interior regions have been experiencing for the last three decades, past economic policies must be changed.

—In order to achieve this, I proposed that the 1980s should be declared the decade for the development of all secondary cities of the interior regions, especially the development of their economic base in general, and the industrial sector and all nonfarm activities in particular.

—Finally, I called for a regional policy that would reexamine completely the "regional question."

These proposals, as this study has shown, are more valid than ever. But I must confess that today, because I didn't pay sufficient attention to political factors (I mentioned them in a sentence or two) I find them somehow naive and ineffective. Years of research on this critical issue have convinced me that economic problems must have political solutions. As a political question, the "regional question" must, therefore, have a political answer. And only a radical regional reform that focuses on the redistribution of *power* between the *State* and the *Region* would bring about an acceptable answer.

As we saw in the first section of Chapter 3, the current Tunisian political-administrative system represents a classic anti-democratic, Jacobin system, familiar, as Nellis put it, "to any student of colonial government."[4] I explained in Chapters 3 and 5 some of the reasons that pushed this nondevelopmental system to its paroxysm by an elite which, in the name of a certain conception of "national unity," have used it for its "self-enrichment." This was further illustrated in Chapter 6, where we saw why and how a promising experience of true regional self-development has failed. My conclusions from all this are that the political significance of this failure is that current officials, despite all the rhetoric about decentralization, do not want to hear about the kind of approach that the CTDA has proposed. The creation of the CGDR confirmed this belief, with the return to the gouvernorat as the main operational unit for regional development policy. My other conclusion is that even the word "region" seems to scare the current leadership. For example, in the *Note d'Orientation*, the important document of the Ministry of Plan that I mentioned several times, among the many reforms announced for the Sixth Plan and the Third Decade of Development, administrative reform is considered as the most important. After having clearly admitted (as we saw in Chapter 1 and 3) the inefficiency, the heaviness, and the anonymous, impersonal and sometimes even inhuman character of the Tunisian administrative system, the authors of the *Note* proposed the following:

> The essential then is, first of all, the redistribution of tasks, functions and power, between the three levels (central administration, regional administration and communal administration).[5]

I can't say how much I agree with this. But we are very quickly disappointed when we see the authors, later, say:

> Certain tasks, without being of a national dimension, are beyond the level of the gouvernorat. They can concern a group of gouvernorats or what is conventionally called "region" ....This is the case for universities, dams, highways, specialized hospitals, etc. Do these tasks justify the creation of an additional level between the central administration and the gouvernorat? Should all the external services of central departments be represented at the regional level as well as at the gouvernorats' one? The answer seems to be negative at this stage of decentralization. A superimposition of new structures at the levels of the region and of the gouvernorats would create the risk of competence conflicts and waste of resources. Moreover, a structure at the regional level would take in "tutelage" the gouvernorats composing it and thus would substitute itself to central administration.[6]

As we can see, this is a classic Jacobin argument! It is a constant characteristic of all "technocratic" reforms, which always tend to incorporate the periphery technocratically.[7] Based on this argument, the authors of the *Note* propose:

> The cell at the level of the "region" must not manage. It must not control either. Its main task must be, with the help of the governors of the region and their services, to conceive of the programs and the development strategy for the region....This task can be accomplished by the

"Commissariat au Développement Régional" and its decentralized units.[8]

Here are, very briefly, the major elements of the reform proposed by the *Note d'Orientation*. We have here not only the explanation for the failure of the Central Tunisia Development Project, but the explanation for regional underdevelopment in Tunisia: the refusal by central officials to propose a political solution to a highly political problem . If "*le temps du mépris*" is to be ended, if "national reconciliation" is to become true, we must get away from this kind of argumentation. Solutions exist. And the objective of the last section of Chapter 2 was to show that these are realistic and feasible.[9] But today in Tunisia the sina qua non condition for these or any solutions to be implemented is the clear recognition of the region's right to existence. If this political condition is met then the search for ways to find an adequate redistribution of power between the State and the region and all other sociospatial entities will begin. This would require, of course, further and careful research about the most effective and most democratic possible distribution of power in order to achieve a self regional and local development. What I can, however, propose right now is this:

—To begin with, if the objective of a self regional and local development is to be achieved, we must start from the level of the *commune*. In this respect a "rural commune" must be created. In the current system only urban communes exist. This means that about 48 percent of the Tunisian population are governed by the administration (the *délégués* and the *omdas*, appointed officials). These new rural communes, along with the existing urban communes (the number of which must be extended), would constitute the foundation of the whole system. Then we have the délégations and the gouvernorats, which have to be transformed into democratic (independent from the administration) and, thus, developmental territorial entities. A group of gouvernorats would then constitute a *region*. There are six "economic" (for planning purposes) regions currently. They must be transformed into real socioeconomic entities; they don't need to be invented or defined. All they need is to be *recognized.* They have existed for hundreds of years. They are more than a "pure economic space." They have historical, cultural and geographical existence. Instead of spending money (not to mention the waste of time) in fussy studies defining them, I propose simply to recognize them as history has made them.

—This recognition of the regions and of their rights to existence, in addition to the creation of rural communes and the transformation of the other entities into democratic and developmental sociospatial territorial units, would consequently, among other things, imply that the whole current fiscal and planning system has to change too. In order to transform all these communities, from the rural/urban communes to the regions, into real democratic, effective sociospatial entities, a "bottom-up" fiscal and planning system must replace the current one. This would end the current "charitable" redistributional system from above and would allow the new territorial entities to have a first-hand control over their resources and the ways to use them.

—The fundamental objective of the regional reform proposed here is to create political-territorial structures of a federalist type that would guarantee, first, a system of reciprocal obligations between the different sociospatial entities, as well as the stability of the whole system by getting rid of, once for all, a system that, after 30 years of independence, disintegrated the unity and began to seriously threaten the stability of the country.

—Now what is left to the State? may argue the "unshakeable" Jacobin! My answer: to the commune, communal affairs; to the délégation and the gouvernorat, délégation and gouvernorat affairs; to the region, regional affairs. To the State?—national affairs! What else?! There is so much to do that I do not see how and why the State, (and the Party!) must put its nose in others' affairs. If we had had a federalist structure, the defense, foreign trade, and foreign policy, to mention just a few (all areas, by the way, that none of the other structures can, or in any case, should, take care of) of Tunisia would be in better shape today (see Chapter 3)! Therefore, the historical reform I call for today, is not intended at all to suppress the State, but rather to reduce it to its necessary, and inevitable, minimum.

These are, very briefly, the major elements of the regional reform that this study calls for in order to get away from today's regional disparities dilemmas.

Now, and I can hear it, Jacobin and Stalinists alike would argue: "You Proudhonists are hopeless! Always coming up with the same eclectic foolishness";[10] or that "...regional equality requires a strong centralized socialist State with strong redistributive powers."[11]

What I can say to this, more than what I tried to say in my concluding remarks about the critique of the new approaches I reviewed in Chapter 2. I really don't know how to explain to "unshakeable" Jacobin-Stalinists that the issue is not to replace "Humpty-Dumpty" with "Dumpty Humpty" (or "Blanc-Bonnet" with "Bonnet-Blanc!") but to suggest a political approach to a political question that seeks first of all to reconcile an African country with its great societal communal traditions through regional pluralism and decentralized local development. It is an approach that, as Ahmed Baba Miské put it, seeks to build for a society "a system that it is rooted in the very life of this society in its realities and felt as its own."[12] Is a "strong centralized socialist State" a guarantee to more justice, to self-regional and local development and above all to what John Agnew has recently called a "strong democracy?"[13] But of course, for "bureaucrats," approaches that advocate changes from "below" (as those we saw in Chapter 2), rather than from "above," are not developmerit, but rather, a new and unacceptable form of "utopianism." The debate will continue.

## NOTES

1. H. Attia, *Propositions pour l'Elaboration d'un Plan de Développement Régional pour la Région du Centre-Ouest de la Tunisie Centrale* (Tunis: Commissariat Général au Développement Régional, 1982), p. 1.

2. H. Attia, *Proposition pour l'Elaboration d'un Plan de Développement Régional pour la Région du Nord-Ouest de la Tunisie* (Tunis: Commissariat Général au Développement Régional, 1983), p. 14.

3. E. Moudoud, "L'Urbanisation et la Politique du Logement Social en Tunisie," MA Thesis, Institut d'Urbanisme de l'Académie de Paris, Université de Paris VIII, May 1980, pp. 115-19.

4. J. Nellis, "Decentralization in North Africa: Problems of Policy Implementation," in *Decentralization and Development: Policy Implementation in Developing Countries*, edited by G.S. Cheema and D.A. Rondinelli (Beverly Hills, CA: Sage, 1983), p. 159.

5. RT/MPF, *Note d'Orientation pour la IIIème Décennie de Développement et le VIème Plan* (Tunis, 1980), pp. 11-12.

6. Ibid, p. 14.

7. The literature is vast on this issue, especially in French. But to mention just a few: J. Martay, *La Région pour un Etat Moderne* (Paris: Eds. France Empire, 1969); J.J. Servan-Schreiber, *Le Pouvoir Régional* (Paris: Grasset, 1971); R. Lafont, *Décoloniser en France* (Paris: Gallimard, 1971); R. Dulong, *Les Régions, L'Etat et la Société Locale* (Paris: PUF, 1978); J.F. Gravier, *Paris et le Désert Français* (Paris: Flammarion, 1972); in 1981, the French review, *Pouvoirs*, devoted an entire issue to "Régions." Among the many very interesting articles that best illustrate the debate between Jacobin ideas and their critiques see: J. Hayward, "Incorporer la Péripherie: L'Essor et la Chute de la Régionalisation Fonctionnelle en France," *Pouvoirs*, no. 19 (1981), pp. 103-18; V. Wright, "Questions d'un Jacobin Anglais aux Régionalistes Français," *Pouvoirs*, no. 19 (1981), pp. 119-30.

8. RT/MPF, op. cit., p. 14.

9. Some other examples of solutions are found in T. Michalon, *Quel Etat pour l'Afrique?* (Paris: L'Harmattan, 1984).

10. In a recent article, C. Weaver gives an overview of these typical Jacobin-Stalinist arguments. See his "Romance of the Roses: A Discourse on the Path to Regional Reconstruction," *Society and Space*, no. 2 (1985), p 249).

11. Ibid., p. 244.

12. A.B. Miské, *Lettre Ouverte aux Elites du Tiers-Monde* (Paris: Ed. Le Sycomore, 1981), p. 87.

13. John Agnew, *The Intellectual Devaluation of Place and the Possibility of Strong Democracy*, Occasional Paper Series, no. 5, Center for the Study of Citizenship, Maxwell School, Syracuse University, October 1985.

# EPILOGUE

Since the study for this book was completed in 1986, an historical event, the lasting consequences of which cannot yet be fully envisioned, has occurred in Tunisia: the deposition of President Habib Bourguiba by his Prime Minister Zine El Abidine Ben Ali on the night of November 6-7, 1987. In what follows, a few remarks will be made on this event—a turning-point in the post-independence history of Tunisia[1], as it relates to the substance of this study.

First and foremost, a few words must be said about the reasons that compelled Prime Minister Ben Ali to remove President Bourguiba. As it was widely reported, it is true that what triggered the "constitutional coup," as it was called by most of the press[2], is the quasi obsession of the former president with the Islamic threat and his pressing demands of first, a new trial of 90 militants of the "Mouvement de la Tendance Islamique" (MTI), and second, and especially, that a number of them, including Mr. Rached Gannouchi, the "Emir" of the MTI, should be hanged[3]. All of this is of course true. And in this perspective, there is no doubt that Prime Minister Ben Ali's swift move has saved the country from a bloody civil war, the consequences of which cannot be imagined.

Having said that, I still believe, however, that the real reasons that compelled Prime Minister Ben Ali to act, reportedly with the support of the moderate wing of the ruling P.S.D. and the backing of the military, are far more important and much more complex, as this book has attempted to show. In my view, the Islamist militants' retrial was simply, so to speak, the "final straw" that triggered the "Revolution du Jasmin" as Tunisians have called it.

President Bourguiba was removed, I believe, because he was, and has been in years since, the major obstacle to the urgent and radical reforms that the profound crisis, inherited from the Nouira period, called for. A crisis, the aggravation of which, since—first, the general strike of January 1978, then, the "Gafsa Affair" of January 1980, and finally the "Bread Revolt" of December-January 1984—has seriously threatened the stability and unity of the country.

This view is strongly supported now by all the events and news we received from Tunisia during the last nine months or so. For example, and in his first public statement as president, known now as the "Declaration of November," President Ben Ali, in a national radio broadcast where he announced his takeover to the Tunisian people, revealed the reasons that compelled him to act in these terms:

> The age in which we live can no longer permit a presidency for life nor automatic succession as head of state from which

> the people are excluded. Our people are worthy of a developing and institutionalized political life, founded in reality on a multi-party system and plurality of popular organization[4].

And that is why he adds, the revision of the constitution has become today "an imperative." In a recent interview to the French daily news Le Monde, the new president revealed in more explicit terms the reasons that forced him to act:

> Since my return to the Ministry of Interior in 1984, or what was called the bread revolt, I witnessed the degeneration of the state. The institutions were dismantled or emptied of their substance. The country was thus plunged in a quasi-anarchy and to the development of violence[5].

Then, and after he listed all the factors that contributed the most to the dislocation of the Tunisian society, the new president summarizes in one sentence the tragedy that the majority of Tunisians were living during the last decade or so: "We were ashamed of our country[6]," said he. No single word here about the Islamic threat, except when talking about the senility and erratic behavior of the former president (which rendered his removal constitutionally possible as article 57 of the constitution stipulates), he says:

> The country was not governed and it was running the risk to become more so. I was also witnessing the unmeasured development of the repressive obsession of this man who was a great politician. In a like manner he insisted to retry the Islamists in order to obtain their death. I was terribly sad for my country and for this man who was, no question about it, a great leader and a prestigious head of state[7].

In brief, here are what I believe the real reasons behind the "Revolution du Jasmin" which was met with widespread support and sight of relief, for it has permitted the country to move into the post-Bourguiba era without a drop of blood shed, as it was feared by many.

Now, how may this historical event relate to the substance of this study? The significant question for us here, of course, is how the ongoing radical changes in the Tunisian political system will affect directly or indirectly the regional question, the major concern of this book?

I think that the best way to answer these questions is to look first at the nature of the concrete actions undertaken so far by the new leadership to fulfill its promises of democratization as outlined in the "Declaration of November," and second, to try to evaluate their impact on the current political situation of Tunisia.

The concrete actions undertaken by the new leadership so far (at the time of this writing) are numerous[8].. I will therefore present only the most important of them.

To begin with, between November 8, 1987 and July 22, 1988, nearly 7,000 political and common law prisoners were granted amnesty. Among these were Mr. Habib Achour, leader of the "Union Generale des Travailleurs Tunisiens" (UGTT), the most important Labor Union in Tunisia (November); Mr. Ahmed Mestiri, leader of a legalized opposition political party, the "Mouvement des Démocrates Socialistes" (December); Mr. Mohamed Mzali, the former Prime Minister between April 1980 and July 1986 (December); Mr. Khemais Chamari, the Secretary General of the Tunisian League of Human Rights (January 1988); and finally in May 1988, two pardons of a particular significance: first that of Mr. Ahmed Ben Salah, with whom the reader of this book is now familiar, and who returned in Tunisia last June after 15 years in exile; then that of Mr. Rached Gannouchi, the leader of the MTI.

The second set of actions undertaken by the new leadership that further translate its commitment towards national reconciliation and the democratization of the regime, are first, the abolition by a law, ratified by the Chamber of Deputies on December 1987, of the State Security Court. Then, on March 8, 1988, and as promised in the "Declaration of November," the submission to the Chamber of Deputies of a constitutional reform bill dismantling the "presidency for life" (introduced by the former president in 1974) and the automatic succession of the president by the prime minister, the limitation of the presidential mandates to three mandates in all, and the age of the president to 70 at maximum. The bill was adopted on July 12, 1988. Finally, and with regard to this particular issue, President Ben Ali announced, in the interview to Le Monde mentioned earlier, that there will be anticipated presidential as well as parliamentary elections in November 1989, fulfilling therefore the wishes of the opposition parties to give to the people the opportunity to express their choice and not to wait until the current presidential mandate ends in 1992.

Right in line with this democratization process, engaged firmly by the new leadership, three major new laws of a capital importance for the political life and habits of Tunisia, have been passed. First, on April 26, 1988, a law regulating the organization of the new multi-party system has been passed with the proviso that no party can be organized on the basis of language, race or religion (excluding therefore, for the moment, the "Mouvement de la Tendance Islamique"). More recently (in July) two new parties ("Le Parti Social pour le Progrés" and "Le Rassemblement Socialiste Progressiste") have been authorized. The second law, concerning the freedom of the press and the third, the freedom of association, were both promulgated by the Chambers of Deputies on July 21, 1988. These two laws will place the press and associative life under the jurisdiction of the courts and not under that of the government (Ministry of Interior) as was the case before November 1987.

Last but not least, the final concrete action I would like to mention concerns the restructuring by the new leadership of the fossilized P.S.D., in power for 32 years, which has been transformed through this process in February 1988, into the "Rassemblement Constitutionnel Democratique." This move has been interpreted as a clear determination of President Ben Ali to rejuvenate the party and to open it to all Tunisians, especially the youth. This, in addition, has been followed in July 1988, few days before the extraordinary conference of the party (called by the way, the "Conference of Salvation," "Le Congres du Salut"), by an important reshuffling of the cadres of the party and the administration at the gouvernorats and the delegations levels.

Finally, on the economic front, soon after the removal of President Bourguiba, the current Seventh Five Year Plan (1987-1992) was slightly revised and, interestingly, more attention was paid to: unemployment, agriculture and.regional and rural development. Furthermore, and despite the declared commitment of the new leadership to pursue the very unpopular and I.M.F.-World Bank inspired "structural adjustment" economic program (which was at the origins of the "Bread Revolt" in 1984, but has, however, been continued by the Sfar's government—July 1986-October 1987), minimum wages have been increased by 5% in April 1988. Notwithstanding the fact that this increase will not of course compensate for inflation, it should be remembered, however, that this measure concerns about two million or near 20% of the Tunisian population, most of them in the rural areas of the interior.

To sum up, these are therefore some of the concrete actions that, at the time of writing, signal very clearly I think, that the country is finally heading in the right direction. Of course, it is impossible to predict what may happen in a year or two. And one may reasonably ask: how far is the new leadership willing to go in the right direction? How far will it be willing to accept being challenged on its left and, especially, on its right? Is it willing to accept and to respect the popular verdict in November 1989—in other words, the principal of alternation, the foundation of any true democracy? How long it will be able to pursue its political liberalization while maintaining the harsh and very unpopular "structural adjustment" economic policy?

It is impossible to answer these questions with certainty at this stage. One can only speculate. But, and as far as the regional question is concerned, I can only say this: since November 1987, a new situation has been created; a new dynamic in which all hopes are now permitted. And what we have here is not only the "spirit of the reforms," but the reforms themselves. What has been accomplished in just nine months, the previous regime refused to do for 32 years. What we are seeing today in Tunisia is not just the replacement of "Humpty Dumpty" by "Dumpty Humpty" (or "Blanc Bonnet" par "Bonnet Blanc") but the beginning of a new era: the post-Bourguiba era. An era where peaceful solutions are finally possible. An era in which at last national reconciliation and the consolidation of national unity became suddenly in reach. And it is in this new environment that the historical regional reform that this book has called for can no longer appear less "realistic," less "feasible" than all what we have seen for the last nine months. It is matter of conviction and will. Who would have believed, a year ago, that Tunisia would undergo a peaceful transition to the post-Bourguiba era? But it has happened. My final remark, in this regard, is that the new leadership has no other alternative than to continue in the right direction, if the new spirit of optimism created by the "Revolution du Jasmin" is to continue, if national reconciliation is to advance further and if, and as far as the regional question is concerned, the danger of a radical separatism is to be totally eliminated. Otherwise, I sincerely believe that the root causes of the explosive situation that prevailed before November 1987 will not be eliminated and that the country will again be facing the same threats and perhaps, as Mr Ben Salah has recently put it in an interview to Africa Report a few weeks before his return to Tunisia,:

> We don't want this change to be condemned to failure because this would have serious repercussions for the future. If there is no real change in the style of power, and Tunisian people cannot democratically participate in shaping the future of their country, then disillusionment will set in. This could turn very quickly to despair and lead to violence. A group of Tunisians were intelligently able to eliminate Bourguiba, but if nothing changes, there are many other intelligent Tunisians who can in turn eliminate them. And that's what we want to avoid because it could lead to an endless cycle of violence[9].

It must be hoped that the new leadership will therefore continue in the right direction and that all those who feel threatened in their power and their privileges by "La Revolution du Jasmin" and would be attempted therefore to undermine it, would very carefully listen to Mr. Ben Salah's fear. It is the only way for Tunisia to overcome the challenges of the post-Bourguiba era.

## NOTES

1. President Habib Bourguiba is the first, and only, president of Tunisia since independence of the country from France in 1956. In 1974, he changed the constitution in order to become "president for life."

2. Referring here to the invocation by Prime Minister Ben Ali of Article 57, which allows the Prime Minister to succeed automatically the President in the event that the later, for whatever reasons, can no longer assume the duties of head of State.

3. A few words of background are necessary here. Following a period of almost one year of direct confrontation between the government and the M.T.I. that culminated in the Spring of 1987 by a massive crackdown on the M.T.I., 90 of its militants, including its leader Mr. Rached Gannouchi, were arrested and brought to trial on August 1987, on the charges, among others things, of conspiring with the Iranians to overthrow by violence Mr. Bourguiba's regime. The trial, and the fear that most of the 90 militants of the M.T.I. could face the death penalty, if convicted, became the major concern of all Tunisians and the focus of international attention, especially among the friends and allies of the Bourguiba's regime, for this would have plunged the country in a bloody civil war. But, and despite the clear desire of the former president to obtain the heads of the M.T.I.'s militants, the State Security Court rendered on September 27, 1987, an unexpected verdict: seven of the accused were sentenced to death, and the "Emir" of the M.T.I., Mr. Gannouchi received a sentence of forced labor in perpetuity. Tunisia was relieved. But President Bourguiba was furious, and threatened to dismiss the president of the State Security Court and insisted that the M.T.I.'s militants be retried and that at least 16 of them, including Mr. Gannouchi, should be hanged.

4. Quoted from the *New York Times*, November 10, 1987. For the French version of the Declaration, see *Jeune Afrique*, November 18, 1987, No. 1402.

5. *Le Monde*, of September 10, 1988 (translation mine)

6. Ibid.

7. Ibid.

8. For an overview and a detailed chronology of these measures undertaken so far see the following: *Jeune Afrique*: No. 1421, March 1988; No.1434, June 1988; No.1440, August, 1988; *Le Monde*: March 1 and 10, 1988; May 17,1988; June 18,1988; July 22, 24-25, 28, 30, 1988; August 1 and 29, 1988; and September 10,1988. See also the Economist Intelligence

Unit, *Quarterly Economic Review of Tunisia and Malta.Country Report, No.1* (London: The Economist,1988).

9. See *Africa Report*, Vol.33, No.3, May-June 1988, pp.56-59.

## BIBLIOGRAPHY


Abou Tarak. "Tunisie: la Satellisation." *Les Temps Modernes*, no. 375 bis (1977), pp. 95-112.

Abu-Lughod, J. *Rabat: Urban Apartheid in Morocco*. Princeton, NJ: Princeton University Press, 1980.

Adedej, A. "Foreign Debt and Prospects for Growth in Africa during the 1980s." *Journal of Modern African Studies*, no. 1 (1985), pp. 53-74.

Agence de Promotion des Investissements. *1973-1983: Une Décennie au Service du Développement Industriel de la Tunisie*. Tunis: API, 1984.

Agnew, John. "Technology Transfer and Theories of Development: Conceptual Issues in the South Asian Context." *Journal of Asian and African Studies*, nos. 1-2 (1982), pp. 16-31.

Agnew, J. and Moudoud, E.: "Modernization Theories, African Development Plans and the Question of Transition," *Cultures et Developpement*, no. 1, 1985, pp. 71-96.

_________. *The Intellectual Devaluation of Place and the Possibility of "Strong Democracy."* Occasional Paper Series, no. 5. Center for the Study of Citizenship, Maxwell School, Syracuse University, October 1985.

Amin, Samir. *Le Développement du Capitalisme en Côte d'Ivoire*. Paris: Les Editions de Minuit, 1967.

_________. *Croissance et Développement*. Douala: Publications de l'Institut Panafricain de Développement, 1971.

_________. *Unequal Development: An Essay on the Social Formations of Peripheral Capitalism*. New York and London: Monthly Review Press, 1976.

_________. "A Critique of the World Bank Report Entitled 'Accelerated Development in Sub-Saharan Africa.'" *Africa Development*, nos. 1-2 (1982), pp. 23-30.

_________. "Expansion or Crisis of Capitalism?" *Third World Quarterly*, no. 2 (1983), pp. 360-80.

Apthorpe, R. "Peasants and Planistrators: Rural Cooperatives in Tunisia." *The Maghreb Review*, no. 1 (1977), pp. 1-18.

Asamoa, A. "On Bourgeois Development Theory: A Critique of Behrendt." *Africa Development*, no. 3 (1982), pp. 87-108.

Ashford, D. "Organization of Cooperatives and the Structures of Power in Tunisia." *The Journal of Developing Areas*, no. 1 (1967), pp. 317-32.

Attia, H. "L'Evolution des Structures Sociales et Economiques dans les Hautes Steppes Tunisiennes." *Revue Tunisienne des Sciences Sociales*, no. 6 (1966), pp. 5-41.

_________. "L'Urbanisation de la Tunisie." *Revue Tunisienne des Sciences Sociales*, nos. 28-29 (1972), pp. 9-32.

________. *Propositions pour l'Elaboration d'un Plan de Développement Régional pour la Région du Centre-Ouest de la Tunisie Centrale.* Tunis: Commissariat Générale au Développement Régional, 1982.

________. *Propositions pour l'Elaboration d'un Plan de Développement Régional pour la Région du Nord-Ouest de la Tunisie.* Tunis: Commissariat Générale au Développement Régional, 1983.

Avineri, S. *Karl Marx on Colonialism and Modernization.* New York: Anchor Books, 1969.

Aydalot, Ph. "La Structuration de l'Espace Economique Tunisien." *Revue Tunisienne des Sciences Sociales*,no. 5 (1966), pp. 65-93.

Baduel, P.R. "Gafsa Comme Enjeu." *Annuaire de l'Afrique du Nord* 19 (1980): 485-511.

Bahroun, S. "La Plannification: Outils et Techniques." In *La Politique Economique de la Tunisie*, edited by Ecole Nationale d'Administration, pp. 57-112. Tunis and Paris: Centre de Recherche et d'Etudes Administratives, 1974.

Bassett, A., et al. *Initiation à la Tunisie.* Paris: Adrien-Maisonneuve, 1950.

Bdira, M. *Relations Internationales et Sous-Développement: la Tunisie 1857-1864.* Uppsala: Almquist and Wiksell International, 1978.

Béji, H. *Désenchantement National. Essai sur le Décolonisation.* Paris: Maspero, 1982.

Belhadi, A. *Le Chemin de Fer et l'Espace Tunisien.* Tunis: Publications de l'Université de Tunis, 1980.

________. "Le Programme de Développement Rural: Les Illusions et la Realité." *Revue Tunisienne de Géographie*, no. 7 (1981), pp. 9-45.

Belhassen, S. "Kasserine ou le Sud Oublié." *Jeune Afrique Economie*, no. 61 (April 1985), pp. 97-106.

________. "Tunisie: Un Métro Nommé Scandale." *Jeune Afrique*, no. 1306 (1986), pp. 43-46.

Benachenou, A. "La Coopération Sud-Sud: Le Plan Lagos et l'Indépendance de l'Afrique." *Africa Development*, nos. 1-2 (1982), pp. 6-22.

Ben Achour, Y., and Moussa, F. "Réformes, Election Municipales et Discours Décentralisateur en Tunisie." *Annuaire de L'Afrique du Nord.* vol. 16. Paris: Editions du CNRS, 1979.

Bennouna, N. "Primary Capital Accumulation in Colonial Tunisia." *Dialectical Anthropology*, no. 2 (1979), pp. 87-88.

Ben Salem, L. "L'Encadrement des Unités de Production Agricole." *Revue Tunisienne des Sciences Sociales*, no. 26 (1971), p. 115-62.

Berdoulay, V. *La Formation de l'Ecole Française de Géographie (1870-1914).* Paris: Bibliothèque Nationale, 1981.

Bernard, A. "Afrique du Nord." In *Géographie Universelle*, edited by P. Vidal de la Blache and L. Gallois, vol. 11, pp. 1-284. Paris: Armand Colin, 1937.

Bernard, Ch., ed. *La Politique de l'Emploi-Formation au Maghreb 1970-1980*. Paris: Centre National de la Recherche Scientifique, 1982.

Berry, B.J.L., ed. *Urbanization and Counter-Urbanization*. Beverly Hills: Sage, 1976.

Bessis, S., and Belhassen, S. "Les Elites Tunisiennes," *Jeune Afrique*, nos. 1284-85 (1985), p. 51-65.

Bonnefant, P. "Béjà, de la Conquête Musulmane à 1881." *Revue de L'Institut des Belles Lettres Arabes*, no. 127 (1971), pp. 3-33.

Bonnefant, P., and Laudy, R. "Gammouda: Essor d'un Centre Urbain dans la Steppe Tunisienne," *Revue de l'Institut des Belles Lettres Arabes*, no. 130 (1972), pp. 332-34.

Boudeville, R.J. *Les Espaces Economique*. Paris: PUF, 1961.

________. *Problems of Regional Economic Planning*. Edinburgh: Edinburgh University Press, 1966.

Brant, E.D. *Railways of North Africa*. Newton Abbot: David and Charles Publishers, 1971).

Braudel, F. *The Mediterranean and the Mediterranean World in the Age of Philip II*. vol. 1. London: Collins, 1972.

British Government, Naval Intelligence Division. *Tunisia*. Geographical Handbook Series. Oxford: Oxford and Cambridge University Presses, 1945.

Brookfield, H. *Interdependent Development*. London: Methuen, 1975.

Brutzkus, E. "Centralized Versus Decentralized Patterns of Urbanization in Developing Countries: An Attempt to Elucidate A Guideline Principle." *Economic Development and Cultural Change* 23, no. 4 (1975): 633-52.

Bugnicourt, J. *Disparités Régionales et Aménagement du Territoire en Afrique*. Paris: Armand Colin, 1974.

Bujra, A. "Editorial Note." *Africa Development*, nos. 1-2 (1982), pp. I-VI.

Camau, M. "Le Discours Politique de Légitimité des Elites Tunisiennes." *Annuaire de l'Afrique du Nord*. vol. 10. Paris: Editions du CNRS, 1972.

________. "L'Etat Tunisien de la Tutelle au Désengagement." *Maghreb-Machrek*, no. 103 (1984), pp. 8-38.

Cao-Pinna, V. "Regional Policy in Italy." In *Public Policy and Regional Economic Development: The Experience of Nine Western Countries*, edited by N. Hansen, pp. 137-79. Cambridge: MA: Ballinger, 1974.

Chaker, M. "La Problématique de la Régionalisation en Tunisie." *Servir*, nos. 25-26 (1980), pp. 7-26.

Chamari, K. "L'Alerte Tunisienne." *Le Monde Diplomatique*, no. 312 (March 1980).

Charraod-Rouissi, H. "Le Commissariat Générale au Développement Régional." *Servir*, nos. 31-32 (1983), pp. 55-81.

Cheema, G.S., and Rondinelli, D., eds. *Decentralization and Development: Policy Implementation in Developing Countries*. Beverly Hills: Sage, 1983.

Chesnaux, J. "Le Mode de Production Asiatique. Quelques Perspectives de Recherche." *La Pensée*, no. 114 (1964), pp. 35-55.

Chipaux, Françoise. "Intrigues et Disgrâce au Palais de Carthage." *Le Monde*, January 20, 1986.

Conroy, M. "Rejection of Growth Center Strategy in Latin America Regional Development Planning." *Land Economics*, no. 4 (1973), pp. 371-80.

Coquery-Vidrovitch, C. "L'Afrique Coloniale Française et la Crise de 1930: Crise Structurelle et Génèse du Sous-Développement." *Revue Française d'Histoire d'Outre-Mer*, nos. 232-233 (1976), p. 395.

Corragio, J.L. "Polarization, Development and Integration." In *Regional Development and Planning: International Perspectives*, edited by A. Kuklinski, pp. 353-74. Leyden: Sijthoff, 1975.

COSDERIA. "Accelerated Development in Sub-Saharan Africa: An Assessment by the OAU, ECA, and ADB Secretariats." *Africa Development*, no. 3 (1982), p. 109-37.

________. "Declaration of Tripoli on the World Bank Report Entitled 'Accelerated Development in Sub-Saharan Africa: An Agenda for Action.'" *Africa Development*, no. 3 (1982), p. 137-38.

Darkoh, M. "Growth Poles and Growth Centers with Special Reference to Developing Countries—A Critique." *Journal of Tropical Geography*, no. 44 (1977), pp. 12-22.

Darwent, D.F. "Growth Poles and Growth Centers in Regional Planning: A Review." *Environment and Planning*, no. 1 (1969), pp. 5-31.

De Epalza, M., and Petit, R. *Etudes sur les Moriscos Andalous en Tunisie*. Tunis: Société Tunisienne de Diffusion, 1973.

Demongeot, P.D. *The Central Tunisia Rural Development Project: Lessons of Experience*. Tunis: USAID-Tunis, 1982.

De Souza, A.R., and Porter, Ph.W. *The Underdevelopment and the Modernization of the Third World*. Comm. of College Geography, Resource Papers, no. 28. Washington, DC: Association of American Geographers, 1974.

Despois, J. *L'Afrique du Nord*. Paris: Payot, 1949.

DeViney, S., and Crowley, J. "Universality of Modernization: An Empirical Critique." *Studies in Comparative International Development*, no. 2 (1978), pp. 23-39.

Djait, H. "Tunisie: Dérive ou Renouveau." *Jeune Afrique*, no. 1207 (1984), pp. 42-44; no. 1208 (1984), pp. 32-33.

Dlala, H. "Développement Economique et Action Régionale en Tunisie." *Revue Tunisienne de Géographie*, no. 6 (1980), pp. 67-85.

________ *L'Economie Industrielle dans les Villes-Ports du Nord-Est Tunisien*. Tunis: Publications de l'Université de Tunis, 1981.

Dulong, R. *Les Regions, L'Etat et la Societe Locale*. Paris: PUF, 1978.

Dumont, D. *Paysanneries aux Abois*. Paris: Le Seuil, 1972.

Durieu, Y. *L'Impossible Regionalisation Capitaliste: Temoignages de Fos et du Languedoc*. Paris: Ed. Anthropos, 1973.

Economist Intelligence Unit. *Quarterly Economic Review of Libya, Tunisia and Malta. Annual Supplement 1982*. London: The Economist, 1982.

________. *Quarterly Economic Review of Tunisia and Malta*. no. 3. London: The Economist, 1985.

El Manoubi, K. "Le Pole Industriel de Gabes et Son Impact sur le Developpement du Sud Tunisien." *Revue Tunisienne des Sciences Sociales*, nos. 48-49 (1977), pp. 115-36.

Entelis, J.P. *Comparative Politics of North Africa*. Syracuse, NY: Syracuse University Press, 1980.

Fakhfakh, M., et al. *Atlas of Tunis*. Paris: Editions Jeune Afrique, 1979.

Federation Anarchiste de Paris. *Centralisme and Federalisme*. Paris: Publications de la Federation Anarchiste, 1983.

Findlay, A. "Tunisia: The Vicissitudes of Economic Development." In *North Africa: Contemporary Politics and Economic Development*, edited by R. Lawless and A. Findlay, pp. 217-40. London: Croom Helm/New York: St. Martin's Press, 1984.

Findlay, A., et al. *Tunisia*. World Bibliographical Series. vol. 33. Oxford: Clio Press, 1982.

Frank, Andre G. *Latin America: Underdevelopment or Revolution*. New York: Monthly Review Press, 1969.

Frey, M.G., ed. *Freedom and Change*. Toronto: MacMelland, 1975.

Friedmann, John. "A Spatial Framework for Rural Development: Problems of Organization and Implementation." *Economie Appliquee*, nos. 2-3 (1975), pp. 519-44.

________. "Basic Needs, Agropolitan Development, and Planning from Below." *World Development*, no. 6 (1979), pp. 607-13.

________. "The Active Community: Toward a Political-Territorial Framework for Rural Development in Asia." *Economic Development and Cultural Change*, no. 2 (1981), pp. 235-61.

________. *Urban Bias in Regional Development Policy*. School of Architecture and Urban Planning, UCLA Working Paper, CU 29, 1981.

________. "Regional Planning for Rural Mobilization in Africa." *Rural Africana*, nos. 12-13 (1982), pp. 3-20.

________. "Political and Technical Moments in Development: Agropolitan Development Revisited." *Society and Space*, no. 2 (1985), pp. 155-67.

Friedmann, John, and Alonso, W., eds. *Regional Development and Planning: A Reader*. Cambridge, MA: MIT Press, 1964.

________. *Regional Policy: Readings in Theory and Applications.* Cambridge, MA: MIT Press, 1975.

Friedmann, J., and Douglas, M. "Agropolitan Development: Towards a New Strategy for Regional Planning in Asia." In *Growth Pole Strategy and Regional Development Policy: Asian Experience and Alternative Approaches*, edited by F. Lo and K. Salih, pp. 163-92. Oxford: Pergamon Press, 1978.

Friedmann, John, and Weaver, Clyde. *Territory and Function: The Evolution of Regional Planning*. Berkeley and Los Angeles: University of California Press, 1979.

Gabsi [pseud.]. "Le Vent a Tourne en Tunisie." *Jeune Afrique*, no. 1295 (October 1985), p. 36.

Ganiage, J. *Les Origines du Protectorat Francais en Tunisie*. Paris: Press Universitaires de France, 1959.

Gauthier, E.F. *L'Islamisation de l'Afrique du Nord: Les Siecles Obscurs du Maghreb*. Paris: Payot, 1927.

Gilbert, A., ed. *Development Planning and Spatial Structure*. London: Wiley, 1976.

Gilbert, A., and Gugler, J. *Cities, Poverty and Development: Urbanization in the Third World*. Oxford: Oxford University Press, 1982.

Gonidec, P.F. *Les Systemes Politiques Africains*. Paris: Librairie Generale de Droit et de Jurisprudence, 1978.

Gore, Ch. *Regions in Question: Space, Development Theory and Regional Planning*. London and New York: Methuen, 1984.

Granotier, B. *La Planete des Bidonvilles: Perspectives de l'Explosion Urbaine dans les Pays du Tiers-Monde*. Paris: Le Seuil, 1980.

Gravier, J.F. *Paris et le Desert Francais: Decentralisation, Equipement, Population*. Paris: Le Portulan, 1947 (Reprinted as *Paris et le Desert Francaise en 1972*. Paris: Flammarion, 1972).

________. *La Question Regionale*. Paris: Flammarion, 1972.

Guen, M. *La Cooperation de l'Etat en Tunisie*. Tunis: UGTT, 1964.

Gurvitch, G. *Proudhon, Sa Vie, Son Oeuvre*. Paris: PUF, 1965.

________. "Proudhon et Marx." *Cahiers Internationaux de Sociologie* (January-June 1966), pp. 7-17.

Hansen, N. *French Regional Planning*. Bloomington: Indiana University Press, 1968.

________, ed. *Human Settlement Systems*. New York: Ballinger, 1977.

Hayward, J. "Incorporer la Peripherie: l'Essor et la Chute de Regionalisation Fonctionelle en France." *Pouvoirs*, no. 19 (1981), pp. 103-18.

Hermassi, E. *Leadership and National Development in North Africa*. Berkeley: University of California Press, 1972.

________. *The Third World Reassessed*. Berkeley: University of California, 1980.

Higgins, B. "Development Poles: Do They Exist?" In *Growth Pole Strategy and Regional Development Policy: Asian Experiences and Alternative Approaches*, edited by F. Lo and K. Salih, pp. 229-43. Oxford: Pergamon Press, 1978.

Hirschman, A.O. *The Strategy of Economic Development*. New Haven, CT: Yale University Press, 1958.

Holland Stuart. *Capital Versus the Regions*. London: Macmillan, 1976.

________. *The Regional Problem*. New York: St. Martin's Press, 1976.

Holt, P.M., et al., eds. *The Cambridge History of Islam: The Further Islamic Lands, Islamic Society and Civiliza-tion*. vol. 2. London: Cambridge University Press, 1970.

Hoogvelt, A. *The Sociology of Developing Societies*. London: Macmillan, 1979.

Hopkins, N. *Social Soundness Analysis: A Report on Central Tunisia Rural Development Project*. Tunis: USAID, 1978.

Hyden, G. *Beyond Ujamaa. Underdevelopment and Uncaptured Peasantry*. Berkeley: University of California Press, 1980.

Illich, I. *Liberer l'Avenir*. Paris: Ed. du Seuil, 1971.

________. *La Convivialite*. Paris: Ed. du Seuil, 1973.

Inkeles, A. "The Modernization of Man." In *Urbanism in World Perspective: A Reader*, edited by S. Fara, pp. 360-69. New York: TY Crowell, 1968.

Inkeles, A., and Smith, D.H. *Becoming Modern*. Cambridge, MA: Harvard University Press, 1974.

Jakobson, L. *An Illustrative Strategic Plan for Central Tunisia*. Regional Planning and Area Development Project, Country Report no. 6. Madison: University of Wisconsin, 1981.

Jazy, D. "Le Mal Tunisien." *Jeune Afrique*, no. 1264 (1986), pp. 68-69.

Jorgenson, D.W. "The Development of a Dual Economy." *Economic Journal*, no. 71 (1961), pp. 309-34.

Judet, P. "Ben Salah et le Developpement Tunisien." *Esprit*, no. 397 (1970), pp. 805-16.

Kafka, F. *The Trial*. New York: Knoff, 1960.

Kamelgarn, D. "Tunisie (1970-1977), le Developpement d'un Capitalisme Dependant." *Peuples Mediterraneens*, no. 4 (1978), pp. 113-45.

Kassab, A., and Sethom, H. *Geographie de la Tunisie: le Pays et les Hommes*. Tunis: Publications de l'Universite de Tunis, 1980.

King, R. "Italy." In *Regional Development in Western Europe*, edited by H.D. Clark, pp. 81-112. London: Wiley, 1975.

Kongstadt, P. "Growth Poles and Urbanization: A Critique of Perroux and Friedmann." *Antipode*, no. 2 (1974), pp. 114-22.

Kropotkine, Pierre. *L'Etat: Son Role dans l'Histoire*. Paris: Publico, 1983.

Kuklinski, A., ed. *Regional Development and Planning: International Perspectives*. Leyden: Sijthoff, 1975.

________, ed. *Polarized Development and Regional Policies*. The Hague: Mouton, 1981.

Lacoste, Y. *Ibn Khaldoun: Naissance de l'Histoire Passe du Tiers-Monde*. Paris: Maspero, 1969.

________. *La Geographie du Sous-Developpement*. Paris: PUF, 1976.

________. "General Characteristics and Fundamental Structures of Mediaeval North African Society." *Economy and Society*. no. 1 (1974), pp. 1-17.

Laffont, R. *Decoloniser en France*. Paris: Gallimard, 1971.

Langlois, J. *Défense et Actualité de Proudhon*. Paris: Payet, 1976.

Laroui, A. *The History of the Maghrib: An Interpretative Essay*. Princeton, NJ: Princeton University Press, 1977.

Latham I.D. "Towns and Cities in Barbary: The Andalusians Influence." *The Islamic Quarterly*, nos. 3-4 (1972), pp. 189-204.

Lausen, J.R. "On Growth Poles." *Urban Studies*, no. 2 (1969), pp. 137-64.

Lawless, R., and Findlay, A., eds. *North Africa: Contemporary Politics and Economic Development*. London: Croom Helm / New York: St. Martin's Press, 1984.

Lefebre, H. *La Proclamation de la Commune*. Paris: Gallmiad, 1965.

Lewis, W.A. "Economic Development with Unlimited Supplies of Labor." *Manchester School of Economic and Social Studies*, no. 2 (1954), pp. 139-91.

Liauzu, C. "Un Aspect de la Crise en Tunisie: La Naissance des Bidonvilles." *Revue Française d'Histoire d'Outre-Mer*, nos. 232-233 (1976), p. 610.

Lipietz, Alain. *Le Capital et Son Espace*. Paris: Maspero, 1977.

. "Marx or Rostow?" *New Left Review*, no. 132 (1982), pp. 48-58.

Lipton, M. *Why Poor People Stay Poor: Urban Bias in World Development*. Cambridge, MA: Harvard University Press, 1977.

Lo, F., and Salih, K. "Growth Poles, Agropolitan Development and Polarization Reversal: The Debate and Search for Alternatives." In *Development from Above or from Below? The Dialectics of Regional Planning Developing Countries*, edited by W. Stöhr and D.R.F. Taylor, pp. 123-52. New York: Wiley, 1981.

________, eds. *Growth Pole Strategy and Regional Development Policy: Asian Experiences and Alternative Approaches*. Oxford: Pergamon Press, 1978.

Lombard, M. "L'Evolution Urbaine pendant le Haut Moyen Age." *Annales: Economies, Sociétés, Civilisations*, no. 1 (1957), pp. 7-28.

Luxembourg, R. *The Accumulation of Capital*. New York: Monthly Review Press, 1968.

Mahjoub. "Analyse Historique du Sous-Développement en Tunisie." *Annuaire de l'Afrique du Nord 1979*. vol. 18. Paris: CNRS, 1980, pp. 443-56.

________. "Analyse Historique du Sous-Développement en Tunisie." *Annuaire de l'Afrique du Nord 1981*. vol 20. Paris: CNRS: 1982, pp. 509-22.

Makhlouf, E. "Les Cooperatives en Tunisia: Structures et Difficultés." *Revue Tunisienne des Sciences Sociales*, no. 26 (1971), pp. 79-114.

Marseille, J. "L'Industrialisation des Colonies: Affaiblissement ou Renforcement de la Puissance Française." *Revue Française d'Histoire d'Outre-Mer*, no. 252 (1982), pp. 23-34.

Martay, J. *La Région pour un Etat Moderne*. Paris: Eds. France Empire, 1968.

Marx, Karl. *Capital*. vol. 1. New York: International Publishers, 1967.

Marx, Roland. *La Révolution Industrielle en Grande-Bretagne*. Paris: Armand Colin, 1970).

Maschino, M.T., and Mrabet, F. "La Tunisie Vingt Ans Après." *Le Monde Diplomatique*, December 1975.

Matteacioti, A. *Diversité Régionale et Coherence Nationale: L'Exemple des Régions Méditerranéenes*. Paris: Economica, 1981.

Matthews, R. *The Creation of Regional Dependency*. Toronto: University of Toronto Press, 1983.

McGee, T.G. *The Urbanization Process in the Third World*. London: Bell and Sons, 1971.

McNulty, M.C. "West African Urbanization." In *Urbanization and Counter-Urbanization*, edited by B.J.L. Berry, pp. 213-32. Beverly Hills: Sage, 1976.

Mehretu, A., and Campbell, D.J. "Regional Planning for Small Communities in Rural Africa: A Critical Survey." *Rural Africana*, nos. 12-13 (winter-spring 1982), pp. 91-110.

Melotti, U., Marx and the Third World. Atlantic Highlands, N.J.: Humanities Press, 1977.

Mennasemay, M. "Political Theory, Political Science and African Development." *Canadian Journal of African Studies*, no. 2 (1982), p. 225.

Micaud, C., et al. *Tunisia: The Politics of Modernization*. New York: Praeger, 1964.

Michalon, T. *Quel Etat pour L'Afrique?* Paris: Les Editions L'Harmaton, 1984.

Miské, A.B. *Lettre Ouverte aux Elites du Tiers Monde*. Paris: Ed. Le Sycomore, 1981.

Mkandawire, T. "The Lagos Plan of Action and the World Bank on Food and Agriculture in Africa: A Comparison." *Africa Development*, nos. 1-2 (1982), pp. 166-77.

Monsted, M. "François Perroux's Theory of 'Growth Pole' and 'Development Pole': A Critique." *Antipode*, no. 2 (1974), pp. 106-14.

Moseley, M.J. "The Impact of Growth Centers in Rural Regions." *Regional Studies*, no. 7 (1973), pp. 57-94.

Moudoud, E. "L'Urbanisation et la Politique du Logement Social en Tunisie." MA thesis, Institut d'Urbanisme de l'Académie de Paris, Université de Paris VIII, May 1980.

________. "La Politique du Logement Social en Tunisie." *Revue Algérienne des Sciences Sociales*, nos. 4-5 (October-November 1980), pp. 169-98.

________. "Le Développement Régional en Tunisie: Le Cas du Gouvernorat de Kasserine." Memoire de "Diplome D'Etude Approfondie." Institut de Géographie, Université de Paris IV-Sorbonne, Paris, 1981.

________. *Le Développement Régional en Tunisie: Le Projet de Développement de la Tunisie Central*. UBC Planning Papers, no. 2. School of Community and Regional Planning, University of British Columbia, Vancouver, May 1982.

________. *Modernisation, Centralisation et Destruction de l'Economie Rurale: L'Expérience des Cooperatives Agricoles en Tunisie, 1962-1969*. UBC Planning Papers, no. 7. School of Community and Regional Planning, University of British Columbia, May 1983.

________. "L'Impossible Régionalisation 'Jacobine' et le Dilemme des Disparités Régionales en Tunisie." *Canadian Journal of Regional Science*, no. 3 (1985), pp. 413-58.

________. The Rise and Fall of the Growth Pole Approach. Discussion Paper, no. 89. Department of Geography, Syracuse University, Syracuse November 1986.

Myrdal, G. *Economic Theory and Underdeveloped Regions*. Oxford: Duckworth, 1957.

Nellis, J.R. "Rural Development, Technical Assistance and Migration. A Tunisian Case Study." Paper presented at the Conference on Rural Development and the Retention of the Rural Population in the Countryside of Developing Countries, Institute for International Development and Cooperation, University of Ottawa, Ottawa, Canada, October 1981.

________. "A Comparative Assessment of the Development Performances of Algeria and Tunisia." *The Middle East Journal*, no. 3 (summer 1983), pp. 370-93.

________. "Decentralization in North Africa: Problems of Policy Implementation." In *Decentralization and Development: Policy Implementation in Developing Countries*, edited by D.A. Rondinelli and G.S. Cheema, pp. 127-82. Beverly Hills, CA: Sage, 1983.

________. *Decentralization, Regional Development and Local Public Finance in Tunisia*. Occasional Paper no. 79. Metropolitan Studies Program, Maxwell School, Syracuse University, Syracuse, NY, March 1984.

Nerfin, M. *Entretiens avec Ahmed Ben Salah sur la Dynamique Socialiste dans la Tunisie des Années 1960*. Paris: Maspero, 1974.

Nichols, V. "Growth Poles: An Evaluation of Their Propulsive Effects." *Environment and Planning*, no. 1 1969), pp. 193-208.

Noushi, A. "North Africa in the Period of Colonization." In *The Cambridge History of Islam*, edited by P.M. Holt, et al., vol. 2, pp. 299-326. London: Cambridge University Press, 1970.

Oakes, J.B. "Youth's Threat to Tunisia." New York *Times*, April 13, 1984, p. A35.

Obudho, R.A., and El-Shakhs, S., eds. *Development of Urban Systems in Africa*. New York: Praeger, 1979.

Obudho, R.A., and Taylor, D.R.F., eds. *The Spatial Structure of Development: A Study of Kenya*. Boulder, CO: Westview, 1979.

Parrain, C. "Le Mode de Production Asiatique: une Etape Nouvelle dans une Discussion Fondamentale." *La Pensée*, no. 114 (1964), pp. 3-7.

Patel, S.J. "The Age of the Third World." *Third World Quarterly*, no. 1 (1983), pp. 58-71.

Perrin, J.C. *Le Développement Regional*. Paris: PUF, 1974.

Perroux, F. "Economic Space: Theory and Applications." *Quarterly Journal of Economics*, no. 64 (1950), pp. 89-104.

________. "Note sur la Notion de 'Pôle de Croissance.'" *Economie Appliquée*, nos. 1-2 (1955), pp. 307-20.

________. *L'Economie du XXe Siècle*. Paris: P.U.F., 1964.

Pletsch, Carl E. "The Three Worlds or the Division of Social Scientific Labor, Circa 1950-1975." *Comparative Studies in Society and History*, no. 4 (1981), pp. 565-90.

Poncet, J. *La Colonisation et l'Agriculture Européennes en Tunisie depuis 1881*. Paris/La Haye: Mouton, 1961.

________. *Paysages et Problèmes Ruraux en Tunisie*. Paris: Presses Universitaires de France, 1962.

________. "Le Mythe de la Catastrophe Hilalienne." *Annales, Economies, Sociétés, Civilisations*, no. 5 (1967), pp. 1099-1120.

________. "La Régionalisation en Tunisie." *Tiers-Monde*, no. 55 (1972), pp. 597-614.

________. *La Tunisie à la Recherche de Son Avenir: Indépendance ou Neo-Colonialisme*. Paris: Les Editions Sociales, 1974.

Portes, A. "Modernity and Development: A Critique." *Studies in Comparative International Development*, no. 3 (1973), pp. 247-79.

Raymond, A. "North Africa in the Precolonial Period." In *The Cambridge History of Islam*, edited by P.M. Holt, et al. vol. 2, pp. 266-98. London: Cambridge University Press, 1970.

Raymond, A., and Poncet, J. *La Tunisie*. Paris: Presses Universitaires de France, Collection Que-Sais-Je?, 1971.

Reclus, E. *The Earth and Its Inhabitants*. vol. 2. New York: D. Appleton and Cie, 1887.

Republic of Tunisia, Ministry of Agriculture/USAID-Tunis. *An Evaluation of the Area Development Sub-Project: Central Tunisia Development Project*. Tunis. 1981.

Republic of Tunisia, Ministry of Public Works, "Direction de l'Aménagement du Territoire" DAT). "Organisation de l'Espace Tunisien." Mimeographed. Tunis: DAT, 1979.

_________. *Rapport du Comité de Réflexion sur l'Aménagement du Territoire et de la Décentralisation Industrielle.* Tunis, 1979.

_________. *Schéma National et Schémas Régionaux d'Aménagement du Territoire.* vols. 1, 2, and 12. Tunis, 1983, 1984.

Republic of Tunisia, Ministry of National Economy. "Industrial Decentralization Policy." *Conjoncture*, no. 59 (1981), p. 4.

Republic of Tunisia, Ministry of Plan and Finance. *Fourth Plan 1973-1976.* Tunis, 1973.

_________. *Fifth Five Year Plan 1977-1981.* Tunis, 1977.

_________. *Note d'Orientation pour la IIIème Décennie de Développement et le VIème Plan.* Tunis, 1980.

_________. *Note sur le Nouveau Programme de Développement Rural Integré.* Tunis, 1983.

_________, Commissariat Général au Développement Régional. *Note sur la Décentralisation et le Développement Régional.* Tunis, 1983.

_________. *Sixth Five Year Plan 1982-1986.* Tunis: Imprimerie Officielle, 1982.

Republic of Tunisia, Sécrétariat d'Etat au Plan et à l'Economie Nationale. *Perspectives Décennales de Développement 1962-1971.* Tunis, 1962.

Richardson, H.W., and Richardson, M. "The Relevance of Growth Center Strategies to Latin America." *Economic Geography*, no. 51 (1975), pp. 163-78.

Rodney, Walter. *How Europe Underdeveloped Africa.* Washington, DC: Howard University Press, 1982.

Rodwin, L. "Choosing Regions for Development." In *Regional Development and Planning: A Reader*, edited by J. Friedmann and W. Alonso, pp. 37-58. Cambridge, MA: MIT Press, 1964.

Rondinelli, D. "Regional Disparities and Investment Allocation Policies in the Philippines: Spatial Dimension of Poverty in a Developing Country." *Canadian Journal of Development Studies*, no. 2 1980), pp. 262-87.

_________. "Intermediate Cities in Developing Countries: A Comparative Analysis of Their Demographic, Social and Economic Characteristics." *Third World Planning Review*, no. 4 (1982), pp. 357-86.

_________. *Secondary Cities in Developing Countries.* Beverly Hills, CA: Sage, 1983.

_________. "The Dynamics of Growth of Secondary Cities in Developing Countries." *The Geographical Review*, no. 1 (1983), pp. 42-57.

_________. "Towns and Small Cities in Developing Countries." *The Geographical Review*, no. 4 (1983), pp. 379-95.

_________. "Population Distribution and Economic Development in Africa: The Need for Urbanization Policies." *Population Research and Policy Review*, no. 2 (1985), pp. 173-96.

_________. "The Crisis of Urbanization in Asia: Finding Alternatives to Megapolitan Growth." *The Journal of Social, Political and Economic Studies*, no. 1 (1985), pp. 69-86.

_________. "Regions in Question: A Critical Review." *Third World Planning Review*, no. 3 (1985), pp. 263-68.

Rondinelli, D.A., and Ruddle, K. *Urbanization and Rural Development: A Spatial Policy for Equitable Growth*. New York: Praeger, 1978.

Rondinelli, D., Nellis, J.R., and Cheema, G.S. *Decentralization in Developing Countries. A Review of Recent Experiences*. World Bank Working Papers, no. 581. Washington, DC: World Bank, 1983.

Rostow, W. *The Stages of Economic Growth: A Non-Communist Manifesto*. Cambridge: Cambridge University Press, 1960.

Rouillé, P. *Le Tourisme en Tunsisie*. Tunis: Ecole Nationale d'Administration, 1970.

Roxborough, I. *Theories of Underdevelopment*. London: Macmillan, 1979.

*La Rue* (*Revue Culturelle et Littéraire d'Expression Anarchiste*) "L'Autogestion," no. 29, 1981 (dossier).

Sachs, Ignacy. "Ecodevelopment." *CERES*, no. 48 (1974), pp. 8-12.

_________. *The Discovery of the Third World*. Cambridge: MIT Press, 1976.

Sahli, M. *Décoloniser l'Histoire*. Paris: Maspero, 1965.

Salih, K., et al., "Decentralization Policy, Growth Pole Approach, and Resource Frontier Development: A Synthesis of the Response in Four Southeast Asian Countries." In *Growth Pole Strategy and Regional Development Policy: Asian Experiences and Alternative Approaches*, edited by F. Lo and K. Salih, pp. 79-119. Oxford: Pergamon Press, 1978.

Sammut, C. *L'Impérialisme Capitaliste Française et le Nationalisme Tunisien*. Paris: Publisud, 1983.

Santos, M. *Les Villes du Tiers-Monde*. Paris: M.Th. Ghenin, 1971.

_________. "Underdevelopment, Growth Poles and Social Justice," Civilisations, no. 1-2 (1975) pp. 18-30.

Sbih, M. *Les Institutions Administratives du Maghreb*. Paris: Hachette, 1977.

Schwarz, A. *Les Dupes de la Modernisation*. Montreal: Nouvelle Optique, 1983.

Schumacker, E. *Small Is Beautiful*. New York: Harper and Row, 1973.

Seers, Dudley. "The Meaning of Development." *International Development Review*, no. 4 (1969), pp. 2-6.

_________. "What Are We Trying to Measure?" In *Measuring Development*, edited by N. Basta, pp. 21-36. London: CASC, 1972.

_________. "The New Meaning of Development." *International Development Review*, no. 3 (1977), pp. 2-7.

Seklani, M. *Economie et Population du Sud*. Paris: CNRS, 1976.

Serinsky, J. "The Anti-Communist Manifesto of Mr. Rostow." *U.S. Joint Publications Research Service*. Washington, DC, 1962.

Servan-Schreiber, J.J. *Le Pouvoir Régional*. Paris: Grasset, 1971.

Sethom, H. "Les Tentatives de Remodelage de l'Espace Tunisien depuis l'Indépendance." *Méditerranée*, nos. 1-2 (1979), pp. 119-25.

Sethom, H., and Kassab, A. *Les Régions Géographiques de la Tunisie*. Tunis: Publications de l'Université de Tunis, 1981.

Shaw, Timothy. "Debates about Africa's Future: The Brandt, World Bank and Lagos Plan Blueprints." *Third World Quarterly*, no. 2 (1983), pp. 330-44.

Signoles, P. "L'Armature Urbaine Tunisienne: Forces et Faiblesses, et Son Rôle dans le Développment National." *Revue Tunisienne des Sciences Sociales*, no. 1 (1978), p. 86.

________. "Les Déséquilibres Urbains en Tunisie." *Aujourd'hui l'Afrique*, no. 20 (1980), pp. 21-30.

Simmons, J.L. "Agricultural Cooperatives and Tunisian Development." *The Middle East Journal*, no. 4 1970), pp. 455-65.

________. "Agricultural Cooperatives and Tunisian Development." *The Middle East Journal*, no. 1 (1971), pp. 45-57.

Société Nationale de Cellulose et de Papier Alfa. "Le Complexe Industriel de Pâte et de Papier Eteint Sa 20ème Bougie." *Journal du Papier*, no. 11 (1983), pp. 28-29.

Slater, D. "Colonialism and the Spatial Structure of underdevelopment - Outlines of an Alternative Approach with Special Reference to Tanzania" Progress is Planning, no. 2 (1975) pp. 137-167.

Soja, E.W. "Territorial Idealism and the Political Economy of Regional Development." *City and Region: Journal of Spatial Studies*, no. 6 (1983), pp. 55-73.

________. "Regions in Context: Spatiality, Periodicity, and the Historical Geography of the Regional Question." *Society and Space*, no. 2 (1985), pp. 175-90.

Soja, E., and Weaver, C. "Urbanization and Underdevelopment in East Africa." In *Urbanization and Counter-Urbanization*, edited by B.J.L. Berry, pp. 233-66. Beverly Hills: Sage, 1976.

Sraïeb, N. "Mutations et Réformes des Structures de l'Enseignement en Tunisie." *Annuaire de l'Afrique du Nord 1968*, vol. 8. Paris: CNRS, 1968.

Stambouli, F. "Sous-Emploi et Espace Urbain: les Bidonvilles au Maghreb." *Espaces et Sociétés*, nos. 6-7 1972), pp. 165-80.

Stambouli, F., and Zghal, A. "Urban Life in Precolonial North Africa." *British Journal of Sociology*, no. 1 (1976), pp. 1-20.

Stöhr, W., and Todtling, F. "An Evaluation of Regional Policies: Experiences in Market and Mixed Economies." In *Human Settlement Systems*, edited by N. Hansen, pp. 85-119. New York: Ballinger, 1977.

Stöhr, W., and Taylor, D.R.F., eds. *Development from Above or from Below? The Dialectics of Regional Planning in Developing Countries*. New York: Wiley, 1981.

Stone, R. "Tunisia: A Single Party System Holds Change in Abeyance." In *Political Elites in Arab North Africa*, edited by I.W. Zartman, et al. pp. 144-76. New York and London: Longman, 1982.

Suret-Canale, J. "Les Sociétés Traditionnelles en Afrique Tropicale et le Concept du Mode de Production Asiatique." *La Pensée*, no. 117 (1964), pp. 21-47.

Sutton, K. "Algeria: Centre-Down Development, State and Capitalism, and Emergent Decentralization." In *Development from Above or from Below? The Dialectics of Regional Planning in Developing Countries*, edited by W. Stöhr and D.R.F. Taylor, pp. 351-75. New York: Wiley, 1981.

Taylor, D.R.F. "Spatial Organization and Rural Development." In *Freedom and Change*, edited by M.G. Frey, pp. 21-36. Toronto: MacMelland, 1975.

_________. *The Role and Functions of Lower Order Centers in Rural Development*. UNCRD, Working Papers, no. 70, Nagoya, 1979.

_________. "Spatial Aspects of the Development Process." In *The Spatial Structure of Development: A Study of Kenya*, edited by R.A. Obudho and D.R.F. Taylor, pp. 1-27. Boulder, CO: Westview, 1979.

_________. "Conceptualizing Development Space in Africa." *Geografiska Annales*, no. 63 (1980), pp. 87-93.

_________. "Some Observations on Theory and Practice in Regional Development in Africa." In *Polarized Development and Regional Policies*, edited by A. Kuklinski, pp. 327-39. The Hague: Mouton, 1981.

Thoman, R.S., ed. *Methodology and Case Studies*. Proceedings of the Commission on Regional Aspects of Development of the International Geographical Union, vol. 1. Toronto: IGU, 1974.

Thomson, D. *France: Empire and Republic, 1850-1940*. New York: Walker and Cie, 1968.

Tipps, D. "Modernization Theory and the Comparative Study of Societies: A Critical Perspective." *Comparative Studies in Society and History*, no. 2 (1973), pp. 199-226.

Toumi, M. *Tunisie: Pouvoirs et Luttes*. Paris: Les Editions le Sycomore, 1978.

Valensi, L. *On the Eve of Colonialism: North Africa before the French Conquest*. New York: Africana Publishing, 1972.

Vidal de la Blache, P., and Gallois, L., eds. *Géographie Universelle*. Paris: Armand Colin, 1937.

Voyenne, B. *Le Fédéralisme de P.J. Proudhon*. Paris: Presses d'Europe, 1973.

_________. *Histoire de l'Idée Fédéraliste: les Lignées Proudhoniennes*. Paris: Presses d'Europe, 1981.

Warren, B. *Imperialism: Pioneer of Capitalism*. London: New Left Books, 1980.

Weaver, Clyde. "Legitimizing Use-Value Production in a Mixed Economy." Paper presented at the Sixth Annual Meeting of the Canadian Regional Science Association, June 1982, University of Ottawa. (Also as UBC Planning Papers, DP #1. Vancouver: School of Community and Regional Planning, University of British Columbia, 1982).

_________ . Review of "Regions in Question." *Society and Space*, no. 2 (1985), pp. 265-70.

_________. "Romance of the Roses: A Discourse on the Path to Regional Reconstruction." *Society and Space*, no. 2 (1985), pp. 239-58.

Weaver, C.; Jessop, J.; and Das,V. "Rationality in the Public Interest: Notes Toward a New Synthesis." In *Rationality in Planning: Critical Essays on the Role of Rationality in Urban and Regional Planning*, edited by M.J. Breheney and A.J. Hooper, pp. 145-65. London: Pion, 1983.

Williams, R. "towards Many Socialisms," Socialist Review, no. 85 (1986) pp. 45-65.

Wolf, Eric. *Europe and the People Without History*. Berkeley: University of California Press, 1982.

World Bank. *Tunisia: Social Aspects of Development*. Washington, DC: World Bank, 1980.

_________. *Accelerated Development in Sub-Saharan Africa: An Agenda for Action*. Washington, DC: World Bank, 1981.

_________. *Tunisia: Country Economic Memorandum*. Washington, DC: World Bank, 1981.

_________. *Aménagement du Territoire et Développement Régionale: Quelle Approche pour Les Pays en Développement*. Washington, DC: World Bank, 1982.

_________. *World Development Report 1983*. Washington, DC: World Bank, 1983.

_________. *Tunisia: Review of the VIth Development Plan 1982-1986*. vol. 1. Washington, DC: World Bank, 1983.

Wright, V. "Questions d'un Jacobin Anglais aux Régionalistes Françaises," *Pouvoirs*, no. 19 (1981), pp. 119-30.

Young, Frank W., Bertoli, Fernando, and Bertoli, Sandra. *A Baseline for Rural Development in Central Tunisia*. Macrosocial Accounting Project. Ithaca, NY: Cornell University, 1981.

Zamiti, K. "Les Freins Idéologiques du Développement." *Cahiers Internationaux de Sociologie* 41 (1966): 105-15.

_________. "Les Obstacles Matériels et Idéologiques à l'Evolution Sociale des Campagnes Tunisiennes." *Revue Tunisiennes des Sciences Sociales*, no. 21 (1970), pp. 9-50.

Zartman, W. "Political Elites in Arab North Africa: Origin, Behavior and Prospects." In *Political Elites in Arab North Africa*, edited by I.W. Zartman, et al, pp. 1-34. New York and London: Longman, 1982.

Zartman, W., et al. *Political Elites in Arab North Africa*. New York: Longman, 1982.

Zghal, A. "Changements de Systèmes Politiques et Réformes des Structures Agraires en Tunisie." *Revue Tunisienne des Sciences Sociales*, no. 12 (1968), pp. 9-32.

_________. "L'Economie Paysanne de la Tunisie Pré-Coloniale." *Revue Tunisienne des Sciences Sociales*, no. 61 (1980), pp. 11-30.

Ziegler, J. *Le Pouvoir Africain*. Paris: Le Seuil, 1979.

# INDEX

Abu-Lughod, J. *104, 105, 108*
Adedej, A. *29, 33*
Agence de Promotion des Investissements (API) *155, 156*
Agnew, J. *17, 23, 198*
agropolises *41*
agropolitan district *41, 42*
Amin, S. *22, 27, 32, 62, 63, 64, 75, 86*
Andalous *105*
Apthorpe, R. *146*
Arrighi, G. *62*
Ashford, D. *146*
asiatic mode of production *6, 17, 114*
Attia, H. *179, 181, 194*
Avineri, S. *18, 19*
Belhadi, A. *164*
Belhassen, S. *76*
Ben Salah, A. *135, 136, 139, 142, 145, 147, 149, 150, 154, 155, 157, 159, 165, 168, 178, 179*
—and regional development policy *135-154*
Berdoulay, V. *105*
bidonvilles *115, 150, 167*
Bizerte *78, 117, 118, 119, 122, 188*
Boudeville, J. *35, 36, 37*
Bourguiba, H. *4, 144, 148*
Braudel, F. *104, 105, 108*
Bujra, A. *28*
Béji, H. *59*
Béjà *136, 137, 150, 153*
Camau, M. *189*
Cambon, P. *112*
Carthage *181*
Central Tunisia *118, 137, 142, 167, 178, 179*
Central Tunisia Development Authority (CTDA) *182, 183, 184, 185, 195*
Chaker, M. *155*
Charrad-Rouissi, H. *187*
Commissariat Général au Développement Régional (CGDR) *5, 165, 186, 187, 196*
Conference of Berlin *109, 111*
Corragio, L. *39*
Crowley, J. *33*
Darwent, D.F. *35*
de Bernis, G.D. *35, 37*
Decentralized development—
agropolitan development *40-43*
and federalism *42*
transformational approach *43-46*
Demongeot, P. *186*
DeViney, S. *33*
Djait, H. *175*
Douglas, M. *41, 42*
Dumont, R. *114, 115*
Economic Commission for Africa (ECA) *29, 33*
Engels *17, 18*
Entelis, J.P. *72, 74, 156*
European Economic Community *74*
Ferry, J. *111, 116*
feudal mode of production *114*
Fonds de Promotion et de Décentralisation Industrielle (FOPRODI) *156*
Frank, A. *22, 26, 27*
French colonization—

and precolonial Tunisia *103-109*
destruction of social formation and space economy *110-119*
land colonization policy *112-116*
regime of capitulation *110-112*
Friedmann, J. *20*, *40*, *41*, *42*, *43*, *44*
Gabes *78*, *118*, *119*
Gafsa *86*, *152*, *153*
Ganiage, J. *110*, *111*
Gramsci, A. *189*
Gravier, J.F. *35*
Growth without development (concept) *62-64*
Habous Association *112*, *113*
Hammam-lif *118*
Hermassi, E. *33*, *115*, *147*
Higgins, B. *38*
Hirschman, A. *35*
Hopkins, N. *178*
Ifriqiya *104*
Illich, I. *17*
International Monetary Fund (IMF) *64*, *162*
Isard, W. *34*
Jacobin—
and regionalization *175-187*
argumentation *194-197*
political-administrative system *43*, *66-70*
Jakobson, L. *179*, *181*
Jazy, D. *76*
Jendouba *85*, *153*
Jeune Afrique *188*
Kafka, F. *147*
Kairouan *76*, *86*, *104*, *108*, *109*, *119*, *122*, *152*, *153*, *181*
Kasserine *76*, *118*, *137*, *139*, *152*, *153*, *181*, *183*, *184*
Kebili *85*
Lagos Plan *15*, *28*, *29*, *30*, *31*, *32*, *33*
Lajugie, J. *35*
Laroui, A. *112*
Le Kef *153*
Lewis, W.A. *21*, *22*
Lipietz, A. *33*
Lösch, A. *34*
L'Union Douanière Française *111*
Mahdia *166*
Mahjoub, A. *122*
Marseille, J. *116*
Marx, K. *17*, *18*, *19*, *24*, *25*, *27*, *33*, *47*
Marxist, orthodox *17*
Matteaccioti, A. *39*
Matthews *126*
Mednine *78*
Mennasemay, M. *24*, *33*
Menzel-Bourguiba, H. *139*
Micaud, C. *148*
Miské, A.B. *1*, *198*
Modernization theories—
bourgeois theories *20-37*
growth pole theory *37-40*
marxist-stalinist theories *17-20*
Monastir *166*
Moriscos *105*
Moseley, M. *38*
Moulares *118*
Myrdal, G. *35*
Mzali, M. *9*, *166*
National Assembly *155*, *161*
Nebeur *118*
Nefza *118*
Nellis, J. *69*, *71*, *183*, *184*, *185*, *187*, *188*, *189*, *195*
Nichols, V. *38*
Nouira, H. *9*, *135*, *155*, *156*, *157*, *165*, *166*, *168*, *177*, *185*, *186*
—and regional development policy *155-167*
Noushi, A. *115*
Organization of African Unity (OAU) *15*, *28*, *30*
oriental despotism *6*, *19*, *114*

Parti Socialiste Destourien
(P.S.D.) *61, 70, 143, 164*
Perroux, F. *34, 35, 36, 37, 39*
Poncet, J. *105, 112, 114*
Proudhon, P. *33, 47, 146*
Raymond, A. *111, 114*
Reclus, E. *108, 122*
Richardson, H. *38*
Richardson, M. *38*
Rodney, W. *116*
Rodwin, L. *34*
Rondinelli, D. *38, 43, 44, 45, 46*
Rostow, W. *25, 26, 27, 33*
Ruddle, K. *38, 43, 44, 45, 46*
Sachs, I. *15, 17, 22, 25, 27*
Sammut, C. *114*
Sbeitla *181*
Schawrz, A. *145*
Schumacker, E. *17*
Seers, D. *17, 62, 63, 64, 86*
selective territorial closure *42*
Sfax *78, 117, 118, 119, 122, 158, 181, 189*
Shaw, T. *32*
Sidi Bouzid *166*
Siliana *166*
Simmons, J. *145*
slums *115, 167*
Société Hotelière et Touristique de Tunisie (SHTT) *152*
Souatir *118*
Sousse *78, 118, 119, 122, 158, 181*
Stalin, J. *33*
State—
and elites hegemony *193-198*, (see also political-administrative system of Tunisia)
and regionalism *184-186*
development strategy *64-74*, (see also regional policy)
political elites and the *70-72*
privatization of *186*
regional question and *195-197*
role of *135-136, 155-156, 198*
Stone, R. *188*
Tabarka *118*
Tataouine *85*
Tebessa *118*
Torrens system *112*
Treaty of La Marsa *112*
Treaty of Le Bardo *112*
Tunis *78, 117, 118, 119, 126, 137, 150, 158, 181, 183, 187*
Tunisia—
development performance of *64-75*
political-administrative system *66-70*
regional disparities in *75-92*
urbanization and urban network *75, 76-86*
underdevelopment/dependency theory *62*
United States Agency for International Development (USAID) *141, 177, 178, 183, 185*
–Tunis *184, 186*
University of Wisconsin-Madison *183*
utopianism *4, 198*
Von Thünen, S. *34*
Weaver, C. *20*
Wolf, E. *145, 194*
World Bank *5, 8, 15, 30, 31, 32, 33, 64, 67, 75*
Zaghouan *166*
Zamiti, K. *148*
Zarzis *188*

For Product Safety Concerns and Information please contact our EU representative GPSR@taylorandfrancis.com Taylor & Francis Verlag GmbH, Kaufingerstraße 24, 80331 München, Germany

**Batch number: 10726013**

Printed by Printforce, the Netherlands